# THE ROUGH GUIDE TO
# USA:THE SOUTH

This first edition was written by Greg ~~Ward~~

This book includes extractions from *The Rough Guide to the USA* written by Maria Edwards, Stephen Keeling, Todd Obolsky, Annelise Sorensen, Georgia Stephens and Greg Ward, updated and published in 2021 by Apa Publications Ltd. A big thank you to all the contributing authors of *The Rough Guide to the USA*.

**ROUGH GUIDES**

# Contents

# Introduction to
# The South

No two people may agree on the precise boundaries of the southern United States, but you'll know when you get there. This book takes in the eight southern heartland states of North Carolina, South Carolina, Georgia, Kentucky, Tennessee, Alabama, Mississippi and Arkansas. Take a road trip through the region, and you'll face so many reminders that you're in a world apart – a land within a land, with its own food, its own music, its own architecture, its own landscapes, its own traditions, and above all its own history.

Mark Twain put it best, as early as 1882: "In the South, the [Civil] war is what AD is elsewhere; they date everything from it". Several generations later, the legacies of slavery and "The War Between the States" remain evident throughout. The eight states covered in this book were in fact joined in the Confederacy by five other states that also seceded from the Union – Virginia, Florida, Louisiana, Missouri and Texas. To this day, however, they continue to form the core of the South. That said, more than 150 years on from the end of the fighting, there's much more to the South than the Civil War.

While there's been talk of the emergence of the so-called "New South" ever since the war, there's no denying that change has finally come. Much of that is due, of course, to the other epic historical clash that shaped the destiny of the South: the Civil Rights movement of the 1950s and 1960s. The extraordinary intertwined history of those struggles, a century apart, makes any tour of the South fascinating: it's simply impossible to travel any distance without encountering endless echoes of the two. Tracing the footsteps of Martin Luther King, Jr. from his birthplace in **Atlanta** to his ministry in Montgomery and his tragic death in **Memphis** is an inspirational, and potentially transformative, pilgrimage.

Let's not forget the sheer joy of visiting the South. For many travellers, the most exciting aspect of touring the region has to be the chance to immerse oneself in its magnificent **music**. It was the South that gave the world rock'n'roll, and the blues before that, and its contribution to music in general cannot be overstated. There's something very compelling about entering the shotgun house where Elvis Presley grew up in Tupelo, **Mississippi**, or exploring Graceland in Memphis, or standing at the very crossroads outside Clarksdale in the **Mississippi Delta** where Robert Johnson supposedly sold his soul to the devil. The real thrill, though, comes when you realise that the music of the South is still alive, and still means something to people, whether you get that from a honky-tonk in **Nashville**, a juke joint deep in the Delta, from a backwoods barn dance in rural Appalachia, or Rev Al Green preaching the gospel at his church in Memphis.

And then there's the **food**. Succulent, smoky, aromatic barbecue is the obvious stand-out, with each state and city boasting its own fiercely-cherished favourite recipe, but there's also the wonderful seafood of the Atlantic coast, especially the Low Country Boils of the sea islands, and the general glories of soul food, as found in cities like Atlanta and Memphis. You can even visit the first-ever KFC in, you guessed it, Kentucky.

The Southern experience is also reflected in a rich regional **literature**, documented by the likes of William Faulkner, Carson McCullers, Eudora Welty, Toni Morrison and Harper Lee.

# Where to go

Unless you have three weeks or more to spare, you won't be able to attempt anything like a comprehensive tour of the South, and you'll have to focus instead on a few

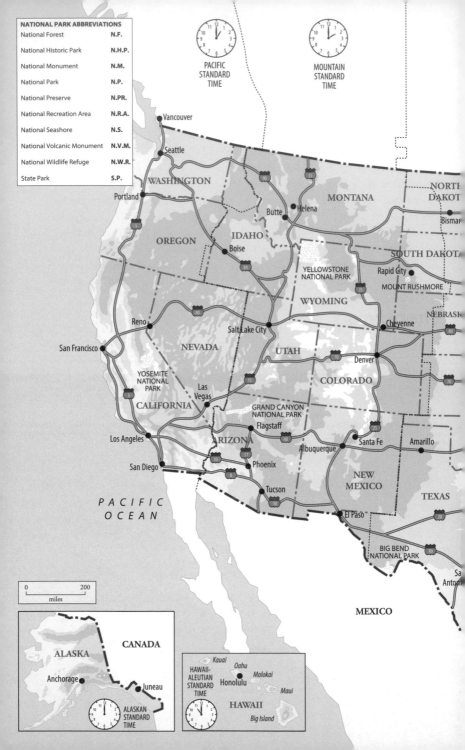

**NATIONAL PARK ABBREVIATIONS**

| National Forest | N.F. |
| National Historic Park | N.H.P. |
| National Monument | N.M. |
| National Park | N.P. |
| National Preserve | N.PR. |
| National Recreation Area | N.R.A. |
| National Seashore | N.S. |
| National Volcanic Monument | N.V.M. |
| National Wildlife Refuge | N.W.R. |
| State Park | S.P. |

PACIFIC STANDARD TIME

MOUNTAIN STANDARD TIME

Vancouver

Seattle

WASHINGTON

Portland

OREGON

IDAHO

Boise

Butte
Helena
MONTANA

NORTH DAKOTA

Bismarck

SOUTH DAKOTA

YELLOWSTONE NATIONAL PARK

Rapid City

MOUNT RUSHMORE

WYOMING

NEBRASKA

Reno

NEVADA

Salt Lake City

UTAH

Cheyenne

Denver

COLORADO

San Francisco

YOSEMITE NATIONAL PARK

CALIFORNIA

Las Vegas

GRAND CANYON NATIONAL PARK

Flagstaff

ARIZONA

Albuquerque

Santa Fe

Amarillo

Los Angeles

Phoenix

San Diego

Tucson

NEW MEXICO

TEXAS

El Paso

PACIFIC OCEAN

BIG BEND NATIONAL PARK

San Antonio

MEXICO

0    200
miles

ALASKA

CANADA

Anchorage

Juneau

ALASKAN STANDARD TIME

HAWAII-ALEUTIAN STANDARD TIME

Kauai

Oahu

Honolulu

Molokai

Maui

HAWAII

Big Island

specific states. The good news is, each state is rewarding in its own way, and each also embodies the full diversity and richness of the region as a whole. Away from the urban areas, perfumed with delicate magnolia trees, the classic scenery of the Southern consists of fertile but sun-baked farmlands, with undulating hillsides dotted with wooden shacks and rust-red barns, and broken by occasional forests.

**North Carolina**, for a start, encompasses several utterly different regions. The windswept **Outer Banks**, the wispy skein of barrier islands that protect and parallel the Atlantic shoreline, have a remote and timeless atmosphere that can barely have changed since the Wright Brothers first took to the skies, or indeed since the lost colonists of Roanoke vanished into thin air. Inland, the dynamic communities of the "**Research Triangle**" – Raleigh, Durham and **Chapel Hill** – have an appealing cultural energy, while further west still the tail end of the Appalachian mountains offers spectacular scenery, along the **Blue Ridge Parkway** in particular, and vibrant, liberal-leaning, beer-chugging towns like **Asheville**. Keep heading west beyond the state's southwestern corner, and you can dip through **Great Smoky Mountains National Park** en route to Tennessee or Kentucky.

Continue south along the coast from North Carolina, on the other hand, and, logically enough, you'll find yourself in **South Carolina**. Assuming you're not twenty years old and new to the delights of alcohol, you may not choose to linger in Myrtle Beach, but tranquil **Georgetown**, in the heart of the rice-growing Low Country, make a relaxing stop. Further south, South Carolina's sea islands – **St Helena Island** for example, reached via a bridge from Beaufort – are quite delightful, and home to the Gullah-speaking descendants of African Americans left to build their own communities at the end of the Civil War. The state's real highlight, though, is the elegant city of **Charleston**, which built its fortunes on slavery and was appropriately where the first shots of the war were fired.

Another hundred miles southwest, just across the state line in **Georgia**, **Savannah** is even more beautiful, with its dreamy squares draped in Spanish moss. Strolling its cobbled riverfront quayside, you could almost be in Portugal or some sleepy Mediterranean port, while the town itself has a seductive, laidback charm. Quite a contrast with state capital **Atlanta**, a go-getting metropolis of six million people that has spearheaded the growth, and redefined the image, of the entire South. Its Sweet Auburn district stands as a haunting memorial to the city's greatest son, **Martin Luther King, Jr.** but with its museums and galleries, vibrant neighbourhoods and sheer energy, Atlanta has its eyes very much focussed on the twenty-first century. Georgia has its fair share of stimulating smaller towns too, like **Athens** and **Macon**, and also some dramatic scenery, from the **Dahlonega** district in the north to the **Okefenokee Swamp** in the south.

**Kentucky** offers a different vision again, its rolling rural splendour encapsulated by its shimmering, bucolic Bluegrass Downs. It's best known these days for its horses, with stud farms peppering the meadows around **Lexington**, and **Louisville** hosting the iconic **Kentucky Derby**. Further attractions range from **Jim Beam's** whiskey distillery in Clermont and **Colonel Sanders'** first-ever fried chicken diner in Corbin to the birthplaces of American heroes **Abraham Lincoln** and **Muhammad Ali**.

## THE BIG MUDDY

"I do not know much about gods; but I think that the river
Is a strong brown god – sullen, untamed and intractable."
St Louis-born T.S. Eliot, *The Four Quartets*

North America's principal waterway, the Mississippi – the name comes from the Algonquin words for "big" and "river" – starts just ninety miles south of the Canadian border at Lake Itasca, Minnesota, and winds its way nearly 2400 miles to the Gulf of Mexico, taking in over one hundred tributaries en route and draining all or part of thirty-one US states and two Canadian provinces.

The "Big Muddy" – it carries 2lb of dirt for every 1000lb of water – is one of the busiest commercial rivers in the world, and one of the least conventional. Instead of widening toward its mouth, like most rivers, the Mississippi grows narrower and deeper. Its delta, near Memphis, more than three hundred miles upstream from the river's mouth, is not a delta at all, but an alluvial flood plain. Furthermore, its estuary deposits, which extend the land six miles out to sea every century, are paltry compared to other rivers; gulf currents disperse the sediment before it has time to settle.

The Mississippi is also, in the words of Mark Twain, who spent four years as a riverboat pilot, "the crookedest river in the world." As it weaves and curls its way extravagantly along its channel, it continually cuts through narrow necks of land to shape and reshape oxbow lakes, meander scars, cutoffs, and marshy backwaters. A bar could operate one day in Arkansas and then find itself in dry Tennessee the next, thanks to an overnight cutoff.

A more serious manifestation of the power of the Mississippi is its propensity to flood. Although the river builds its own levees, artificial embankments have, since as early as 1717, helped to safeguard crops and homes. After the disastrous floods of 1927, the federal government installed a wide range of flood-protection measures; virtually the entire riverfront from Cape Girardeau, Missouri, to the sea is now walled in, and it's even possible to drive along the top of the larger levees.

While it's no longer feasible to sail Twain's route for yourself, riverboat excursions operate in most sizeable river towns. The Delta Queen Steamboat Company (ⓦ deltaqueen.com) offers longer cruises on a reconstructed paddlewheeler. Some trips start on the Ohio, Cumberland and Tennessee rivers, potentially allowing passengers to board in Louisville, Nashville or Chattanooga before joining the Mississippi to cruise past Memphis, Vicksburg and Natchez en route to New Orleans.

For music lovers, **Tennessee** is arguably the most rewarding state of all. Sprawling superbly beside the Mississippi, **Memphis** lives up to every expectation. Even when you've toured **Sun Studio**, listening to Elvis' original recordings in the very room where the stardust descended, and swooned over the precious relics on display in **Graceland**, you've only scraped the surface. Still to come: an evening in the clubs of legendary Beale Street; a sermon in Al Green's church; soaking up the vibes in the Stax Museum. **Nashville** too is electrifying, from the **Country Music Hall of Fame** to the **Grand Ole Opry**, by way of countless unsung honky-tonks. And Tennessee has its own share of natural treasures, including the nation's most-visited national park, **Great Smoky Mountains**. Be sure to pay your respects to Dolly Parton in **Dollywood** en route.

**Alabama** owes its primary role on tourist itineraries to the legacy of the Civil Rights era. It was in state capital **Montgomery** that **Martin Luther King, Jr.** served as pastor of his first church, and took on leadership of the bus boycott prompted by **Rosa Parks** – it brings home the raw courage of those days to see quite how close King's church stood to the capitol itself. In nearby **Selma** you walk the fearsome bridge where marchers confronted state troopers in 1965, while **Birmingham** in the north has its own share of evocative memorials. Of course, there's more than that to visiting Alabama than that, including plenty of wonderful **soul food**, and charming **Mobile**, a miniature New Orleans down on the Gulf Coast.

While **Mississippi** may have the most tainted history of any southern state – in the words of Nina Simone, "Everybody knows about Mississippi Goddam" – it too holds a proud place in the story of popular music. It was the haunting flatlands of the **Mississippi Delta** that spawned the delta blues, which as Muddy Waters memorably put it "… had a baby, and they named the baby rock'n'roll". The delta's main town, **Clarksdale**, is filled with shrines to blues greats, while in every direction sleepy time-forgotten settlements hold further memories. To the west, **Natchez** and **Vicksburg** are venerable river ports, while to the east Oxford was home to the definitive Southern novelist, William Faulkner, and **Tupelo** gave the world Elvis himself.

Finally, **Arkansas** has its own share of Delta ports, most notably **Helena**, and its own Civil Rights legacy too, most conspicuous at **Little Rock**, but it also the holds the one-of-a-kind spa town of **Hot Springs**, and some gorgeous untrammelled scenery in the (jagged) shape of the **Ozark Mountains**.

As a rule, **public transport** in the rural South is poor to the point of non-existence. You'll see far more if you **rent a car**, which will also enable you to explore to the backwaters – the Blue Ridge Parkway, the Cape Hatteras National Seashore and Outer Banks of North Carolina, the Ozarks and the Mississippi Delta to mention but a few. In any case, it's best to take things at your own pace – you'll find things to see and do in the most unlikely places. Incidentally, if you harbour fantasies of travelling through the South by boat along the Mississippi, note that only luxury craft make the trip these days.

# When to go

It's well worth visiting the South any time of year, but if you're free to go whenever you choose, then spring and fall have to be the top picks. At the height of summer, in July and August, the daily high temperature throughout the region is mostly a very humid 90°F, and while almost every public building is air-conditioned, the heat can be debilitating. May and June are much more bearable, and tend to see a lot of local festivals, while spring wildflowers are at their most spectacular somewhat earlier. Great Smoky Mountains National Park, for example, is ablaze with colour in April, while Macon celebrates its ravishing Cherry Blossom Festival in mid-March.

The fall colours in the South are every bit as beautiful as in New England, and visiting in that season is a lot less expensive and congested. On the Blue Ridge Parkway in North Carolina the fall foliage is generally at its multihued best in the middle two weeks of October, while further south, on the Natchez Trace Parkway in Tennessee and Mississippi for example, displays have peaked in recent years during the first two weeks in November.

Daily minimum temperatures in the depths of midwinter can drop pretty low – freezing January nights are not unusual in Atlanta and Memphis, for example – but the cold is seldom likely to impact on travel plans. Only in the Smokies is there much risk of roads being closed by snow. While you'd have to be unlucky to coincide with a hurricane, on the other hand, the hurricane season along the Atlantic seaboard does lasts a full six month. In principle, between June and November, a tropical storm might hit anywhere from Mobile on the Gulf Coast up to Charleston, South Carolina.

## AVERAGE TEMPERATURE (°F) AND RAINFALL

To convert °F to °C, subtract 32 and multiply by 5/9

|  | Jan | Feb | March | April | May | June | July | Aug | Sept | Oct | Nov | Dec |
|---|---|---|---|---|---|---|---|---|---|---|---|---|
| **ATLANTA, GA** | | | | | | | | | | | | |
| Max/Min temp | 51/35 | 55/39 | 63/46 | 73/53 | 81/61 | 88/68 | 91/72 | 89/71 | 84/65 | 73/54 | 61/44 | 54/40 |
| Days Rainfall | 9 | 7 | 8 | 6 | 7 | 7 | 9 | 7 | 5 | 5 | 6 | 7 |
| **CHARLESTON, SC** | | | | | | | | | | | | |
| Max/Min temp | 57/44 | 61/48 | 65/53 | 73/60 | 80/68 | 86/75 | 88/77 | 87/77 | 84/73 | 76/64 | 66/53 | 61/49 |
| Days Rainfall | 6 | 5 | 6 | 5 | 5 | 7 | 8 | 9 | 7 | 4 | 4 | 6 |
| **MEMPHIS, TN** | | | | | | | | | | | | |
| Max/Min temp | 47/34 | 51/38 | 61/45 | 70/53 | 79/63 | 87/70 | 89/72 | 88/71 | 83/66 | 73/54 | 59/44 | 51/39 |
| Days Rainfall | 7 | 7 | 9 | 8 | 8 | 6 | 7 | 5 | 5 | 5 | 7 | 8 |
| **MOBILE, AL** | | | | | | | | | | | | |
| Max/Min temp | 59/43 | 63/48 | 70/54 | 77/60 | 84/67 | 90/75 | 91/76 | 91/77 | 87/72 | 79/62 | 68/51 | 62/48 |
| Days Rainfall | 6 | 6 | 6 | 5 | 5 | 9 | 10 | 10 | 6 | 4 | 5 | 7 |

# Author picks

Our hard-travelling author has visited every corner of this huge, magnificent region and picked out his personal highlights.

**One-of-a-kind accommodations** The South holds some totally out-of-the-ordinary lodging options. Take the *Hike Inn* at Georgia's dramatic Amicalola Falls (see page 79), which can only be reached by a five-mile hike into the Appalachians, or the *Shack Up Inn* outside Clarksdale, MS (see page 123), where you sleep in a sharecroppers' cabin on a Delta cotton plantation.

**Round table restaurants** At least once, you've got to eat Southern specialities like fried chicken with some real-life Southerners. At "round table" restaurants like *Mrs Wilkes'* in Savannah, GA (see page 86), *Monell's* in Nashville, TN (see page 110), and *Walnut Hills* in Vicksburg, MS (see page 126), diners share meals at large communal tables.

**Best beaches** The southern states may be not as famous for beaches as neighbouring Florida, but superb strands abound if you know where to look. Try Hammocks Beach, NC (see page 52); St Simons Island in Georgia's Golden Isles (see page 88); and wonderful Hunting Island, SC (see page 69) for a sublimely peaceful beach day.

**Most evocative Civil Rights memorials** There's no separating the inspirational story of the Civil Rights struggle from the personal journey of Martin Luther King, Jr. Visit his birth home and final resting place in Atlanta, GA (see page 70), then continue to his first church in Montgomery, AL (see page 118), before paying tribute at the site of his assassination in Memphis, TN, now home to the uplifting National Civil Rights Museum (see page 98).

**Classic diners** The South has to be the spiritual home of the much-loved all-American diner. Prime specimens include *Big Ed's* in Raleigh, NC (see page 55), and *Weaver D's* in Athens, GA (see page 80), but how about two from the movies? The *Arcade*, a former haunt of Elvis in Memphis, TN (see page 103), played itself in Jim Jarmusch's Mystery Train, while the *Whistle Stop Café* in Juliette, GA (see page 81), starred in *Fried Green Tomatoes at the Whistle Stop Café*.

> Our author recommendations don't end here. We've flagged up our favourite places – a perfectly sited hotel, an atmospheric café, a special restaurant – throughout the Guide, highlighted with the ★ symbol.

CHARLESTON, SC

ALABAMA STATE CAPITOL

# 15
# things not to miss

It's obviously not possible to see everything that the South has to offer in one trip. What follows is a selective and subjective taste of the region's highlights: unforgettable cities, spectacular drives, magnificent parks, spirited celebrations and stunning natural phenomena. All highlights are colour-coded by chapter and have a page reference to take you straight into the Guide, where you can find out more.

### 1 SAVANNAH, GA
See page 81
Mint juleps on wide verandas, horse-drawn carriages on cobbled streets, romantic garden squares draped with Spanish moss; this historic cotton port remains the South's loveliest town.

### 2 THE KENTUCKY DERBY, LOUISVILLE, KY
See page 93
Even if the race itself lasts just two minutes, Derby Day, at the start of May, is the culmination of a wild and unforgettable two-week spree.

### 3 MARTIN LUTHER KING, JR. NATIONAL HISTORIC SITE, ATLANTA, GA
See page 72
Georgia's dynamic capital is home to its most evocative sight, encompassing King's birth home and the church that witnessed his baptism and funeral.

### 4 BLUE RIDGE PARKWAY, NC
See page 58
The South's most spectacular drive meanders through the North Carolina mountains, taking in stunning vistas, wildflower-studded hiking trails and Appalachian bluegrass shows.

### 5 CAPE HATTERAS NATIONAL SEASHORE, NC
See page 50
Windswept dunes and saltwater marshes flank sun-dappled beaches at this wild North Carolina barrier island.

### 6 THE MISSISSIPPI DELTA, MS

See page 122

The birthplace of the blues holds an irresistible appeal, with the legendary crossroads where Robert Johnson sold his soul, outside funky little Clarksdale, as the obvious first port of call.

### 7 ASHEVILLE, NC

See pages 59

A great base for adventures amid North Carolina's wild western mountains, this hip outdoors-oriented town is at the centre of a buzzing craft-beer scene.

### 8 SPOLETO FESTIVAL, CHARLESTON, SC

See pages 67

Historical Charleston, on the South Carolina coast, takes on a festive air during its extravagant early-summer celebration of the performing arts.

### 9 MEMPHIS, TN

See page 96

This sleepy city on the Mississippi is especially thrilling for music fans: quite apart from Elvis, you could spend days checking out Beale Street, Sun Studio, the Stax Museum, and Al Green's church.

### 10 HOT SPRINGS, AK

See page 130

A fascinating slice of Americana, Hot Springs is a hugely enjoyable throwback to an earlier kind of tourism – and yes, its springs are still active.

### 11 BARBECUE
See page 29
There's no better place to
sample the quintessential
American cuisine – be it
smoked ribs, pulled pork or
brisket – than the southern
states.

### 12 IN THE FOOTSTEPS OF ELVIS, MS & TN
See page 125 and 100
Walk a mile in the King's
shoes – blue suede, naturally
– by making a pilgrimage
from his birthplace in Tupelo,
MS, to his home and burial
site in Memphis, TN.

### 13 GREAT SMOKY MOUNTAINS NATIONAL PARK, TN & NC
See page 112
At its most colourful in
spring, this dramatic forested
wilderness welcomes more
than twice as many visitors
as any other national park.

### 14 MONTGOMERY, AL
See page 117
Alabama's state capital,
where Rosa Parks refused
to sit at the back of the
bus, is filled with haunting
reminders of the Civil Rights
era.

### 15 COUNTRY MUSIC HALL OF FAME, NASHVILLE, TN
See page 107
At once a fascinating
interactive museum
and a treasure trove of
memorabilia, including
Elvis's gold Cadillac.

11

12

13

14

CHET ATKINS

15

# Itineraries

With eight separate states to discover, the South does not lend itself to quick visits. If you only have a week, you can't hope to much more than cover a couple of cities and a bit of coastline or countryside in between – Memphis and Nashville with a taste of the Delta, perhaps, or Charleston and Savannah plus some of the sea islands. Two weeks will give you a whole lot more scope, to follow the Civil Rights or Civil War trails, for example, while three weeks or more and you can hope to explore the region in all its glory.

## SOUTHERN SHORELINES AND SCENIC SPLENDOURS

Only if you drive will you be able to complete this stunning loop through some of the South's wildest and most spectacular scenery. You could do it in ten days, if you're not seduced to linger in the two gorgeous towns en route, Savannah and Charleston.

**❶ Charlotte, NC** With its international airport, North Carolina's largest city makes a convenient gateway to the South. See page 57

**❷ The Outer Banks, NC** Head straight for this remote coastal wilderness, a tracery of long flat islands strung with historic landmarks. See page 48

**❸ Cape Hatteras National Seashore, NC** Deserted beaches, lonely lighthouses, and seabirds in the salt marshes combine to shape a gloriously haunting experience. See page 50

**❹ Charleston, SC** One of the best preserved old cities in North America, enriched by the culture of the nearby Sea Islands. See page 63

**❺ Savannah, GA** A little further south, across the river in Georgia, Charleston's raffish but equally ravishing cousin abounds in moss-swaddled squares and historic homes. See page 81

**❻ Dahlonega, GA** A relic of Georgia's very own Gold Rush, up in the Appalachian foothills, Dahlonega stands at the edge of some dramatic landscapes. See page 78

**❼ Great Smoky Mountains, TN** As you cross the Smokies from western Tennessee, you're confronted by a vast expanse of forested mountains. See page 112

**❽ Blue Ridge Parkway, NC** Take a small detour as you return to Charlotte to drive one of America's most fabulous, and peaceful, scenic roads. See page 58

---

**Create your own itinerary with Rough Guides**. Whether you're after adventure or a family-friendly holiday, we have a trip for you, with all the activities you enjoy doing and the sights you want to see. All our trips are devised by local experts who get the most out of the destination. Visit **www.roughguides.com/trips** to chat with one of our travel agents.

# A MUSIC PILGRIMAGE

Music permeates southern culture, so there's no escaping it wherever you go, but whether it's Dolly, Elvis, Hank or Otis who most touches your buttons, certain shrines are absolutely unmissable. Allow at least ten days, and more if you plan to enjoy some long nights of live music.

❶ **Nashville, TN** Country music heaven… still the centre of a vibrant music industry, Nashville celebrates its heritage every day in every way. See page 105

❷ **Memphis, TN** The birthplace of rock'n'roll, home to Stax and Sun, Al Green and Elvis, Memphis is the place to fall in love with music all over again. See page 96

❸ **Mississippi Delta** Spend a night or two soaking up the essence of the blues in Clarksdale, and exploring the Delta's eerie backroads. See page 122

❹ **Tupelo, MS** Who can resist walking through the tiny cottage where Elvis was born? See page 125

❺ **Athens, GA** College towns have made many extraordinary contributions to American music, but few more so than Athens. See page 79

❻ **Dollywood, TN** Dolly Parton's exuberant theme park is alive with country and bluegrass music. Catch a show at one of the many stages dotted around the park. See page 111

# THE GRAND TOUR

You'll need a good three weeks to complete a full grand tour of the South, but you'll be rewarded with an amazing array of experiences, from splendid historic cities to memorable music, and a sobering sense of the Civil Rights struggle to some magnificent landscapes.

❶ **Atlanta, GA** There's no better place to get a flavour of today's South than the region's buzzing capital, birthplace of Martin Luther King, Jr, and Coca-Cola. See page 70

❷ **Montgomery, AL** Alabama's capital is laced with monuments to Martin Luther King, Jr, civil rights and Hank Williams. See page 117

❸ **Vicksburg, MS** Perched above the Mississippi, this crucial river port was the scene of a dramatic Civil-War siege. See page 125

❹ **Mississippi Delta** An iconic American landscape, the much-fabled Delta spawned many of music's most celebrated innovators. See page 121

❺ **Memphis, TN** Named for an Egyptian capital, and even boasting its own pyramid, this atmospheric river city is the highlight of any Southern road trip. See page 96

❻ **Nashville, TN** Still going strong after a century of developing and promoting country music, Nashville rewards fans with pleasures galore. See page 105

❼ **Great Smoky Mountains, TN** America's most popular national park preserves some of the South's most pristine mountain scenery. See page 112

❽ **Cape Hatteras National Seashore, NC** A windswept wonderland of bracing coastal breezes and wild walks. See page 50

❾ **Charleston, SC** Charleston's historic core remains little changed since the slave trade shaped the state's economy, and Civil War started just offshore. See page 63

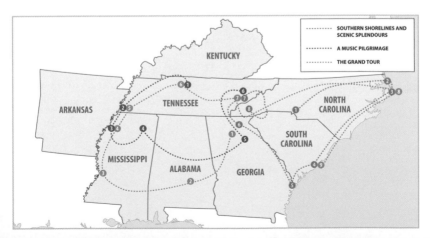

ATLANTA, GA

# Basics

# Getting there

If you're travelling to the USA from abroad, even if you're only planning to explore the southern states, the region is so vast that it makes a huge difference which airport you fly into. Only a handful of southern cities welcome non-stop flights from Europe, while many others can be easily reached if you transfer onto a domestic connection at any of those cities, or an international hub such as New York, Boston or Washington DC.

In general, ticket prices are highest from July to September, and around Easter, Thanksgiving and Christmas. Fares drop during the shoulder seasons – April to June, and October – and even more so in low season, from November to March (excluding Easter, Christmas and New Year). Prices depend more on when Americans want to head overseas than on the demand from foreign visitors. Flying at weekends usually costs significantly more; prices quoted below assume midweek travel and include taxes.

## Flights from the UK and Ireland

Four southern US cities are accessible via nonstop flights from the UK – Atlanta in Georgia, Charlotte and Durham in North Carolina, and Nashville in Tennessee, with services in every instance departing from London Heathrow. Both Atlanta and Charlotte also have nonstop connections with Dublin in Ireland. At each of these gateway cities, you can connect with onward flights to other southern destinations.

Nonstop flights from London to Atlanta or other southern cities take around nine hours, while following winds ensure that return flights take an hour or two less. Journey times from Ireland are very similar.

As for fares, Britain remains one of the best places in Europe to obtain flight bargains, though prices have risen in the wake of the Covid pandemic, and vary widely. In low or shoulder season, you should be able to find a return flight to southern destinations for around £600, while high-season rates can reach over £1000. These days the fares available on the airlines' own websites are often just as good as those you'll find on more general travel websites.

With an open-jaw ticket, you can fly into one city and out of another, though if you're renting a car remember that there's usually a high drop-off fee for returning a rental car in a different state than where you picked it up.

## Flights from Australia, New Zealand and South Africa

For passengers travelling from Australasia to the USA, the most expensive time to fly has traditionally been during the northern summer (mid-May to end Aug) and over the Christmas period (Dec to mid-Jan), with shoulder seasons covering March to mid-May and September, and the rest of the year counting as low season. Fares no longer vary as much across the year as they used to, however.

Instead, fares on the regular Air New Zealand, Qantas and United flights from eastern Australian cities to the southern states, which will entail a transfer in Los Angeles, the main US gateway airport, tend to start at around Aus$1700 in low season, or more like Aus$22500 in summer. Flying from Western Australia can add around Aus$300–400.

From New Zealand, the cost of flying from Auckland or Christchurch to the South, via LA or San Francisco, ranges from roughly NZ$1500–2000 across the year.

From South Africa, transatlantic flights from Cape Town or Johannesburg cost around 18,000R to East Coast destinations, depending on the time of year.

### AIRLINES

**Aer Lingus** Ⓦ aerlingus.com
**Air Canada** Ⓦ aircanada.com
**Air India** Ⓦ airindia.com
**Air New Zealand** Ⓦ airnewzealand.com
**American Airlines** Ⓦ aa.com
**British Airways** Ⓦ ba.com
**Delta Air Lines** Ⓦ delta.com

## A BETTER KIND OF TRAVEL

At Rough Guides we are passionately committed to travel. We believe it helps us understand the world we live in and the people we share it with – and of course tourism is vital to many developing economies. But the scale of modern tourism has also damaged some places irreparably, and climate change is accelerated by most forms of transport, especially flying. We encourage all our authors to consider the carbon footprint of the journeys they make in the course of researching our guides.

**Emirates** ⓦ emirates.com
**Frontier Airlines** ⓦ flyfrontier.com
**JAL (Japan Airlines)** ⓦ jal.com
**JetBlue** ⓦ jetblue.com
**KLM** ⓦ klm.com
**Qantas Airways** ⓦ qantas.com.au
**Singapore Airlines** ⓦ singaporeair.com
**South African Airways** ⓦ flysaa.com
**Southwest** ⓦ southwest.com
**United Airlines** ⓦ united.com
**Virgin Atlantic** ⓦ virgin-atlantic.com

### AGENTS AND OPERATORS

**Adventure World** Australia ⓦ adventureworld.com.au, New
Zealand ⓦ adventureworld.co.nz
**American Holidays** Ireland ⓦ americanholidays.com
**Wotif?** Australia ⓦ wotif.com

# Getting around

**Distances in the USA are so great that it's essential to plan in advance how you'll get from place to place. Amtrak provides a skeletal but often good bus links between the major cities. Even in rural areas, with advance planning, you can usually reach the main points of interest without too much trouble by using local buses and charter services.**

That said, travel between cities is almost always easier if you have a car. Many worthwhile and memorable US destinations lie far from the cities: even if a bus or train can take you to the general vicinity of a national park, for example, it would be of little use when it comes to enjoying the great outdoors.

## By rail

Travelling on the national Amtrak network (☎800 872 7245, ⓦ amtrak.com) is rarely the fastest way

to get around, though if you have the time it can be a pleasant and relaxing experience. The Amtrak system is far from comprehensive. Broadly speaking, routes in the South run north–south rather than east–west. Thus the line south from Washington DC to Florida calls at Charleston and Savannah, while another service connects Washington DC with New Orleans via Atlanta and Birmingham, and there's a train from Memphis down to New Orleans, but there's no link between Atlanta and Memphis to the west or Savannah to the east, and no trains at all serve Nashville. What's more, long-distance routes tend to be served by one or at most two trains per day, so in large areas there's always the possibility that the only train of the day passes through at three or four in the morning. Amtrak also runs the coordinated, but still limited, Thruway bus service which connects certain cities – on the North Carolina coast, for example – that their trains don't reach.

For any one specific journey, the train is usually more expensive than taking a Greyhound bus, or even a plane – the standard rail fare from Washington DC to Birmingham, for example, starts at around $121 one-way by booking online at least a month in advance – though special deals, especially in the off-peak seasons (Sept–May, excluding Christmas), can bring the cost of return trips down. Money-saving passes are also available.

Even with a pass, you should always reserve as far in advance as possible; all passengers must have seats, and some trains are booked solid. Sleeping compartments start at around $400 per night, including three full meals, in addition to your seat fare, for one or two people. However, even standard Amtrak quarters are surprisingly spacious compared to aeroplane seats, and there are additional dining cars and lounge cars.

## By bus

If you're travelling on your own and plan on making a lot of stops, buses are by far the cheapest way to get

---

## PACKAGES AND TOURS

Although independent travel is usually cheaper, countless flight and accommodation packages allow you to bypass all the organizational hassles. A typical package from the UK, might be a return flight with a rental car and a week's hotel accommodation in Atlanta, costing in the region of £1400 at peak periods.

Fly-drive deals, which give cut-rate car rental when a traveller buys a transatlantic ticket from an airline or tour operator, are always cheaper than renting on the spot, and give great value if you intend to do a lot of driving. They're readily available through general online booking agents such as Expedia, as well as through specific airlines. Several of the operators listed here also book accommodation for self-drive tours.

around. The main long-distance operator, Greyhound (☎800 231 2222, ⓦgreyhound.com, international customers without toll-free access can also call ☎214 849 8100 open 24/7), links all major cities and many towns. Out in the country, buses are fairly scarce, sometimes appearing only once a day, if at all. However, along the main highways, buses run around the clock to a full timetable, stopping only for meal breaks (almost always fast-food chains) and driver changeovers.

To avoid possible hassle, travellers should take care to sit as near to the driver as possible, and to arrive during daylight hours – many bus stations are in dodgy areas, at least in large cities. In many smaller places, the post office or a gas station doubles as the bus stop and ticket office. Reservations can be made in person at the station, online or on the toll-free number. Oddly they do not guarantee a seat, so it's wise to join the queue early – if a bus is full, you may have to wait for the next one, although Greyhound claims it will lay on an extra bus if more than ten people are left behind. For long hauls there are plenty of savings available – check the website's discounts page.

In addition, Trailways (☎877 908 9330, ⓦtrailways. com), and Megabus (☎877 462 6342; ⓦus.megabus. com), provide extensive and often cheaper coverage of the southern states.

## By plane

Despite the presence of good-value discount airlines – most notably Southwest and JetBlue – air travel is not a very practical or appealing way of getting around the South. Air fuel costs have been escalating even faster than gas costs, while airlines have cut routes, demanded customers pay for routine services and jacked up prices across the board. To get any kind of break on price, you'll have to reserve well ahead of time (at least three weeks), preferably not embark in the high season, and be firm enough in your plans to buy a "non-refundable" fare – which if changed can incur costs of $100 or more. Nonetheless, flying can still cost less than the train – though still more than the bus.

## By car

For many, the concept of cruising down the highway, preferably in a convertible with the radio blasting, is one of the main reasons to set out on a tour of the Deep South. The romantic images of countless road movies are not far from the truth, though you don't have to embark on a wild spree of drinking, drugs and sex to enjoy driving across America. Apart from anything else, a car makes it possible to choose your own itinerary and to explore the spectacular landscapes that may well provide your most enduring memories of the country.

Driving in the cities, on the other hand, is not exactly fun, and can be hair-raising. Yet in larger places a car is by far the most convenient way to make your way around, especially as public transport tends to be spotty outside the major cities. Many urban areas have grown up since cars were invented. As such, they sprawl for so many miles in all directions – Atlanta springs to mind – that your hotel may be fifteen or twenty miles from the sights you came to see, or perhaps simply on the other side of a freeway that can't be crossed on foot.

### Renting a car

To rent a car, you must have held your licence for at least one year. Drivers under 25 may encounter problems and have to pay higher than normal insurance premiums. Rental companies expect customers to have a credit card; if you don't, they may let you leave a cash deposit (at least $500), but don't count on it. All the major rental companies have outlets at the main airports but it can be cheaper to rent from a city branch. Reservations are handled centrally, so the best way to shop around is either online, or by calling their national toll-free numbers. Potential variations are endless; certain cities and states are consistently cheaper than others, while individual travellers may be eligible for corporate, frequent-flier or AAA discounts. In low season you may find a tiny car (a "subcompact") for as little as $185 per week, but a typical budget rate would be more like $35–40 per day or around $245 per week including taxes. You can get some good deals from strictly local operators, though it can be

---

### DRIVING FOR FOREIGNERS

Foreign nationals from English-speaking countries can drive in the USA using their full domestic driving licences (International Driving Permits are not always regarded as sufficient). Fly-drive deals are good value if you want to rent a car (see above), though you can save up to fifty percent simply by booking in advance with a major firm. If you choose not to pay until you arrive, be sure you take a written confirmation of the price with you. Remember that it's safer not to drive right after a long transatlantic flight – and that most standard rental cars have automatic transmissions.

risky as well. Make reading up on such inexpensive vendors part of your pre-trip planning.

Even between the major operators – who tend to charge $50–100 per week more than the local competition – there can be a big difference in the quality of cars. Industry leaders like Alamo, Hertz and Avis tend to have newer, lower-mileage cars and more reliable breakdown services. Always be sure to get unlimited mileage and remember that leaving the car in a different city from the one where you rented it can incur a drop-off charge of $200 or more. It normally costs quite a bit extra – on the scale of $25 per day – to rent a Sat-Nav or GPS system; if you're planning a long trip, it can work out cheaper simply to buy a new one.

**Small print and insurance**

When you rent a car, read the small print carefully for details on Collision Damage Waiver (CDW), sometimes called Liability Damage Waiver (LDW). This form of insurance specifically covers the car that you are driving yourself – you are in any case insured for damage to other vehicles. At $12–25 a day, it can add substantially to the total cost, but without it you're liable for every scratch to the car – even those that aren't your fault. Increasing numbers of states are requiring that this insurance be included in the weekly rental rate and are regulating the amounts charged to cut down on rental-car company profiteering. Some credit card companies offer automatic CDW coverage to customers using their card; contact your issuing company for details. Alternatively, European residents can cover themselves against such costs with a reasonably priced annual policy from Insurance4CarHire (Ⓦ insurance4carhire.com).

The American Automobile Association, or AAA (Ⓣ 800 222 4357, Ⓦ aaa.com), provides free maps and assistance to its members and to members of affiliated associations overseas, such as the British AA and RAC. If you break down in a rented car, call one of these services if you have towing coverage, or the emergency number pinned to the dashboard.

### CAR RENTAL AGENCIES

**Alamo** USA Ⓣ 844 354 6962, Ⓦ alamo.com

**Avis** USA Ⓣ 800 633 3469, Ⓦ avis.com
**Budget** USA Ⓣ 800 218 7992, Ⓦ budget.com
**Dollar** USA Ⓣ 800 800 5252, Ⓦ dollar.com
**Enterprise** USA Ⓣ 855 266 9565, Ⓦ enterprise.com
**Hertz** USA Ⓣ 800 654 3131, Ⓦ hertz.com
**Holiday Autos** USA Ⓣ 312 843 5783, Ⓦ holidayautos.com
**National** USA Ⓣ 844 382 6875, Ⓦ nationalcar.com
**Thrifty** USA & Canada Ⓣ 800 847 4389, Ⓦ thrifty.com

## Cycling

Cycling is another realistic mode of transport. An increasing number of big cities have cycle lanes and local buses equipped to carry bikes (strapped to the outside), while in country areas, roads have wide shoulders and fewer passing motorists. Unless you plan to cycle a lot and take your own bike, however, it's not especially cheap. Bikes can be rented for $20–50 per day, or at discounted weekly rates, from outlets that are usually found close to beaches, university campuses and good cycling areas. Local visitor centres have details.

The national non-profit Adventure Cycling Association, (Ⓣ 406 721 1776 or Ⓣ 800 755 2453, Ⓦ adventurecycling.org), publishes maps of various lengthy routes – including for example an Underground Railroad itinerary that heads north from Mobile, AL – detailing campgrounds, motels, restaurants, bike shops and places of interest. Many individual states issue their own cycling guides; contact the state tourist offices (see page 37). Before setting out on a long-distance cycling trip, you'll need a good-quality, multispeed bike, panniers, tools and spares, maps, padded shorts and a helmet (legally required in many states and localities). Plan a route that avoids interstate highways (on which cycling is unpleasant and usually illegal) and sticks to well-maintained, paved rural roads. Of problems you'll encounter, the main one is traffic: RVs, huge eighteen-wheelers and logging trucks can create intense backdraughts capable of pulling you out into the middle of the road.

Backroads Bicycle Tours (Ⓣ 800 462 2848, Ⓦ backroads.com), and the HI-AYH hostelling group (see page 28) arrange multi-day cycle tours, with

---

### HITCHHIKING

Hitchhiking in the United States is generally a bad idea, making you a potential victim both inside (you never know who you're travelling with) and outside the car, as the odd fatality may occur from hitchers getting a little too close to the highway lanes. At a minimum, in the many states where the practice is illegal, you can expect a steep fine from the police and, on occasion, an overnight stay in the local jail. The practice is still fairly common, however, in more remote rural areas with little or no public transport.

camping or stays in country inns; where appropriate we've also mentioned local firms that offer this.

Greyhound, Amtrak and major airlines will carry passengers' bikes – dismantled and packed into a box – for a small fee.

# Accommodation

**The cost of accommodation is significant for any traveller exploring the USA, especially in the cities, but wherever you travel, you're almost certain to find a good-quality, reasonably priced motel or hotel. If you're prepared to pay a little extra, wonderful historic hotels and lodges can offer truly memorable experiences.**

The prices we give in the Guide represent the cheapest double room in high season. Typical rates in motels and hotels start at $65 per night in rural areas, more like $90 in major cities, though substantial discounts are available at slack times. Unsurprisingly, the sky's the limit for luxury hotels, where exclusive suites can easily run into four figures. Many hotels will set up a third single bed for around $15–25 extra, reducing costs for three people sharing. For lone travellers, on the other hand, a "single room" is usually a double at a slightly reduced rate at best. A dorm bed in a hostel usually costs $25–40 per night, but standards of cleanliness and security can be low, and for groups of two or more the saving compared to a motel is often minimal. In certain parts of the USA, camping makes a cheap – and exhilarating – alternative. Alternative methods of finding a room online include via Ⓦairbnb.com and the free hosting site Ⓦcouchsurfing.org.

Wherever you stay, you'll be expected to pay in advance, at least for the first night and perhaps for further nights, too. Most hotels ask for a credit card imprint when you arrive, but many still accept cash for the actual payment. Reservations – essential in busy areas in summer – are held only until 6pm, unless you've said you'll be arriving late. Note that some cities – probably the ones you most want to visit – tack on a hotel tax that can raise the total tax for accommodation to as much as fifteen percent.

Note that as well as the local numbers we give in the Guide, many hotels have freephone numbers (found on their websites), which you can use within the USA.

## Hotels and motels

The term "hotels" refers to most accommodation in the Guide. Motels, or "motor hotels", tend to be found beside the main roads away from city centres, and are thus much more accessible to drivers. Budget hotels or motels can be pretty basic, but in general standards of comfort are uniform – each room comes with a double bed (often two), a TV, phone and usually a portable coffeemaker, plus an attached bathroom. You don't get a much better deal by paying, say, $100 instead of $75. Above $100 or so, the room and its fittings simply get bigger and include more amenities, and there may be a swimming pool and added amenities such as irons and ironing boards, or premium cable TV (HBO, Showtime, etc). It's very unusual these days to find a hotel or motel that doesn't offer wi-fi.

The least expensive properties tend to be family-run, independent "mom'n'pop" motels, but these are rarer nowadays, in the big urban areas at least. When you're driving along the main interstates there's a lot to be said for paying a few dollars more to stay in motels belonging to the national chains. These range from the ever-reliable and cheap Super 8 and Motel 6 (from $70) through to the mid-range Days Inn and La Quinta (from $85) up to the more commodious Holiday Inn Express and Marriott (from $100).

During off-peak periods, many motels and hotels struggle to fill their rooms, so it's worth bargaining to get a few dollars off the asking price, especially at independent establishments. Staying in the same place for more than one night may bring further reductions. In addition to using booking sites such as Ⓦbooking.com, it's worth looking out for discount coupons, especially in the free magazines distributed by local visitor centres and welcome centres near the borders between states. These can offer amazing value – but read the small print first.

Few budget hotels or motels bother to compete with the ubiquitous diners by offering full breakfasts,

---

### ACCOMMODATION PRICE CODES

Throughout the guide, accommodation is categorized according to a price code, which roughly corresponds to the following price ranges. Price categories reflect the cost of a double room, with breakfast, in peak season.

§ Up to $70
§§ $71–150
§§§ $151–250
§§§§ over $250

although most will provide free self-service coffee, pastries and if you are lucky, fruit or cereal, collectively referred to as "continental breakfast".

## B&Bs

Staying in a B&B is a popular, sometimes luxurious, alternative to conventional hotels. Some B&Bs consist of no more than a couple of furnished rooms in someone's home, and even the larger establishments tend to have fewer than ten rooms, sometimes without TV or phone, but often laden with potpourri, chintzy cushions and an assertively precious Victorian atmosphere. If this cosy, twee setting appeals to you, there's a range of choices throughout the region, but keep a few things in mind. For one, you may not be an anonymous guest, as you would in a chain hotel, but may be expected to chat with the host and other guests, especially during breakfast. Also, some B&Bs enforce curfews, and take a dim view of guests stumbling in after midnight after an evening's partying. The only way to know the policy for certain is to check each B&B's policy online – there's often a lengthy list of do's and don'ts.

The price you pay for a B&B – which varies from around $85 to $275 for a double room – always includes breakfast (sometimes a buffet on a sideboard, but more often a full-blown cooked meal). The crucial determining factor is whether each room has an en-suite bathroom; most B&Bs provide private bath facilities, although that can damage the authenticity of a fine old house. At the top end of the spectrum, the distinction between a "boutique hotel" and a "bed-and-breakfast inn" may amount to no more than that the B&B is owned by a private individual rather than a chain.

## Hostels

Hostel-type accommodation is not as plentiful in the USA as it is in Europe, but provision for backpackers and low-budget travellers does exist. Unless you're travelling alone, most hostels cost about the same as motels; stay in them only if you prefer their youthful ambience, energy and sociability. Many are not accessible on public transport, or convenient for sightseeing in the towns and cities, let alone in rural areas.

These days, most hostels are independent, with no affiliation to the HI-AYH (Hostelling-International-American Youth Hostels; ☎ 240 650 2100, http://hiusa.org) network. Many are no more than converted motels, where the "dorms" consist of a couple of sets of bunk beds in a musty room, which is also let out as a private unit on demand. Most

expect guests to bring sheets or sleeping bags. Rates range from $25 to about $45 for a dorm bed, and from $50–80 for a double room, with prices in the major cities at the higher end. Those few hostels that do belong to HI-AYH tend to impose curfews and limit daytime access hours, and segregate dormitories by sex.

# Food and drink

**There's so much more to eating in the USA than fast food, and the South especially can claim all sorts of wonderful treats and delicacies as its very own. Even the least promising roadside shack may turn out to surprise and delight you with its time-honoured family recipe for pit-roast barbecued pork, soft-shell crab, or, of course, Southern fried chicken.**

In the big cities, you can pretty much eat whatever you want, whenever you want, thanks to the ubiquity of restaurants, 24-hour diners, and bars and street carts selling food well into the night. Also, along all the highways and on virtually every town's main street, restaurants, fast-food joints and cafés try to outdo one another with bargains and special offers. Whatever you eat and wherever you eat it, service is usually prompt, friendly and attentive – thanks in large part to the institution of tipping. Waiters depend on tips for the bulk of their earnings; fifteen to twenty percent is the standard rate, and giving anything less is sure to be seen as an insult.

## Down-home southern cooking

The varied cuisine of the southern states ranges from creamy, cheese-topped grits (maize porridge), often served topped with shrimp, to highly calorific, irresistible soul food: fried chicken, smothered pork chops and the like, along with collard greens, sweet

---

### SIX OF THE BEST: CLASSIC SOUTHERN BARBECUE RESTAURANTS

**12 Bones Smokehouse** Asheville, NC see page 61
**Fox Bros. Bar-B-Q** Atlanta, GA see page 77
**Southern Soul Barbeque**, St Simons, GA see page 88
**Central BBQ** Memphis, TN see page 103
**Abe's** Clarksdale, MS see page 123
**McClard's Bar-B-Q** Little Rock, AR see page 132

---

**EATING PRICE CODES**

Throughout the guide, eating out listings are categorized according to a price code, which roughly corresponds to the following price ranges. Price categories reflect the cost of a two-course meal for one with alcohol.

$ Up to $12
$$ $13–25
$$$ $26–40
$$$$ over $40

---

potatoes, macaroni and all manner of tasty vegetables. Look out for the region's few remaining "round table" restaurants, where diners pay a flat fee of perhaps $20–25 to sit with strangers at shared tables and enjoy an all-you-can-eat spread of traditional Southern specialities; prime examples include Mrs Wilkes' in Savannah, GA (see page 86), and Walnut Hills in Vicksburg, MS (see page 126).

Barbecue is king in the South, and nowhere more so than in Memphis, TN, where every neighbourhood seems to have its own classic 'cue hut, offering anything from dry-rub ribs to sweetly smoky barbecue (generally, the more ramshackle the restaurant, the better the barbecue). That said, each state has its own smoked-meat variations and closely guarded recipes, helping to shape a deep source of regional pride and cultural identity. Seafood is also exemplary, from the wonderful Low Country Boils – fish stews served with rice, traditionally prepared on the sea islands of the Carolinas and Georgia – to succulent catfish, slathered in butter and "blackened" with spices.

## Other cuisines

It's also worth mentioning Cajun food, which originated in the bayous of Louisiana but is widely available throughout the South. This French-inspired country cooking evolved as a way to finish up leftovers, and uses a lot of pork, in such forms as chitlins (pork intestines), and the spicy sausages known as boudin and chaurice abound. Sausages are also prepared with

seafood such as crawfish, or even alligator. Creole cuisine, its urban cousin, stems originally from New Orleans, and often features on the same menus as Cajun dishes. The product of a number of cultures, it's characterized by spicy, fragrant jambalayas, po'boys and gumbos.

## Drink

The South has its fair share of boozing towns – in Savannah, for example, you are even permitted to drink alcohol on the streets – but almost anywhere you shouldn't have to search very hard for a comfortable place to drink. You need to be 21 years old to buy and consume alcohol in the USA, and it's likely you'll be asked for ID if you look under 30.

"Blue laws" – archaic statutes that restrict when, where and under what conditions alcohol can be purchased – are held by many states, and prohibit the sale of alcohol on Sundays; on the extreme end of the scale, some counties (popularly said to be "dry") don't allow any alcohol, ever. The famous whiskey and bourbon distilleries of Tennessee and Kentucky, including Jack Daniel's (see page 111), can be visited – though maddeningly, several are in dry counties, so they don't offer samples.

Note that if a bar is advertising a happy hour on "rail drinks" or "well drinks", these are cocktails made from the liquors and mixers the bar has to hand (as opposed to top-shelf, higher-quality brands).

### Beer

The most popular American beers may be the fizzy, insipid lagers from national brands, but there is no lack of alternatives. The national craze for microbreweries still hasn't waned, several decades in, and in strongholds like Asheville, North Carolina, the number of superb craft breweries continues to grow year after year.

Brewpubs can now be found in virtually every sizeable Southern city and college town. Almost all serve a wide range of good-value, hearty food to help soak up the drink. For more on craft beers, see Ⓦ craftbeer.com.

---

**VEGETARIAN AND VEGAN EATING**

In the big cities at least, being a vegetarian – or even a vegan – presents few problems. However, don't be too surprised in rural areas if you find yourself restricted to a diet of eggs, grilled-cheese sandwiches and limp salads. In the South, most soul food cafés offer great-value vegetable plates (four different veggies, including potatoes), but many dishes will be cooked with pork fat, so ask before tucking in. Similarly, baked beans, and the nutritious-sounding red beans and rice that originated in Louisiana, usually contain bits of diced pork.

# Festivals

In addition to the main public holidays – on July 4, Independence Day, the entire country takes time out to picnic, drink, salute the flag, and watch or participate in fireworks displays, marches, beauty pageants, eating contests and more, to commemorate the signing of the Declaration of Independence in 1776 – there is a diverse multitude of engaging local events in the USA: arts-and-crafts shows, county fairs, ethnic celebrations, music festivals, chilli cookoffs and countless others.

Certain festivities and events, such as Memphis in May or the Spoleto Festival in Charleston, are well worth planning your holiday around but obviously other people will have the same idea, so visiting during these times requires an extra amount of advance effort, not to mention money. Halloween (Oct 31) is also immensely popular. No longer just the domain of masked kids running around the streets banging on doors and demanding "trick or treat", in some bigger cities Halloween has evolved into a massive celebration, with colourful parades, huge block parties and wee-hours partying. Thanksgiving Day, on the fourth Thursday in November, is more sedate. Relatives return to the nest to share a meal (traditionally, roast turkey and stuffing, cranberry sauce, and all manner of delicious pies) and give thanks for family and friends. Ostensibly, the holiday recalls the first harvest of the Pilgrims in Massachusetts, though Thanksgiving was a national holiday before anyone thought to make that connection.

## Annual festivals and events

For further details of the festivals and events listed below, including more precise dates, see the relevant page of the Guide (where covered) or access their websites. The state tourist boards (see page 37) can provide more complete calendars for each area.

### JANUARY

**Ozark Mountain Music Festival** Eureka Springs, AR ⓦ ozarkmountainmusicfestival.com. See page 134.

### MARCH

**Cherry Blossom Festival** Macon, GA ⓦ cherryblossom.com. See page 80.

### APRIL

**Arkansas Folk Festival** Mountain View, AR ⓦ arkansas.com/ events.

**Juke Joint Festival** Clarksdale, MS ⓦ jukejointfestival.com. See page 122.

### MAY

**Kentucky Derby** Louisville, KY ⓦ kentuckyderby.com. See page 93.
**Leaf Festival** (also Oct) Black Mountain, NC ⓦ theleaf.org. See page 61.
**Memphis in May International Festival** Memphis, TN ⓦ memphisinmay.org. See page 104.
**Spoleto Festival** Charleston, SC (into June) ⓦ spoletousa.org. See page 67.

### JUNE

**CMA Music Festival** Nashville, TN ⓦ cmafest.com. See page 109.
**Elvis Festival** Tupelo, MS ⓦ tupeloelvisfestival.com. See page 125.

### AUGUST

**Elvis Week** (Anniversary of Elvis's death) Memphis, TN ⓦ graceland.com. See page 104.
**Mountain Dance and Folk Festival** Asheville, NC ⓦ folkheritage.org.
**Sunflower River Blues & Gospel Festival** Clarksdale, MS ⓦ sunflowerfest.org. See page 122.

### SEPTEMBER

**Mississippi Delta Blues & Heritage Festival** Greenville, MS ⓦ deltabluesms.org. See page 122.
**Moja Arts Festival** Charleston, SC (into Oct) ⓦ mojafestival.com.

### OCTOBER

**Hot Springs Documentary Film Festival** Hot Springs, AR ⓦ hsdfi.org. See page 131.
**King Biscuit Blues Festival** Helena, AR ⓦ kingbiscuitfestival. com. See page 129.
**Leaf Festival** (also May) Black Mountain, NC ⓦ theleaf.org. See page 61.
**Wings Over Water Festival** Lake Muttamuskeet, NC ⓦ fws,gov/ mattamuskeet. See page 48.

### NOVEMBER

**Ozark Folk Festival** Eureka Springs, AR ⓦ ozarkfolkfestival.com. See page 134.

# The outdoors

Coated by dense forests, cut by deep canyons, capped by great mountains and lapped by the Atlantic, the South is blessed with some fabulous backcountry and wilderness areas. It may not boast the most untrammelled wilderness in the nation, but the South has its far share of open space, notably along the Appalachian Trail, which winds south to the southern Appalachians in Georgia, and in the Great Smoky Mountains National Park. On the downside, be warned that in many coastal areas, the shoreline can be disappointingly hard to access, with a high proportion under private ownership.

---

### INFORMATION ON NATIONAL PARKS

The Park Service website, Ⓦ nps.gov, details the main attractions of the national parks, plus opening hours, the best times to visit, admission fees, hiking trails and visitor facilities.

---

## National parks and monuments

The National Park Service administers both national parks and national monuments. Its rangers do a superb job of providing information and advice to visitors, maintaining trails and organizing such activities as free guided hikes and campfire talks.

In principle, a national park preserves an area of outstanding natural beauty, encompassing a wide range of terrain and prime examples of particular landforms and wildlife, while a national monument is usually much smaller, focusing perhaps on just one archaeological site or geological phenomenon. Altogether, the national park system comprises around four hundred units, including national seashores, lakeshores, battlefields and other historic sites.

While national parks tend to be perfect places to hike – almost all have extensive trail networks – they're far too large to tour entirely on foot. Even in those rare cases where you can use public transport to reach a park, you'll almost certainly need some sort of vehicle to explore it once you're there.

Most parks and monuments charge admission fees, ranging from $5 to $25, which cover a vehicle and all its occupants for up to a week. For anyone on a touring vacation, it may well make more sense to buy the Inter-agency Annual Pass, also known as the "America the Beautiful Pass". Sold for $80 at all federal parks and monuments, or online at Ⓦ store. usgs.gov, this grants unrestricted access for a year to the bearer, and any accompanying passengers in the same vehicle, to all national parks and monuments, as well as sites managed by such agencies as the US Fish and Wildlife Service, the Forest Service and the BLM (Bureau of Land Management). It does not, however, cover or reduce additional fees like charges for camping in official park campgrounds, or permits for backcountry hiking or rafting.

Two further passes, obtainable at any park or online, grant free access for life to all national parks and monuments, again to the holder and any accompanying passengers, and also provide a fifty-percent discount on camping fees. The Senior Pass is available to any US citizen or permanent resident aged 62 or older for a one-time fee of $90 ($10 of which is a processing fee), while the Access Pass is issued free to blind or permanently disabled US citizens or permanent residents, with a $10 processing fee. While hotel-style lodges are found only in major parks, every park or monument tends to have at least one well-organized campground. Often, a cluster of motels can be found not far outside the park boundaries, as for example in Gatlinburg and Pigeon Forge, TN. With appropriate permits – subject to restrictions in popular parks – backpackers can also usually camp in the backcountry (a general term for areas inaccessible by road).

## Other public lands

National parks and monuments are often surrounded by tracts of national forest – also federally administered but much less protected. These too usually hold appealing rural campgrounds but, in the words of the slogan, each is a "Land Of Many Uses", and usually allows logging and other land-based industry (thankfully, more likely to be ski resorts than strip mines).

Other government departments administer wildlife refuges, national scenic rivers, recreation areas and the like. The Bureau of Land Management (BLM) has the largest holdings of all, including some enticingly out-of-the-way reaches. Environmentalist groups engage in endless running battles with developers, ranchers and the extracting industries over uses – or alleged misuses – of federal lands.

While state parks and state monuments, administered by individual states, preserve sites of more limited, local significance, many are explicitly intended for recreational use, and thus hold better campgrounds than their federal equivalents.

## Camping and backpacking

The ideal way to see the great outdoors – especially if you're on a low budget – is to tour by car and camp in state and federal campgrounds. Typical public campgrounds range in price from free (usually when there's no water available, which may be seasonal) to around $39 per night. Fees at the generally less scenic commercial campgrounds – abundant near major towns, and often resembling open-air hotels, complete with shops and restaurants – are more like $25–50. If you're camping in high season, either reserve in advance or avoid the most popular areas.

Backcountry camping in the national parks is usually free, by permit only. Before you set off on anything more than a half-day hike, and whenever you're headed for anywhere at all isolated, be sure to inform a ranger of your plans, and ask about weather conditions and specific local tips. Carry sufficient food and drink to cover emergencies, as well as all the necessary equipment and maps. Check whether fires are permitted; even if they are, try to use a camp stove in preference to local materials. In wilderness areas, try to camp on previously used sites. Where there are no toilets, bury human waste at least six inches into the ground and 100ft from the nearest water supply and campground.

### Health issues

Backpackers should never drink from rivers and streams; you never know what acts people – or animals – have performed further upstream. Giardia – a water-borne bacteria that causes an intestinal disease characterized by chronic diarrhoea, abdominal cramps, fatigue and weight loss – is a serious problem. Water that doesn't come from a tap should be boiled for at least five minutes or cleansed with an iodine-based purifier or a giardia-rated filter.

Hiking at lower elevations should present few problems, though near water mosquitoes can drive you crazy; Avon Skin-so-Soft or anything containing DEET are fairly reliable repellents. Ticks – tiny beetles that plunge their heads into your skin and swell up – are another hazard. They sometimes leave their heads inside, causing blood clots or infections, so get advice from a ranger if you've been bitten. One species of tick causes Lyme Disease, a serious condition that can even affect the brain. Nightly inspections of your skin are strongly recommended.

Beware, too, of poison oak, which usually grows among oak trees. Its leaves come in groups of three (the middle one on a short stem) and are distinguished by prominent veins and shiny surfaces. If you come into contact with it, wash your skin (with soap and cold water) and clothes as soon as possible – and don't scratch. In serious cases, hospital emergency rooms can give antihistamine or adrenaline shots. A comparable curse is poison ivy, found throughout the country. For both plants, remember the sage advice, "Leaves of three, let it be".

### Wildlife

Watch out for bears, deer, snakes and other animals in the backcountry, and consider the effect your presence can have on their environment.

Other than in a national park, you're highly unlikely to encounter a bear; Great Smoky Mountains National Park, on the other hand, is home to an estimated 1500 black bears. Even there, it's rare to stumble across one in the wilderness. If you do, don't run, just back away slowly. Most fundamentally, it will be after your food, which should be stored in airtight containers when camping. Ideally, hang both food and garbage from a high but slender branch some distance from your camp. Never attempt to feed bears, and never get between a mother and her young. Young animals are cute; their irate mothers are not.

# Travel essentials

## Costs

When it comes to estimating your travelling expenses, much depends on where you choose to go. A road trip around the backroads of the Deep South won't cost you much in accommodation, dining or souvenir-buying, although the amount spent on gas will add up – this varies from state to state, but at the time of writing the average price was between $3 and $3.50 per gallon.

By contrast, getting around a city such as Atlanta will be relatively cheap, but you'll pay much more for your hotel, meals, sightseeing and shopping. Most items you buy will be subject to some form of state – not federal – sales tax, anywhere from four percent (in Alabama) up to seven percent (in Tennessee and Mississippi). In addition, varying from state to state, some counties and cities may add on another point or two to that rate.

Unless you're camping or staying in a hostel, accommodation will be your greatest expense. A detailed breakdown is given in the Accommodation section, but you can reckon on at least $50–80 per day, based on sharing, and potentially double that if travelling solo. Unlike accommodation, prices for good food don't automatically take a bite out of your wallet, and you can indulge anywhere from the lowliest (but still scrumptious) barbecue shack to the choicest restaurant helmed by a celebrity chef. You can get by on as little as $25 a day, but it's more realistic to aim for something like $50.

Where it exists, and where it is useful (which tends to be only in the larger cities), public transport is usually affordable, with many cities offering good-value travel passes. Renting a car, at $175–250 per week, is a far more efficient way to explore the broader part of the country, and, for a group of two or more, it could well work out cheaper. Drivers staying in larger hotels in the cities should factor in the increasing trend towards charging even for self-parking; this daily fee may well be just a few dollars less than that for valet parking.

For attractions in the Guide, prices are quoted for adults, with children's rates listed if they are significantly lower or when the attraction is aimed primarily at youngsters; at some spots, kids get in for half-price, or for free if they're under six.

### Tipping

In the USA, waiters earn most of their income from tips, and not leaving a fair amount is seen as an insult. Waiting staff expect tips of at least fifteen percent, and up to twenty percent for very good service. When sitting at a bar, you should leave at least a dollar per round for the barkeeper; more if the round is more than two drinks. Hotel porters and bellhops should receive at least $2 per piece of luggage, more if it has been lugged up several flights of stairs. About fifteen percent should be added to taxi fares, rounded up to the nearest 50¢ or dollar.

## Crime and personal safety

No one could pretend that America is crime-free, although away from the urban centres crime is often remarkably low. Even the lawless reputations of certain cities are far in excess of the truth and most parts of such places, by day at least, are safe; at night, however, some areas are completely off-limits. All the major tourist areas and the main nightlife zones in cities are invariably brightly lit and well policed. So long as you plan carefully and take good care of your possessions, you should, generally speaking, have few problems.

### Car crime

Crimes committed against tourists driving rented cars aren't as common as they once were, but it still pays to be cautious. In major urban areas, any car you rent should have nothing on it – such as a particular licence plate – that makes it easy to spot as a rental car. When driving, under no circumstances should you stop in any unlit or seemingly deserted urban area – and especially not if someone is waving you down and suggesting that there is something wrong with your car. Similarly, if you are accidentally rammed by the driver behind you, do not stop immediately, but proceed on to the nearest well-lit, busy area and call ☎911 for assistance. Hide any valuables out of sight, preferably locked in the trunk or in the glove compartment.

## Electricity

Electricity runs on 110V AC. All plugs are two-pronged and rather insubstantial. Some travel plug adapters don't fit American sockets.

## Entry requirements

At the time of writing, the citizens of several countries were not permitted to enter the US, due to measures to limit the spread of Covid-19. The situation may remain subject to specific restrictions for some time to come, and testing or proof of a negative Covid-19 test may be required, even after the border has reopened. For the latest information, visit ⓦtravel.state.gov.

Temporary restrictions aside, citizens of 35 countries – including the UK, Ireland, Australia, New Zealand and most Western European countries – can enter under the Visa Waiver Program if visiting the United States for a period of less than ninety days. To obtain authorization, you must apply online for ESTA (Electronic System for Travel Authorization) approval before setting off. This is a straightforward process – simply go to the ESTA website (ⓦesta.cbp.dhs.gov), fill in your info and wait a very short while (sometimes just minutes, but it's best to leave at least 72hr before travelling to make sure) for them to provide you with an authorization number. You will not generally be asked to produce that number at your port of entry,

### MARIJUANA AND OTHER DRUGS

Over recent years, several US states have legalized the use of marijuana for recreational purposes, and pot, as it is commonly referred to in America, is now on sale at licensed shops in those regions. None of the southern states, however, have so far followed suit, though Alabama, Mississippi and Arkansas allow the usage of medical marijuana with a licence. Note that in states where pot is still illegal, you can be prosecuted even if you have bought it legally elsewhere, so it's wise not to take it across state lines in such cases. Also note that all other recreational drugs remain illegal at both state and federal level, so even simple possession can get you into serious trouble.

but it is as well to keep a copy just in case, especially in times of high-security alerts – you will be denied entry if you don't have one. This ESTA authorization is valid for up to two years (or until your passport expires, whichever comes first) and costs $14, payable by credit card when applying. When you arrive at your port of entry you will be asked to confirm that your trip has an end date, that you have an onward ticket and that you have adequate funds to cover your stay. The customs official may also ask you for your address while in the USA; the hotel you are staying at on your first night will suffice. Each traveller must also undergo the US-VISIT process at immigration, where both index fingers are digitally scanned and a digital head shot is also taken for file.

Prospective visitors from parts of the world not mentioned above require a valid passport and a non-immigrant visitor's visa for a maximum ninety-day stay. How you'll obtain a visa depends on what country you're in and your status when you apply; check ⓦ travel.state.gov. Whatever your nationality, visas are not issued to convicted felons and anybody who owns up to being a communist, fascist, drug dealer or guilty of genocide (fair enough, perhaps). On arrival, the date stamped on your passport is the latest you're legally allowed to stay. The Department of Homeland Security (DHS) has toughened its stance on anyone violating this rule, so even overstaying by a few days can result in a protracted interrogation from officials. Overstaying may also cause you to be turned away next time you try to enter the USA. To get an extension before your time is up, apply at the nearest Department of Homeland Security office, whose address will be under the Federal Government Offices listings at the front of the phone book. INS officials will assume that you're working in the USA illegally, and it's up to you to convince them otherwise by providing evidence of ample finances. If you can, bring along an upstanding American citizen to vouch for you. You'll also have to explain why you didn't plan for the extra time initially.

## FOREIGN EMBASSIES IN THE USA

**Australia** 1601 Massachusetts Ave NW, Washington DC 20036, ☏ 202 797 3000, ⓦ usa.embassy.gov.au
**Canada** 501 Pennsylvania Ave NW, Washington DC 20001, ☏ 202 682 1740, ⓦ international.gc.ca
**Ireland** 2234 Massachusetts Ave NW, Washington DC 20008, ☏ 202 462 3939, ⓦ dfa.ie/irish-embassy/usa
**New Zealand** 37 Observatory Circle NW, Washington DC 20008, ☏ 202 328 4800, ⓦ mfat.govt.nz
**South Africa** 3051 Massachusetts Ave NW, Washington DC 20008, ☏ 202 232 4400, ⓦ saembassy.org
**UK** 3100 Massachusetts Ave NW, Washington DC 20008, ☏ 202 588 6500, ⓦ ukinusa.fco.gov.uk

# Health

If you have a serious accident while in the USA, emergency medical services will get to you quickly and charge you later. For emergencies or ambulances, dial ☏ 911, the nationwide emergency number.

Should you need to see a doctor, you can search online or ask at the reception of your accommodation. A typical basic consultation fee would be $150–200, payable in advance. Tests, X-rays etc cost much more. Medications aren't cheap either – keep all your receipts for later claims on your insurance policy.

Foreign visitors should bear in mind that many pills available over the counter at home – most codeine-based painkillers, for example – require a prescription in the USA. Local brand names can be confusing; ask for advice at the pharmacy in any drugstore.

In general, inoculations aren't required for entry to the USA.

## Covid-19

The global Covid-19 pandemic impacted the US from early 2020 onwards, and by March 2022, it has claimed the lives of almost one million Americans, the highest number in the world by some margin, and a total that was still climbing at time of writing. More positively, the US's vaccination programme to protect citizens from future infections was well underway, with 200 million vaccine shots given before President Biden's 100th day in office, doubling his original pledge.

Visitors should inform themselves as to what health precautions are necessary at both federal and state level, in particular with regards to mask-wearing and social distancing.

## MEDICAL RESOURCES FOR TRAVELLERS

**CDC** ⓦ cdc.gov/travel. Official US government travel health site.
**International Society for Travel Medicine** ⓦ istm.org. Full listing of travel health clinics.

# Insurance

In view of the high cost of medical care in the USA, all travellers visiting from overseas should be sure to buy some form of travel insurance. American and Canadian citizens should check whether they are already covered – some homeowners' or renters' policies are valid on holiday, and credit cards such as American Express often include some medical or other insurance, while most Canadians are covered for medical mishaps overseas by their provincial health plans. If you only need trip cancellation/interruption coverage (to supplement your existing plan), this is generally available at a cost of about six percent of the trip value.

## ROUGH GUIDES TRAVEL INSURANCE

Rough Guides has teamed up with WorldNomads.com to offer great travel insurance deals. Policies are available to residents of over 150 countries, with cover for a wide range of adventure sports, 24hr emergency assistance, high levels of medical and evacuation cover and a stream of travel safety information. Roughguides.com users can take advantage of their policies online 24/7, from anywhere in the world – even if you're already travelling. And since plans often change when you're on the road, you can extend your policy and even claim online. Roughguides.com users who buy travel insurance with WorldNomads.com can also leave a positive footprint and donate to a community development project. For more information go to ⓦroughguides.com/travel-insurance.

## Internet

Almost all hotels and many coffeeshops and restaurants offer free wi-fi for guests, though some upmarket hotels charge for access. State and local visitor centres often offer free wi-fi access too. As a result, cybercafés, where you can use a terminal in the establishment for around $5–10 an hour, are increasingly uncommon. Nearly all public libraries provide free internet access, but often there's a wait and machine time is limited.

## LGBTQ+ travellers

The LGBTQ+ scene in America is huge, albeit heavily concentrated in the major cities. LGBTQ+ public officials and police officers are no longer a novelty, and resources, facilities and organizations are endless.

Most major cities have a predominantly LGBTQ+ area and we've tried to give an overview of local resources, bars and clubs in each large urban area. In the rural heartland of the South, however, life can look more like the Fifties – homosexuals are still oppressed and commonly reviled.

National publications are available from any good bookstore. Bob Damron in San Francisco (ⓦdamron.com) produces the best and sells them at a discount online. These include the Men's Travel Guide, a pocket-sized yearbook listing hotels, bars, clubs and resources for gay men; the Women's Traveller, which provides similar listings for lesbians; the Damron City Guide, which details lodging and entertainment in major cities; and Damron Accommodations, with 1000 accommodation listings for LGBTQ travellers worldwide.

*Gayellow Pages* in New York (ⓦgayellowpages.com) publishes a useful directory of businesses in the USA and Canada, available online in PDF form.

Finally, the International Gay & Lesbian Travel Association in Fort Lauderdale, FL (☎954 776 2626, ⓦiglta.org), is a comprehensive, invaluable source for LGBTQ travellers.

## Mail

Post offices are usually open Monday to Friday from 8.30am to 5.30pm, and Saturday from 9am to 12.30pm, and there are blue mailboxes on many street corners. At time of publication, first-class mail within the USA costs 55¢ for a letter weighing up to 28 grams (an ounce), $1.20 for the rest of the world. Airmail between the USA and Europe may take a week.

In the USA, the last line of the address includes the city or town and an abbreviation denoting the state ("GA" for Georgia; "TN" for Tennessee, for example). The last line also includes a five-digit number – the zip code – denoting the local post office. It is very important to include this, though the additional four digits that you will sometimes see appended are not essential. You can check zip codes on the US Postal Service website, at wusps.com.

Rules on sending parcels are very rigid: packages must be in special containers bought from post offices and sealed according to their instructions, which are given at the start of the Yellow Pages. To send anything out of the country, you'll need a green customs declaration form, available from a post office.

## Maps

The free road maps distributed by each state through its tourist offices and welcome centres are usually fine for general driving and route planning.

Rand McNally produces maps for each state, bound together in the Rand McNally Road Atlas, and you're apt to find even cheaper state and regional maps at practically any gas station along the major highways for around $3–7. Britain's best source for maps is Stanfords, at 7 Mercer Walk, London WC2H 9FA (☎020 7836 1321, ⓦstanfords.co.uk), and 29 Corn St, Bristol BS1 1HT (☎0117 929 9966); it also has a mail-order service.

The American Automobile Association, or AAA ("Triple A"; ☎800 222 4357, ⓦaaa.com) provides free maps and assistance to its members, as well as to British members of the AA and RAC. Call the main

## OPENING HOURS AND PUBLIC HOLIDAYS

The traditional summer holiday period runs between the weekends of Memorial Day, the last Monday in May, and Labor Day, the first Monday in September. Many parks, attractions and visitor centres operate longer hours or only open during this period and we denote such cases as "summer" throughout the Guide. Otherwise, specific months of opening are given.

Government offices (including post offices) and banks will be closed on the following national public holidays:

**Jan 1** New Year's Day
**Third Mon in Jan** Martin Luther King, Jr.'s birthday
**Third Mon in Feb** Presidents' Day
**Last Mon in May** Memorial Day
**July 4** Independence Day
**First Mon in Sept** Labor Day
**Second Mon in Oct** Columbus Day
**Nov 11** Veterans' Day
**Fourth Thurs in Nov** Thanksgiving Day
**Dec 25** Christmas Day

number to get the location of a branch near you; bring your membership card or at least a copy of your membership number.

Highly detailed wilderness and topographical maps are available for parklands and forests all over the south through the Forest Service (W fs.usda.gov). For a detailed, large-format map book for recreational travel in in the Southern Appalachians, contact Benchmark Maps (W benchmarkmaps.com), whose elegantly designed depictions are easy to follow and make even the most remote dirt roads look appealing.

## Money

The US dollar comes in $1, $2, $5, $10, $20, $50 and $100 denominations. One dollar comprises one hundred cents, made up of combinations of one-cent pennies, five-cent nickels, ten-cent dimes and 25-cent quarters. You can check current exchange rates at W x-rates. com; at the time of writing one pound sterling will buy around $1.35 and a euro around $1.13.

Bank hours generally run from 9am to 5pm Monday to Thursday, and until 6pm on Friday; the big bank names are Wells Fargo, US Bank and Bank of America. With an ATM card, you'll be able to withdraw cash just about anywhere, though you'll be charged $2–5 per transaction for using a different bank's network. Foreign cash-dispensing cards linked to international networks, such as Plus or Cirrus, are also widely accepted – ask your home bank or credit card company which branches you can use. To find the location of the nearest ATM, call AmEx (☎ 800 227 4669); Cirrus (☎ 800 424 7787); Accel/The Exchange (☎ 800 519 8883); or Plus (☎ 800 843 7587).

Credit and debit cards are by far the most widely accepted form of payment at major hotels, restaurants and retailers, even though a few smaller merchants still do not accept them. You'll be asked to show some plastic when renting a car, bike or other such item, or to start a "tab" at hotels for incidental charges; in any case, you can always pay the bill in cash when you return the item or check out of your room.

## Phones

The USA currently has well over one hundred area codes – three-digit numbers that must precede the seven-figure number if you're calling from abroad (following the 001 international access code) or from a different area code, in which case you prefix the ten digits with a 1. It can get confusing, especially as certain cities have several different area codes within their boundaries; for clarity, in this Guide, we've included the local area codes in all telephone numbers. Note that some cities require you to dial all ten digits, even when calling within the same code. Numbers that start with the digits 800 – or increasingly commonly 888, 877 and 866 – are toll-free, but these can only be called from within the USA itself; most hotels and many companies have a toll-free number that can easily be found on their websites.

Unless you can organize to do all your calling online via Skype (W skype.com), the cheapest way to make long-distance and international calls is to buy a prepaid phonecard, commonly found in newsagents or grocery stores, especially in urban areas. These are cheaper than the similar cards issued by the big phone companies, such as AT&T, that are usually on sale in pharmacy outlets and chain stores, and will

## CALLING HOME FROM THE USA

For country codes not listed below, dial 0 for the operator, consult any phone directory or log onto ⓦcountrycallingcodes.com.
Australia 011 + 61 + area code minus its initial zero.
New Zealand 011 + 64 + area code minus its initial zero.
Republic of Ireland 011 + 353 + area code minus its initial zero.
South Africa 011 + 27 + area code.
UK 011 + 44 + area code minus its initial zero.

charge only a few cents per minute to call from the USA to most European and other western countries. Such cards can be used from any touchpad phone but there is usually a surcharge for using them from a payphone (which, in any case, are increasingly rare). You can also usually arrange with your local telecom provider to have a chargecard account with free phone access in the USA, so that any calls you make are billed to your home. This may be convenient, but it's more expensive than using prepaid cards.

If you are planning to bring your mobile phone (more often called a cell phone in America) from outside the USA, it will almost certainly work in the country, but it's worth checking with your service provider first: you will need a tri-band or quad-band phone that is enabled for international calls. Using your phone from home will probably incur hefty roaming charges for making calls and charge you extra for incoming calls, as the people calling you will be paying the usual rate. It's also likely to prove expensive if you use it to go directly online, as opposed to signing into local wi-fi access. Depending on the length of your stay, it might make sense to rent a phone or buy a compatible prepaid SIM card from

## STATE TOURISM INFORMATION

Alabama ☎800 252 2262, ⓦtourism. alabama.gov
Arkansas ☎800 628 8725, ⓦarkansas.com
Georgia ☎800 847 4842, ⓦexploregeorgia.org
Kentucky ☎800 225 8747, ⓦkentuckytourism.com
Mississippi ☎601 359 3449, ⓦvisitmississippi.org
North Carolina ☎800 847 4862, ⓦvisitnc.com
South Carolina ☎803 734 0124, ⓦdiscoversouthcarolina.com
Tennessee ☎615 741 2159, ⓦtnvacation.com

a US provider; check ⓦtriptel.com or ⓦtelestial.com. Alternatively, you could pick up an inexpensive pay-as-you-go phone from one of the major electrical shops.

## Senior travellers

Anyone aged over 62 (with appropriate ID) can enjoy a vast range of discounts in the USA. Both Amtrak and Greyhound offer (smallish) percentage reductions on fares to older passengers, and any US citizen or permanent resident aged 62 or over is entitled to free admission for life to all national parks, monuments and historic sites using a Senior Pass (issued for a one-time fee of $10 plus $80 at any such site). This free admission applies to all accompanying travellers in the same vehicle and also gives a fifty-percent reduction on park user fees, such as camping charges.

For discounts on accommodation, group tours and vehicle rental, US residents aged 50 or over should consider joining the AARP (American Association of Retired Persons; ☎888 687 2277, ⓦaarp.org) for an annual $16 fee, or a multi-year deal; the website also offers lots of good travel tips and features. Road Scholar (☎800 454 5768, ⓦroadscholar.org) runs an extensive network of educational and activity programmes for people over 60 throughout the South, at prices in line with those of commercial tours.

## Shopping

Not surprisingly, the South has some great shopping opportunities– from the luxury-lined blocks of Atlanta, or the boutiques of Charleston, to the local markets found in cities both big and small, offering everything from fruit and vegetables to handmade local crafts.

When buying clothing and accessories, inter-national visitors will need to convert their sizes into American equivalents (see box). For almost all purchases, state taxes will be applied (see page 32).

## Time

Although the continental US covers four time zones, only two apply in the South. Georgia, North and South Carolina, Tennessee, and eastern parts of Kentucky are within the Eastern zone, which is five hours behind Greenwich Mean Time (GMT), so 3pm London time is 10am in Atlanta. Alabama, Arkansas, Mississippi and western parts of Kentucky lie in the Central zone, which is an hour behind the east (10am in New York is 9am in Little Rock). The USA puts its clocks forward one hour to daylight saving time on the second Sunday in March and turns them back on the first Sunday in November.

## Tourist information

Each state has its own tourist office (see box). These offer prospective visitors a colossal range of free maps, leaflets and brochures on attractions from overlooked wonders to the usual tourist traps. You can either contact the offices before you set off, or, as you travel around the country, look for the state-run "welcome centres", usually along main highways close to the state borders. In heavily visited states, these often have piles of discount coupons for cut-price accommodation and food. In addition, visitor centres in most towns and cities – often known as the "Convention and Visitors Bureau", or CVB, and listed throughout this Guide – provide details on the area, as do local Chambers of Commerce in almost any town of any size.

## Travelling with children

Children under 2 years old go free on domestic flights and for ten percent of the adult fare on international flights – though that doesn't mean they get a seat, let alone frequent-flier miles. Kids aged between 2 and 12 are usually entitled to half-price tickets. Discounts for train and bus travel are broadly similar. Car-rental companies usually provide kids' car seats – which are required by law for children under the age of 4 – for around $10–15 a day. You would, however, be advised to check, or bring your own; they are not always available. Recreational vehicles (RVs) are a particularly good option for families. Even the cheapest motel will offer inexpensive two-double bed rooms as a matter of course, which is a relief for non-US travellers used to paying a premium for a "family room", or having to pay for two rooms.

Virtually all tourist attractions offer reduced rates for kids. Most large cities have natural history museums or aquariums, and quite a few also have hands-on children's museums; in addition most state and national parks organize children's activities. All the national restaurant chains provide highchairs and special kids' menus; and the trend for more upmarket family-friendly restaurants to provide crayons with which to draw on paper tablecloths is still going strong.

## Travellers with disabilities

By international standards, the USA is exceptionally accommodating for travellers with mobility concerns or other physical disabilities. By law, all public buildings, including hotels and restaurants, must be wheelchair accessible and provide suitable toilet facilities. Most street corners have dropped curbs (less so in rural areas), and most public transport systems include subway stations with elevators and buses that "kneel" to let passengers in wheelchairs board.

### Getting around

The Americans with Disabilities Act (1990) obliges all air carriers to make the majority of their services accessible to travellers with disabilities, and airlines will usually let attendants of more severely disabled people accompany them at no extra charge.

Almost every Amtrak train includes one or more coaches with accommodation for handicapped passengers. Guide dogs travel free and may accompany blind, deaf or disabled passengers. Be sure to give 24 hours' notice. Hearing-impaired passengers can get information on ☎ 800 523 6590 (TTY/TDD).

Greyhound, however, has its challenges. Buses are not equipped with lifts for wheelchairs, though staff will assist with boarding (intercity carriers are required by law to do this), and the "Helping Hand" policy offers two-for-the-price-of-one tickets to passengers unable to travel alone (carry a doctor's certificate). The American Public Transportation Association, in Washington DC (☎ 202 496 4800, ⓦ apta.com), provides information about the accessibility of public transport in cities.

The American Automobile Association (contact ⓦ aaa.com for phone number access for each state) produces the *Handicapped Driver's Mobility Guide*, while the larger car-rental companies provide cars with hand controls at no extra charge, though only on their full-sized (ie most expensive) models; reserve well in advance.

### Resources

Most state tourism offices provide information for disabled travellers (see page 37). In addition, SATH, the Society for Accessible Travel and Hospitality (☎ 212 447 7284, ⓦ sath.org), is a not-for-profit travel-industry group of travel agents, tour operators, hotel and airline management, and people with disabilities. They pass on any enquiry to the appropriate member, though you should allow plenty of time for a response. Mobility International USA (☎ 541 343 1284, ⓦ miusa.org), offers travel tips and operates exchange programmes for disabled people; it also serves as a national information centre on disability.

The "America the Beautiful Access Pass", issued without charge to permanently disabled or blind US citizens, gives free lifetime admission to all national parks. It can only be obtained in person at a federal area where an entrance fee is charged; you'll have to show proof of permanent disability, or that you are eligible for receiving benefits under federal law.

## CLOTHING AND SHOE SIZES

### WOMEN'S CLOTHING

| American | 4 | 6 | 8 | 10 | 12 | 14 | 16 | 18 | | |
|---|---|---|---|---|---|---|---|---|---|---|
| British | 6 | 8 | 10 | 12 | 14 | 16 | 18 | 20 | | |
| Continental | 34 | 36 | 38 | 40 | 42 | 44 | 46 | 48 | | |

### WOMEN'S SHOES

| American | 5 | 6 | 7 | 8 | 9 | 10 | 11 | | | |
|---|---|---|---|---|---|---|---|---|---|---|
| British | 3 | 4 | 5 | 6 | 7 | 8 | 9 | | | |
| Continental | 36 | 37 | 38 | 39 | 40 | 41 | 42 | | | |

### MEN'S SHIRTS

| American | 14 | 15 | 15.5 | 16 | 16.5 | 17 | 17.5 | 18 | | |
|---|---|---|---|---|---|---|---|---|---|---|
| British | 14 | 15 | 15.5 | 16 | 16.5 | 17 | 17.5 | 18 | | |
| Continental | 36 | 38 | 39 | 41 | 42 | 43 | 44 | 45 | | |

### MEN'S SHOES

| American | 7 | 7.5 | 8 | 8.5 | 9 | 9.5 | 10 | 10.5 | 11 | 11.5 |
|---|---|---|---|---|---|---|---|---|---|---|
| British | 6 | 7 | 7.5 | 8 | 8.5 | 9 | 9.5 | 10 | 11 | 12 |
| Continental | 39 | 40 | 41 | 42 | 42.5 | 43 | 44 | 44 | 45 | 46 |

### MEN'S SUITS

| American | 34 | 36 | 38 | 40 | 42 | 44 | 46 | 48 | | |
|---|---|---|---|---|---|---|---|---|---|---|
| British | 34 | 36 | 38 | 40 | 42 | 44 | 46 | 48 | | |
| Continental | 44 | 46 | 48 | 50 | 52 | 54 | 56 | 58 | | |

## Women travellers

A woman travelling alone in America is not usually made to feel conspicuous, or liable to attract unwelcome attention. Cities can feel a lot safer than you might think, though particular care must be taken at night: walking through unlit, empty streets is never a good idea, and, if there's no bus service, take a taxi. Avoid travelling at night by public transport – deserted bus stations, if not actually threatening, will do little to make you feel secure. Hitchhiking is never a good idea in the USA. Similarly, you should never pick up anyone who's trying to hitchhike. If someone is waving you down on the road, ostensibly to get help with a broken-down vehicle, just drive on by or call the highway patrol to help them.

If you have been sexually assaulted the local sheriff's office will arrange for you to get help and counselling. The National Organization for Women (☎ 202 628 8669, ⓦ now.org) has branches listed in local phone directories and on its website and can provide information on rape crisis centres and counselling services.

## Working in the USA

Permission to work in the USA can only be granted by the Immigration and Naturalization Service in the USA itself. Contact your local embassy or consulate for advice on current regulations, but be warned that unless you have relatives or a prospective employer in the USA to sponsor you, your chances are at best slim. Students have the best chance of prolonging their stay, while a number of volunteer and work programmes allow you to experience the country less like a tourist and more like a resident.

### STUDY, VOLUNTEER AND WORK PROGRAMMES

**American Institute for Foreign Study** ⓦ aifs.com. Language study and cultural immersion, as well as au pair and Camp America programmes.

**BUNAC** (British Universities North America Club) ⓦ bunac.org. Working holidays in the USA for international students and young people.

**Camp America** ⓦ campamerica.co.uk. Well-known company that places young people as counsellors or support staff in US summer camps, for a minimum of nine weeks.

**Council on International Educational Exchange (CIEE)** ⓦ ciee.org. Leading NGO offering study programmes and volunteer projects around the world.

**Go Overseas** ⓦ gooverseas.com. Specializes in gap year programmes and internships around the world, including a good number of opportunities in the USA.

# The South

MEMPHIS, TN

# 1 | The South

It's impossible to travel through the southern states of North Carolina, South Carolina, Georgia, Kentucky, Tennessee, Alabama, Mississippi and Arkansas without experiencing constant reminders of the two epic historical clashes that have shaped the entire region: the Civil War, and the civil rights movement of the 1950s and 1960s. The legacy of the turbulent past lives on in its antebellum architecture and its still-charged historical sites. Nowhere does this heritage present itself more strongly, however, than in the spirited culture that defines the South and its people.

Major destinations include the elegant coastal cities of **Charleston** and **Savannah**, college towns **Athens** and **Chapel Hill**, and the historic Mississippi River ports of **Natchez** and **Vicksburg**. Highlights include the misty **Appalachian mountains** of Kentucky, Tennessee and North Carolina; the subtropical **beaches** and tranquil **barrier islands** along the Atlantic and Gulf coasts of Georgia and South Carolina; and the river road through the tiny, time-warped settlements of the flat **Mississippi Delta**.

The cradle of the Civil War and the birthplace of the civil rights movement, the South is home to countless landmarks vital in the history of the long march towards racial equality in the United States. None is more important than the **Martin Luther King, Jr. National Historic Site** in **Atlanta** where you can visit King's home, as well as the Ebenezer Baptist Church where he preached alongside his father and where his mother was assasinated six years after the great activist himself.

The history of the South is raw and divisive. But from its often painful past a rich musical heritage has sprung. The blues was born in **Mississippi**. The King of Rock and Roll ruled in **Memphis**. And you'll find the roots of country in Nashville at the **Country Music Hall of Fame**.

In July and August, the daily high **temperature** is mostly a very humid 90°F, and while almost every public building is air-conditioned, the heat can be debilitating. May and June are more bearable, and tend to see a lot of local festivals, while the fall colours in the mountains – just as beautiful and a lot less expensive and congested than New England – are at their headiest during October.

**Public transport** is not very convenient and in some areas it can be sparse or even non-existent. If you want to make the most of your trip to the South you'll need to **rent a car**, especially if you want to explore the backwaters (highlights include the **Mississippi Delta**, the **Ozarks**, the **Cape Hatteras National Seashore** and the **Blue Ridge Parkway**) and enjoy some of South's mountain routes or coastal drives.

---

## GREAT REGIONAL DRIVES

**Blue Ridge Parkway, NC and VA** Spanning more than four hundred miles, this spectacular mountain route links North Carolina with Virginia and takes in stunning vistas, wild-flower-studded hiking trails and Appalachian bluegrass shows.

**Cape Hatteras National Seashore, NC** Snake down this slender coastal barrier island and you'll be sandwiched between forty miles of ravishing beaches and saltwater marshes, with sunbathing opportunities galore.

**Natchez Trace Parkway, MS and TN** Stretching all the way from Natchez to Nashville, this verdant corridor offers a glimpse into road travel before gas stations and billboards, and intersects with some of Mississippi's most historic towns.

# Highlights

**❶ Cape Hatteras National Seashore, NC**
Snaking your way down this slender barrier
island, you're sandwiched between ravishing
beaches and saltwater marshes. See page 50

**❷ Martin Luther King, Jr. National Historic
Site, Atlanta, GA** Atlanta's historic "Sweet
Auburn" neighborhood is now a monument
to its greatest son, holding King's birth home
and the Baptist church where he and his father
preached. See page 72

**❸ Savannah, GA** With its impossibly romantic
garden squares, gorgeous architecture and
bustling old waterfront, this atmospheric town
also has a trendy cuisine scene. See page 81

**❹ Memphis, TN** Stretching languidly along the
Mississippi waterfront, this timeless city was the
launching pad for music legends from B.B. King
to Otis Redding and Al Green, as well, of course,
as Elvis himself. See page 96

**❺ Country Music Hall of Fame, Nashville,
TN** Nashville's state-of-the-art showcase
celebrates the glitz, glory and glamour of
country music in all its richness. See page 107

**❻ The Mississippi Delta, MS** The land where
the blues began is still imbued with haunting
echoes of the past, and nowhere more so than
Clarksdale. See page 121

**HIGHLIGHTS ARE MARKED ON THE MAP ON PAGE 44**

### Brief history

**1**

The British dominated the region from the seventeenth century, establishing successful agricultural colonies in the Carolinas and Georgia. Massive labour-intensive plantations sprang up, predominantly growing tobacco prior to independence, and then cotton. Eventually, the landowners turned to slavery as the most profitable source of labour. Millions of Africans were brought across the Atlantic, most arriving via the port of Charleston.

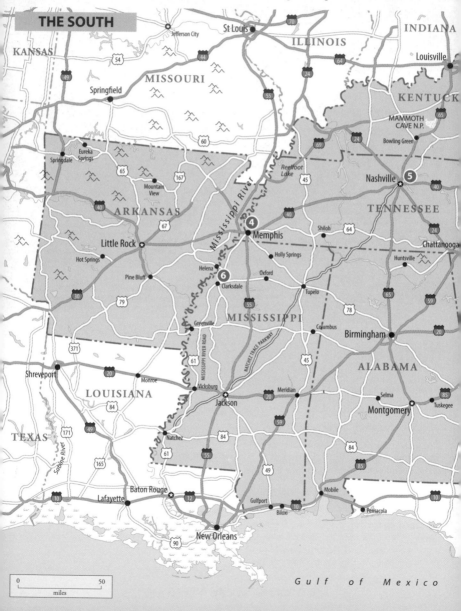

THE SOUTH

## Early nineteenth century

Although the South prospered until the middle of the nineteenth century, there was little incentive to diversify its economy. As a result, the Northern states began to surge ahead in both agriculture and industry; while the South grew the crops, Northern factories monopolized the more lucrative manufacturing of finished goods. So long as there were equal numbers of slave-owning and "free" states, the South continued to play a central role in national politics, and was able to resist **abolitionist** sentiment.

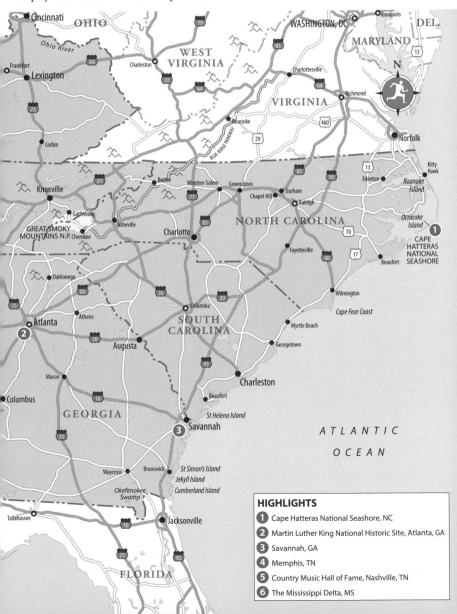

**HIGHLIGHTS**

1. Cape Hatteras National Seashore, NC
2. Martin Luther King National Historic Site, Atlanta, GA
3. Savannah, GA
4. Memphis, TN
5. Country Music Hall of Fame, Nashville, TN
6. The Mississippi Delta, MS

1

However, the more the United States fulfilled its supposed "Manifest Destiny" to spread across the continent, the more new states joined the Union for which plantation agriculture, and thus slavery, was not appropriate. Southern politicians and plantation owners accused the North of political and economic aggression, and felt that they were losing all say in the future of the nation. The election of **Abraham Lincoln**, a longtime critic of slavery, as president in 1860 brought the crisis to a head. South Carolina **seceded** from the Union that December, and ten more southern states swiftly followed. On February 18, 1861, Jefferson Davis was sworn in as president of the **Confederate States of America** – an event for which his vice president shockingly proclaimed that this was the first government in the history of the world "based upon this great physical and moral truth…that the Negro is not equal to the white man".

Civil War (1861–65)

During the resultant **Civil War**, the South was outgunned and ultimately overwhelmed by the vast resources of the North. The Confederates fired the first shots and scored the first victory in April 1861, when the Union garrison at Fort Sumter (outside Charleston) surrendered. The Union was on the military defensive until mid-1862, when its navy blockaded Georgia and the Carolinas and occupied key ports. Then Union forces in the west, under generals Grant and Sherman, swept through Tennessee, and by the end of 1863 the North had taken Vicksburg, the final Confederate-held port on the Mississippi, as well as the strategic mountain-locked town of Chattanooga on the Tennessee–Georgia border. Grant proceeded north to Virginia, while Sherman captured the transport nexus of Atlanta and began a bloody and ruthless march to the coast, burning everything in his way. With 258,000 men dead, the Confederacy's defeat was total, and General Robert E. Lee **surrendered** on April 9, 1865, at Appomattox in Virginia.

Reconstruction and Jim Crow

The war left the South in chaos. A quarter of the South's adult white male population had been killed, and two-thirds of Southern wealth destroyed. From controlling thirty percent of the nation's assets in 1860, the South was down to twelve percent in 1870, while the spur the war gave to industrialization meant that the North was booming. For a brief period of **Reconstruction**, when the South was occupied by Union troops, newly freed Southern blacks were able to vote, and black representatives were elected to both state and federal office. However, unrepentant former Confederates, spurred in part by allegations of profiteering by incoming Northern Republican "carpetbaggers", thwarted any potential for change, and by the end of the century the Southern states were firmly back under white Democratic control. As Reconstruction withered away, "**Jim Crow**" segregation laws were imposed, backed by the not-so-secret terror of the **Ku Klux Klan**, and poll taxes, literacy tests and property qualifications disenfranchised virtually all blacks. Many found themselves little better off as **sharecroppers** – in which virtually all they could earn from raising crops went to pay their landlords – than they had been as slaves, and there were mass migrations to cities like Memphis and Atlanta, as well as to the North.

School desegregation and the Civil Rights movement

Not until the landmark 1954 Supreme Court ruling in **Brown vs Topeka Board of Education** outlawed segregation in schools was there any sign that the federal authorities in Washington might concern themselves with inequities in the South. Even then, individual states proved extremely reluctant to effect the required changes. In the face of institutionalized white resistance, nonviolent black protestors coalesced to form the **Civil Rights movement**, and broke down segregation through a sustained programme of mass action. After tackling such issues as public transport – most famously in the Montgomery bus boycott and the Freedom Rides – and segregated dining facilities, with lunch-counter sit-ins reaching their apex in Greensboro, North

Carolina, the campaign eventually culminated in restoring full black voter registration – not without the loss of many protestors' lives. The Civil Rights movement is an ongoing one: in 2012, the **Black Lives Matter** movement started in response to the acquittal of George Zimmerman, who was on trial in Florida for the fatal shooting of African American teen Trayvon Martin.

Today, one of the most fulfilling itineraries through the Southern states is to trace the footsteps of **Martin Luther King, Jr.** from his birthplace in Atlanta through his church in Montgomery to the site of his assassination in Memphis.

# North Carolina

**NORTH CAROLINA**, the most industrialized of the Southern states, breaks down into three distinct areas – the coast, the Piedmont and the mountains. The **coast** promises stunning beaches, beautiful landscapes and a fascinating history – the world's first powered flight took place here. The inner coast consists largely of the less developed **Albemarle Peninsula**, with colonial **Edenton** nearby. The central **Piedmont** is less appealing, dominated by manufacturing cities and the academic institutions of the prestigious "Research Triangle": **Raleigh**, the state capital, is home to North Carolina State University; **Durham** has Duke; and the University of North Carolina is in trendy **Chapel Hill**. **Winston-Salem** combines tobacco culture and Moravian heritage, while the boomtown of **Charlotte** is distinguished by little but its downtown skyscrapers. In the **Appalachian Mountains**, alternative **Asheville** makes a hugely enjoyable stop along the spectacular **Blue Ridge Parkway**.

## The Albemarle-Pamlico Peninsula

The huge **Albemarle-Pamlico Peninsula**, which unfolds between the Albemarle Sound and Pamlico Sound, is less about big-name sights, and more about sleepy little towns with colonial history, remote plantations and wide swathes of rural farmland. This area is most rewarding for those who like to travel off the beaten path, with a much slower pace of life than elsewhere in North Carolina. The first stop is **Edenton**, a quiet bayside town that makes for a perfect base in discovering the coast.

### Edenton

**EDENTON**, set along the majestic Albemarle Sound waterfront, was established as North Carolina's first state capital in 1722 and was a major centre of unrest in the American Revolution. Nowadays, it's a nostalgically inviting small town, with some good B&Bs and restaurants. Strolling along its main road, **Broad Street**, lined with colonial facades and old-fashioned stores, brings you to the visitor centre.

Among other historic figures, Edenton was home to **Harriet Jacobs**, a runaway slave who hid for seven years in her grandmother's attic. In 1842, she finally escaped to the North through such ruses as disguising herself as a sailor, and was eventually reunited in Boston with the two children she had with a white man in Edenton. She wrote her autobiography as *Incidents in the Life of a Slave Girl*, one of the most famous published slave narratives of the nineteenth century.

**ACCOMMODATION AND EATING** **EDENTON**

**309 Bistro & Spirits** 309 S Broad St ⓦ 309bistro.com. Right in the heart of things, this gussied-up café with a cheerful striped awning is the regional hub for tangy martinis and New American food such as lobster rolls, burgers and grilled portobello sandwiches. $$

**Inner Banks Inn** 103 E Albemarle St ⓦ innerbanksinn.

com. Grand old inn with a variety of unique properties: a Victorian mansion, a tobacco packing house (dating from 1915), the nineteenth-century Tillie Bond Cottage that's great for families and the handsome, early-1800s Saterfield House. Other perks include complementary welcome drinks and snacks, lavish antiques, coal-burning fireplaces and the

1

farm-to-fork restaurant *The Table*. $$$

**Old Colony Smokehouse** 802 W Queen St ⓦ oldcolonysmokehouse.com. Line up at the market-style counter, from 11am on, order from an appetizing array

of freshly coal-smoked meats and homemade desserts, and then settle down on the patio to enjoy a true Southern feast. They only open for lunch, and close once each day's batch sells out. $$

## Somerset Place State Historic Site

Creswell, 28 miles southeast of Edenton on US-64 • Tues–Sat 9am–5pm • Free • ⓦ nchistoricsites.nc.gov

A vivid picture of slave life is painted by **Somerset Place State Historic Site**. The museum here tells the history of the plantation, from its origins in the 1780s to its growth by 1865 into a 100,000-acre enterprise, and its demise after the Civil War. Exhibits detail the accumulation of more than eight hundred enslaved Africans and the work they did; on the grounds, a sweeping waterfront vista of lowland fields and huge oaks, you can walk through reconstructions of the plantation hospital and two typical slave houses.

## The southern shore

On the southern shore of the Albemarle Peninsula, the marshy country roads make for a pleasant drive. **Lake Mattamuskeet Wildlife Refuge** (ⓦ fws.gov/mattamuskeet) is an amazing sight in winter (particularly Dec & Jan), when thousands of swans migrate here from Canada. In October and December (dates vary), the refuge celebrates, along with other nature centres in this area, the annual **Wings Over Water Festival** (ⓦ wingsoverwater.org), with birding tours, kayaking paddles, photography and painting classes, lectures and more. The entrance to the refuge is on Hwy-94, about a mile north of its intersection with US-264.

# The Outer Banks

The **OUTER BANKS**, a string of skinny barrier islands, the remnants of ancient sand dunes, stretch about 180 miles from the Virginia border to Cape Lookout. Easily navigable by bridges, seafood shack-lined avenues and lonely highways, it's a great region to meander, with wonderful wild beaches, otherworldly marshes and attractive small towns such as **Kitty Hawk**, **Kill Devil Hills** and **Nags Head**. **Roanoke Island**, site of the first English settlement in the USA – which vanished inexplicably in 1590 – has obvious historical interest; its village, **Manteo**, is one of the nicest on the Outer Banks. There is no public transport other than the ferries between Ocracoke and the mainland.

## Kitty Hawk, Kill Devil Hills and Nags Head

A melding of salt marshes, beaches and estuaries, the main towns of the Outer Banks are in parts beautifully unspoiled, yet in the high summer season quite touristy. In **Nags Head**, **Jockey's Ridge State Park** (ⓦ jockeysridgestatepark.com) boasts the largest sand dunes on the East Coast – beautiful at sunset. Walking downhill is like clomping through a warm snowbank – a surreal and highly enjoyable experience.

### Wright Brothers National Memorial

1000 N Croatan Hwy (US-158) • Daily 9am–5pm • Charge • ⓦ nps.gov/wrbr

The main feature of the **Wright Brothers National Memorial**, just off the main road at **Kill Devil Hills**, is the Wright Brothers Monument, a 60ft granite fin atop a 90ft dune (which is in fact *the* Kill Devil Hill). The memorial commemorates Orville Wright's **first powered flight**, on December 17, 1903. (Most histories say the flight took place at **Kitty Hawk**, 8 miles north, but that was just the name of the nearest post office.) A boulder next to the memorial's **visitor centre** marks where Orville's first aircraft took off, and numbered markers show the distance of the brothers' four subsequent landings. Exhibits in the visitor centre record their various outlandish experiments.

**1**

### INFORMATION                     KITTY HAWK, KILL DEVIL HILLS AND NAGS HEAD

**Visitor centre** 5230 N Croatan Hwy (US-158), Kitty Hawk  (daily 9am–5pm; ☎ 252 261 4644, ⊛ outerbanks.org).

### ACCOMMODATION AND EATING

#### KILL DEVIL HILLS

**Kill Devil Grill** 2008 S Virginia Dare Trail ⊛ thekilldevilgrill.com. Part 1930s diner car (complete with tabletop jukeboxes), part snug dining room with vinyl booths, this retro favourite dishes up mouth-watering wood-roasted chicken, fish-of-the-day sandwiches, hefty crab cakes, and decadent key lime pie, as well as densely delicious chocolate chip pecan pie. $\overline{\underline{\$\$}}$

#### NAGS HEAD

★ **First Colony Inn** 6715 S Croatan Hwy (US-158) ⊛ firstcolonyinn.com. Luxurious inn in a 1930s beach hotel, with wraparound verandas and a pool. The airy rooms are filled with antique furniture and have a crisp white colour palette. Continental breakfast is included, as well as a daily Afternoon Social (3–5pm), where you can enjoy wine, cheese and lemonade. There's also free access to the water park and exercise rooms of the nearby YMCA. $\overline{\underline{\$\$\$}}$

**Nags Head Beach Inn** 303 E Admiral St ⊛ keesouterbanks.com. Genial small inn that backs onto the beach and is stocked with beach chairs, umbrellas, bikes and coolers. There's a nice modern style, too. Generally open May–Aug. $\overline{\underline{\$\$}}$

**Surfin' Spoon** 3408 S Virginia Dare Trail ⊛ surfinspoon. com. This hip, self-serve frozen yogurt shop scoops up ingenious flavours including strawberry lemonade and tart plain, with a vast range of toppings. Plus, sink your teeth into ice cream sandwiches, like the classic chocolate chip cookie with vanilla ice cream, and the vegan and gluten-free macaroon cookie with pistachio coconut ice cream. $\overline{\underline{\$}}$

**Tale of the Whale** 7575 S Virginia Dare Trail ⊛ taleofthewhalenagshead.com. Soak in views of Roanoke Sound while feasting on fresh seafood, including the ever-popular she-crab soup (a creamy soup made with female crabs with roe), a delicious mound of shrimp and grits topped with an Andouille sausage cream sauce, and juicy seafood skewers, with shrimp, scallops and mahi. $\overline{\underline{\$\$\$}}$

**Tortugas' Lie** 3014 S Virginia Dare Trail ⊛ tortugaslie. com. Rowdy little Caribbean spot with surfboards, licence plates and chilli lights dangling over the tables and horseshoe-shaped bar. The creamy fish tacos, crammed with jack cheese and cabbage, are superb, as is the Coco Loco Chicken, rolled in coconut and served with a lime-curry sauce. The "shark attack" cocktail (vodka lemonade), comes with a plastic fish full of grenadine. $\overline{\underline{\$\$}}$

## Roanoke Island

**ROANOKE ISLAND**, between the mainland and Bodie Island, is accessible from both by bridges. This was the location of the **first English settlement** in North America, founded in 1585, and makes much of its status as Sir Walter Raleigh's so-called "Lost Colony". **Manteo**, the island's commercial centre, is a quaint waterfront village with clapboard cottages clustered under delicate magnolia trees, and a downtown dotted with restaurants, kite shops, parks and art galleries.

### Fort Raleigh National Historic Site

Three miles north of Manteo off US-64 • **Site** Daily 9am–5pm • Free • ⊛ nps.gov/fora • **Elizabethan Gardens** Daily, times vary with season • Charge • ⊛ elizabethangardens.org

Nothing authentic survives of the Roanoke settlement, though **Fort Raleigh National Historic Site** contains a tiny reconstruction of the colonists' earthwork fort, set in a wooded glade. A fascinating museum covers the history of the expeditions and colonization, and an outdoor amphitheatre on the ocean hosts performances of *The Lost Colony* and other productions (June–Aug; $12–45; ⊛ thelostcolony.org). Adjacent to the fort, the **Elizabethan Gardens** are elegantly landscaped with walkways and statues.

### Roanoke Island Festival Park

1 Festival Park • Daily March–Oct 9am–5pm • Charge • ⊛ roanokeisland.com

Across a small footbridge from **Manteo**, the **Roanoke Island Festival Park** has a slew of historical attractions. Highlights include the **adventure museum**, an interactive exhibit

**1**

## ROANOKE: THE LOST COLONY

According to popular myth, the first English attempt to settle in North America – Sir Walter Raleigh's colony at Roanoke – remains an unsolved mystery, in which the "Lost Colony" disappeared without a trace. In 1587, 117 colonists set off from England, intending to farm a fertile site beside Chesapeake Bay; however, after tensions grew between the privateers and their passengers, the ships dumped them at Roanoke Island. Their leader, **John White**, was stranded in England when war broke out with Spain. When White finally managed to persuade a reluctant sea captain to carry him back to Roanoke in 1590, he found the island abandoned. Even so, he was reassured by the absence of the agreed distress signal (a carved Maltese cross), while the word "**Croatoan**" inscribed on a tree seemed a clear message that the colonists had moved south to the eponymous island. However, fearful of both the Spanish and of the approaching hurricane season, White's crew refused to take him any further. There the story usually ends, with the colonists never seen again. In fact, twenty years later, several reports reached the subsequent, more durable colony of Jamestown (in what's now Virginia), of English settlers being dispersed as slaves among the Native American tribes of North Carolina. Rather than admit their inability to rescue their fellow countrymen, and thus expose a vulnerability that might deter prospective settlers or investors, the Jamestown colonists seem simply to have written their predecessors out of history.

on the history of the Outer Banks, the **settlement site**, a living museum peopled with "Elizabethan" soldiers and craftsmen and the *Elizabeth II*, a reconstruction of a sixteenth-century English ship.

### ACCOMMODATION AND EATING                                      ROANOKE ISLAND

**Lost Colony Brewery and Cafe** 208 Queen Elizabeth St ⓦ lostcolonybrewery.com. Casual, friendly, central spot that brews its own beer and serves comfort food such as baked crab dip, warm Brie salad with apples and almonds, and seafood platters such as stuffed flounder drizzled in a lemon-butter sauce. Nice outdoor seating, too. $̄$̄$̄
**Roanoke Island Inn** 305 Fernando St

ⓦ roanokeislandinn.com. Perched on the bay and steps from the town boardwalk, this 1860s cottage with a sun-dappled backyard makes a nice retreat, with several pet-friendly rooms, as well as bike use and baked goods. Spacious rooms are outfitted with antique headboards and cosy quilts; there's also a bungalow and three-bedroom cottage. Breakfast is included. $̄$̄$̄$̄

## Cape Hatteras National Seashore

**CAPE HATTERAS NATIONAL SEASHORE** stretches south from South Nags Head on Bodie Island to **Hatteras** and **Ocracoke** islands, with forty miles of unspoiled beaches on its seaward side. Even in high season you can pull off the road and walk across the dunes to deserted beaches. The salt marshes on the western side are also beautiful. At the northern end of Hatteras Island, the **Pea Island National Wildlife Refuge** (ⓦ fws.gov/peaisland) offers a wide range of guided tours (free), including canoe tours, birding walks and open-air tram tours, as well as trails and observation platforms.

Since the sixteenth century, around a thousand ships have been wrecked along this treacherous stretch of coast. At the south end of Hatteras Island, near the early nineteenth-century black-and-white-striped **Cape Hatteras Lighthouse**, a visitor centre (see below) has exhibits on the island's maritime history; you can climb the 208ft (around twelve-storey) lighthouse (mid-April to mid-Oct daily 9am–4.30pm; charge).

Further south at the village of **Frisco**, the **Native American Museum** is a loving collection of arts and crafts from around the USA, including intricate beadwork and basketry, and a drum from a Hopi *kiva*. It also offers several acres of nature **trails** that wind through maritime forest (Tues–Sun 10.30am–5pm; Jan–March weekends only 10.30am–5pm; charge; ⓦ nativeamericanmuseum.org).

In Hatteras, next to the Ocracoke ferry landing, the **Graveyard of the Atlantic Museum** (April–Oct Mon–Sat 10am–4pm; Nov–March Mon–Fri 10am–4pm; free; ⓦgraveyardoftheatlantic.com) tells the stories of the explorers, pirates and Civil War blockade-runners who perished along this wild stretch of coast.

### INFORMATION                                                        CAPE HATTERAS NATIONAL SEASHORE

**Visitor centre** Cape Hatteras Lighthouse (daily 9am–    4.30pm; ⓦnps.gov/caha).

### ACCOMMODATION AND EATING

**Cape Hatteras Motel** 46556 Hwy-12, Buxton ⓦcapehatterasmotel.com. About a mile from the lighthouse, this faded beach motel has a spectacular location, simple decor, good rates and a pool and hot tub (open May–Sept). $$$

**Diamond Shoals** 46843 Hwy-12, next to Lighthouse Rd, Buxton ⓦdiamondshoalsrestaurant.com. It's a good seafood rule of thumb that if a restaurant has its own fish market, only the freshest crustaceans will make it to your

plate. A long-time Hatteras favourite, *Diamond Shoals* adheres to this principle. Try steamed Ocracoke clams, tomato-based crab bisque and a heaping platter of shrimp and scallops. There's great sushi too. $$$

**National Park Service campgrounds** ⓦnps.gov/caha. The NPS operates first-come, first-served campgrounds at Frisco and Oregon Inlet on Bodie Island, as well as Cape Point near Buxton (late April to Nov). $

## Ocracoke Island

Peaceful **OCRACOKE ISLAND**, a sixteen-mile ribbon of land forty minutes by free ferry from Hatteras, is even more beautiful than its neighbour. Despite the tourist crowds in the tiny village of **Ocracoke**, the southern tip of the island has hung onto its atmosphere and it's easy to find yourself a deserted patch of beach.

### ARRIVAL AND DEPARTURE                                                                OCRACOKE ISLAND

**By ferry** In summer, free ferries run between Hatteras and Ocracoke (40min). There's room for just thirty cars, and it's loaded on a first-come, first-served basis. Ferries from Ocracoke also head south down the coast to Cedar Island on the mainland (2hr 15min; $1/pedestrian, $15/

car) and to Swan Quarter on the Albemarle Peninsula (2hr 30min; same fares). Both require reservations in summer, preferably a day or two in advance. For further information contact ☏800 293 3779 or ⓦncdot.gov/travel/ferryroutes.

### ACCOMMODATION AND EATING

**Captain's Landing Waterfront Inn** 324 Irving Garrish Hwy ⓦthecaptainslanding.com. Rising over the shores of Silver Lake, this cosy hotel has comfortable, cool-toned, waterfront rooms and suites with fully equipped kitchens. Many also have balconies with sweeping views of the lake and the elegant Ocracoke Lighthouse. $$$

★**Dajio** 305 Irving Garrish Hwy ⓦdajiorestaurant. com. Candlelit cottage set back among spindly oak trees, with a patio and outdoor bar. The Southern-accented New American cuisine includes tempura-fried fish tacos (market price), fried green tomato sandwich with cherry-smoked bacon and avocado, and a variety of good vegetarian options like the red curry tofu scramble. Stop by for happy

hour (3–5pm), with baskets of peel-and-eat shrimp. Live music in summer. $$

**Eduardo's Taco Stand** 950 Irvin Garrish Hwy ⓦeduardosocracoke.com. Mouth-watering Mexican food truck with delicious fare such as seafood burritos and cheesy pork tacos, with sliced avocado and *pico de gallo*. Seating consists of a handful of picnic tables. Cash only. $$

**Ocracoke Campground** 4352 Irvin Garrish Hwy ⓦnps. gov/caha. Ocracoke's NPS campground tends to be the first of the Outer Banks sites to fill up – make a reservation before arriving. There are toilets, showers and grills; a quick jaunt over the dunes and you'll be on the beach. Open April–Nov. $

## Cape Lookout National Seashore

The mainland between Cedar Island and Beaufort is a rural backwater, sparsely settled and barely touched by tourists. There are no hotels, and the most likely reason to pass through is to get to the all-but-deserted **CAPE LOOKOUT NATIONAL SEASHORE**, a narrow ribbon of sand stretching south of Ocracoke Island along three Outer Banks with no roads or habitation, a total of around 56 miles of beach. The seashore is only accessible by **ferry** or private boat (see below).

**1**

At the northern tip of the first island, **North Core Banks**, stand the eerie ruins of the abandoned village of **Portsmouth**, whose last two residents left in 1971. To get to the peaceful **Shackleford Banks**, inhabited by wild mustangs since the early 1500s, when they are thought to have swum ashore from shipwrecks, you can catch ferries from Beaufort (see page 52).

### ARRIVAL AND INFORMATION

**CAPE LOOKOUT NATIONAL SEASHORE**

**By ferry** Ferries from Ocracoke arrive at Portsmouth Village (Portsmouth Island Boat Tours; ☎ 252 928 4361). The ferry from Atlantic, south of Cedar Island on the mainland (Morris Marina ferry service; ⓦ portsmouthislandfishing.com), lands at Long Point, 17 miles south of Portsmouth, which you can only reach on foot. South Core Banks is served by private ferry from Davis (south of Atlantic), Beaufort and Harkers Island; see ⓦ nps.gov/calo. Ferries run April–Nov.

**Visitor centre** The visitor centre is at the eastern end of the mainland settlement of Harkers Island (daily 9am–5pm; ⓦ nps.gov/calo).

### ACCOMMODATION

**National Park Service cabins** ⓦ nps.gov/calo. There are two sets of cabins on the island, one apiece on North and South Core. Amenities are basic – think bunk beds, hot water heater, kitchen with propane oven/stove and a charcoal grill – but your reward is total isolation on a stunning, melancholy beach. Cabins sleep at least six. There's also primitive beach camping (generally free) available. Open mid-March to Nov. $$

## Beaufort and around

**BEAUFORT**, about 150 miles southeast of Raleigh, is one of North Carolina's most alluring coastal towns. A good base for visiting the nearby beaches, it has an attractive waterfront that's lively at night. North Carolina's third oldest town, Beaufort also has an appealing **historical district**, centring on Turner Street, off the waterfront. Here you'll find handsome old houses, an apothecary and the city jail.

### The beaches

South of Beaufort, the **beaches** along the twenty-mile offshore **Bogue Banks** are always pretty crowded, especially **Atlantic Beach** at the east end, with **Emerald Isle**, to the west, marginally less so. On **Bear Island** to the south (ferries May & Sept Wed–Sun, April & Oct Fri–Sun), the stunning **Hammocks Beach State Park** has high dunes, a wooded shore and perfect beaches.

### ARRIVAL AND ACTIVITIES

**BEAUFORT AND AROUND**

**By ferry** Ferries (15min; $16) from Beaufort to Shackleford Banks are run by various companies, including Island Express Ferry Services (☎ 252 728 7433, ⓦ islandexpressferryservices.com).

**Parasailing** Beaufort Inlet Watersports (ⓦ beaufort watersports.com) offers 1hr parasailing tours, with fantastic bird's-eye views.

### ACCOMMODATION

**Cedars Inn** 305 Front St ☎ 252 838 1463. Built for a shipwright's son in 1768, this waterfront inn has six light and airy rooms, some with fireplaces, done up with a tasteful blend of modern textiles and antique fixtures. A few of the bathrooms have clawfoot tubs. From the front steps, you can take a quick stroll into town, or watch the sailboats bobbing in the harbour. $$$

**Hammocks Beach State Park** 1572 Hammocks Beach Rd, Swansboro ⓦ ncparks.gov. Accessible only by boat, this pristine campground is fringed by seagrass, tidal pools and the glorious ocean. From late May to Aug, you might spot loggerhead turtles coming ashore to lay their eggs. $

**Inlet Inn** 601 Front St ⓦ inlet-inn.com. In the heart of the historic district, this harbourfront hotel has large balcony rooms, each with a refrigerator, and rocking chairs on the deck, plus a complimentary breakfast basket delivered to your room each morning. $$$

### EATING AND DRINKING

**Beaufort Grocery Co.** 117 Queen St ⓦ beaufortgrocery. com. The inventive Southern food includes a smoked sea salt-seared tuna with truffle oil and fried leeks. and pan-seared shrimp and scallops with Champagne cream. In the heart of downtown, it fills up quickly with locals, especially at lunch. Brunch (Sun 11am–2pm) is also hugely popular – try the Coastal Scramble, with scrambled eggs, shrimp, asparagus tips and scallions. $$$$

**Island Grille** 401 Money Island Drive, Atlantic Beach, 7 miles southwest of Beaufort ⓦislandgrillenc.com. Tropical fans whir over patrons dining on smoked trout with local greens and shrimp and scallop grits at this sophisticated but unintimidating Caribbean-style gem by the beach. Reservations essential (it's tiny). $$$

★ **Moonrakers** 326 Front St ⓦmoonrakersbeaufort. com. The views don't get much better than here. Ascend to the rooftop for cocktails and ocean vistas, and then dig into fresh seafood at this friendly waterfront restaurant. Try the blackened grouper with clams and fennel, and the shrimp and grits. $$$

# Wilmington and around

Even though it's the largest town on North Carolina's coast, **WILMINGTON**, set back along the **Cape Fear River**, fifty miles short of the state's southern border, has these days for a laidback, attractive air. It's notorious, however, as the scene of an appalling incident in 1898, when in what amounted to a coup d'etat, a white supremacist mob overthrew the city's biracial elected government and massacred between 60 and 300 of its black citizens. More recently, as the location for a number of movies and TV shows (including, notably, *Dawson's Creek* and *One Tree Hill*), it has earned the nickname "Wilmywood", and the influx of creative types has led to a certain style that feels very different from the rest of the coast. It's particularly lively after dark, when the tiny riverfront downtown takes on an edgy energy that belies the town's size.

Wilmington's history is on display around every corner, from the ornate **City Hall** to the lovely **Thalian Hall theatre** to the extravagant historic houses, a number of which you can tour, including the handsome **Burgwin-Wright House Museum**, 224 Market St (Tues–Sat 10am–4pm; charge; ⓦburgwinwrighthouse.com). The **Cape Fear Museum**, 814 Market St (Mon–Sat 9am–5pm but until 7pm on Thurs, Sun 1–5pm; charge; ⓦcapefearmuseum.com) – along with the adjoining landscaped park, developed as an outdoor learning environment – gives a lively and broad account of local history. Perhaps the best way to experience Wilmington, though, is outdoors, especially along the weathered, boardwalked **waterfront**, dotted with bars and restaurants.

## The beaches

Wilmington makes a great base for a number of **beaches**: wide and bustling Wrightsville Beach, just nine miles east; Carolina Beach, fifteen miles south, which is also good for hiking; and the laidback white sands of Kure Beach, a popular fishing destination. Local celebs and starlets hang out on rarefied and lovely **Bald Head Island**, around an hour's drive from Wilmington south on Hwy-17.

### Carolina Beach State Park

1010 State Park Rd, Carolina Beach (15 miles south of Wilmington) • Daily: Nov–Feb 8am–6pm; March, April, Sept & Oct 8am–8pm; May–Aug 8am–10pm • Free • ⓦncparks.gov

Honeycombed with wooded trails, the riverfront preserve of **Carolina Beach State Park** is home to a cache of botanical gems: within a 65-mile radius of Wilmington, you'll find the only native-growing Venus flytraps in the world, many right here among the longleaf pines and turkey oaks. The park sustains a number of other splendidly named carnivorous plants; meandering around the grounds, you may stumble upon butterworts, bladderworts, pitcher plants or sundews. The flytraps are smaller and less conspicuous than you'd expect; to make sure you spot them, take a ranger-led tour.

| **ARRIVAL, INFORMATION AND TOURS** | **WILMINGTON AND AROUND** |
|---|---|

**By bus** Greyhound (☏910 791 8040) buses stop at 505 Cando St, 4 miles east of downtown.

**Visitor centre** 505 Nutt St (Mon–Fri 8.30am–5pm, Sat 9am– 4pm, Sun 1–4pm; ☏910 341 4030, ⓦwilmingtonandbeaches. com); there's also an information booth at the foot of Market St by the water.

**1**

**Tours** At the base of Market St, in the small Riverfront Park, you can pick up a horse-drawn carriage tour April–Oct daily 10am–10pm; Nov–March Sun–Thurs 11am–4pm, Fri–Sat 11am–1pm; ⓦ horsedrawntours.com); a sunset harbour cruise (ⓦ cfrboats.com); and a variety of other water tours with Wilmington Water Tours (ⓦ wilmingtonwatertours. net), including sunset cruises with live music (1hr 30min; Thurs–Sun 6.30pm; $35). The Bizzy Bee Water Taxi (all-day pass $15; ☏ 910 338 3134, ⓦ wilmingtonwatertaxi. com) is also a great way to get around, with stops that include the USS *North Carolina* (daily: summer 8am–8pm; rest of year 8am–5pm; charge; ⓦ battleshipnc.com). The battleship participated in every naval offensive in the Pacific during World War II. Wrightsville Beach Scenic Tours (ⓦ wrightsvillebeachscenictours.com) runs superb nature tours to pristine Masonboro Island, including birding and shelling tours– hunt for pretty shells on the beach like the Scotch Bonnet, the state shell of North Carolina. .

## ACCOMMODATION

**Graystone Inn** 100 S 3rd St ⓦ graystoneinn.com. Genteel B&B with lovely rooms – some with fireplaces – and posh comforts including a wine and cheese hour. Peruse books in the library or linger on the veranda; if you do choose to venture out, it's just a few blocks to downtown. $$$
**TownePlace Suites** 305 Eastwood Rd ☏ 910 332 3326, ⓦ marriott.com. While the exterior looks like a ubiquitous chain hotel, the location is supremely convenient (halfway between Wrightsville Beach and downtown Wilmington). Rooms are a compact version of a stylish modern apartment: fluffy beds, flatscreen TVs and kitchens outfitted with dishwashers, fridges and stovetops. $$

## EATING AND DRINKING

★ **Catch** 6623 Market St, ⓦ catchwilmington.com. Helmed by talented local chef Keith Rhodes, this lively restaurant serves superb crab cakes and wonderfully creative seafood dishes, like Firecracker Shrimp, tossed with Vermont maple syrup and sriracha cream, and blackened swordfish with truffle eggs. $$$$
**Copper Penny** 109 Chestnut St ⓦ copperpennync.com. Convivial English pub with excellent bar food – nachos (piled high with steak and sautéed veggies), juicy burgers and overstuffed sandwiches – served amid wooden booths and sports paraphernalia. $$
**Oceanic** 703 S Lumina Ave, Wrightsville Beach ⓦ oceanicrestaurant.com. There's no better place to enjoy seafood treats like she-crab soup, shrimp and cheddar grits, crispy oysters or tuna poke than the outdoor seating at the Atlantic, in a wonderful seafront setting at the iconic Crystal Pier in Wrightsville Beach, 11 miles east of downtown Wilmington. $$
★ **Savorez** 402 Chestnut St ⓦ savorez.com. This colourful restaurant – helmed by chef Sam Cahoon – brings Latin American spice to Wilmington. Start off with the seared tuna tostadas, pineapple salsa and bacon-black bean dip, and then dig into innovative main dishes like flounder crusted in quinoa with coconut-braised greens. $$$

# Raleigh and around

Founded as North Carolina's capital in 1792, **RALEIGH**, part of the "Triangle" along with Durham and Chapel Hill, focuses on the central **Capitol Square**, where the **North Carolina Museum of History**, 5 E Edenton St (Mon–Sat 9am–5pm, Sun noon–5pm; free; ⓦ ncmuseumofhistory.org), provides a far-reaching chronology. Opposite, the **North Carolina Museum of Natural Sciences**, 11 W Jones St (same hours; free; ⓦ naturalsciences.org), looks at local geology, as well as animal and plant life dating back to the dinosaur age. Continue your explorations of nature at beautiful **Pullen Park**, which unfolds west of the museum (daily: May–Aug 10am–9pm; April & Sept 10am–8pm; Oct–March 10am–6pm; ⓦ raleighnc.gov). The first public park in the state, founded in 1887, it abounds with rolling hills, shaded nooks, picnic areas, a glassy pond with pedal boats, the Pullen Park Carousel, a wooden carousel from 1900, and the popular Theatre in the Park, a theatre in the north end of the park that features acclaimed year-round performances.

## City Market

South of the Capitol, the four-block **City Market**, a lamplit, cobbled enclave at Blount and Martin streets, holds a number of good shops and restaurants. Check out the local artists at work in **Artspace**, 201 E Davie St (Wed–Sat 11am–7pm, Sun 11am–4pm; ⓦ artspacenc.org).

1

### North Carolina Museum of Art

2110 Blue Ridge Rd • Wed–Sun 10am–5pm • Free • Docent tours (free) are offered 1–3 times daily • ⓦ ncartmuseum.org

Eight miles northwest of the city (accessed via Rte-1), the **North Carolina Museum of Art** has an eclectic display from the ancient world, Africa, Europe and the USA, along with a smart restaurant, *Iris*. It's surrounded by 160 bucolic acres that are crisscrossed with nature trails and peppered with fanciful sculptures.

### ARRIVAL AND INFORMATION

### RALEIGH AND AROUND

**By plane** Raleigh-Durham airport is off I-40, 15min northwest of town. A taxi into town costs around $30, while a circuitous shuttle service (ⓣ 919 599 8100, ⓦ skyshuttleride. com) will set you back $25–30.

**By bus** The Greyhound station is in a seedy area at 314 W Jones St (ⓣ 919 834 8275).

**By train** Amtrak stops at 320 W Cabarrus St.

**Visitor centre** 500 Fayetteville St (Mon–Sat 9am–5pm; ⓣ 800 849 8499, ⓦ visitraleigh.com).

### ACCOMMODATION AND EATING

**42nd St Oyster Bar** 508 W Jones St ⓦ 42ndstoysterbar. com. This downtown restaurant has been a popular spot for fish and seafood since the 1930s, and retains many original fixtures – the signature neon sign dates from the 1950s, and legend has it that, when in use, the boiler in the lobby cooked more oysters than any other in the country. $$$

**Big Ed's** 220 Wolfe St ⓦ bigedsnc.com. Classic Southern cooking done right at this City Market breakfast hub, with molasses on the table, monstrous hot cakes and French toast, slabs of country ham slathered in gravy and just-like-mom's biscuits. The ceiling is a jumble of dangling lamps, hams, baskets and jugs. $$

★ **Death and Taxes** 105 W Hargett St ⓦ ac-restaurants.com. Chef Ashley Christensen takes Southern cuisine to a high art in a building that has previously been a funeral home and bank (hence the name). The menu celebrates land and sea, including grilled shrimp with avocado and bok choy and roast beets with blue cheese mousse. The inventively named cocktails include Prophets & Loss, made with rum, orange and tonka bean syrup. $$$$

**Neomonde** 3817 Beryl Rd ⓦ neomonde.com. Just off Hillsborough St, the epicentre of Raleigh's student scene, *Neomonde* is a superb Middle Eastern café, bakery and market serving stuffed pitta sandwiches and fava bean salad. $$

**The Pit** 328 W Davie St ⓦ thepit-raleigh.com. North Carolina is famed for its barbecue – particularly smoked pork – and this lively landmark wins accolades for its beef brisket and, of course, its pulled pork. $$

# Durham

Twenty miles northwest of Raleigh, **DURHAM** found itself at the centre of the nation's tobacco industry after farmer Washington Duke came home from the Civil War with the idea of producing cigarettes. By 1890 he and his three sons had formed the **American Tobacco Company**, one of the nation's most powerful businesses.

In 1924, the Duke family's $40 million endowment to Trinity College enabled it to expand into a world-respected medical research facility that became **Duke University**. On campus, the **Nasher Museum of Art** at 2001 Campus Drive (Tues, Wed, Fri & Sat 10am–5pm, Thurs 10am–9pm, Sun noon–5pm; charge; ⓦ nasher.duke.edu) has good African, pre-Columbian, medieval and contemporary collections.

### Duke Homestead Historic Site

North of I-85 at 2828 Duke Homestead Rd • Tues–Sat 9am–5pm • Free • ⓦ historicsites.nc.gov

The **Duke Homestead Historic Site** is an absorbing living museum covering the social history of tobacco farming, with demonstrations of early farming techniques and tobacco-rolling. It centres on the former home of Washington Duke, a modest pine farmhouse that he built in 1852. After fighting in the Civil War, Duke walked 135 miles to return to his country home.

### Historic Stagville

5828 Old Oxford Rd (10 miles north of downtown) • Hourly tours Tues–Sat 10am–5pm • Free • ⓦ historicsites.nc.gov

The fascinating **Historic Stagville** illustrates North Carolina plantation life, in particular the slave experience, from the early 1800s to Reconstruction. The grounds have

**1**

preserved the small two-storey homes of its residents, as well as the plantation owners' house and a colossal barn built by skilled slave carpenters.

## ARRIVAL AND INFORMATION                                                          DURHAM

**By bus** Greyhound buses (☎ 919 687 4800) stop at 515 W Pettigrew St.

**Visitor centre** 212 W Main St (Mon–Fri 10am–5pm; ☎ 919 687 0288, ⓦ discoverdurham.com).

## ACCOMMODATION AND EATING

★ **21c Museum Hotel Durham** 111 N Corcoran St ⓦ 21cmuseumhotels.com/durham. Durham's downtown revitalization is embodied by this chic hotel, which is part of the innovative *21c Museum Hotels* chain. Operating as a hybrid boutique hotel and contemporary art museum, it's set in the restored 1935 Hill Building, designed by the New York architects behind the Empire State Building. The spacious rooms have tall ceilings and terrazzo floors. $$$

**Arrowhead Inn** 106 Mason Rd ⓦ arrowheadinn.com. Dating from 1775, this inviting B&B – set on six acres of gardens and greenery – pampers with fresh flowers, whirlpool tubs and a fireplace in every room. If you're feeling flush, book a night in the delightfully modern log cabin. Sip your morning coffee on the private veranda,

surrounded by gardens. Doubles $$$, cabin $$$$

**Dame's Chicken & Waffles** 530 Foster St ⓦ dameschickenwaffles.com. Leave your diet at the door for this Durham favourite specializing in a truly American, culinary hybrid: sweet, syrupy waffles (try the gingerbread variety) topped with savoury fried chicken. Wait times can be outrageous (upwards of an hour), and reservations are a must. $$

**Parker & Otis** 324 Blackwell St ⓦ parkerandotis.com. At the heart of an upbeat shopping area, stylish *Parker & Otis* serves organic gourmet sandwiches and breakfasts, like the shrimp BLT (with juicy shrimp, Havarti cheese and bacon on toasted sourdough), using local ingredients. $

# Chapel Hill

**CHAPEL HILL**, on the southwest outskirts of Durham, is a charming liberal little college town with a strong music scene – having given birth to bands like Superchunk and Archers of Loaf, and musicians including Ben Folds, not to mention James "*Carolina on My Mind*" Taylor, it's a regular on the indie band tour circuit. It's a pleasant place to hang out, joining the students in the bars and cafés along **Franklin Street**, which fringes the north side of campus. Franklin continues west into the community of **Carrboro**, where it becomes **Main Street**, with a slightly hipper, post-collegiate edge.

## The University of North Carolina

The **University of North Carolina**, dating from 1789, was the nation's first state university. On campus, the splendid **Morehead Planetarium & Science Center**, 250 E Franklin St (Tues–Sat 10am–3.30pm, Sun 1–4.30pm; charge; ⓦ moreheadplanetarium. org), served as an early NASA training centre, while the **Ackland Art Museum**, 101 S Columbia St (Wed–Sat 10am–5pm, Sun 1–5pm; free; ⓦ ackland.org) is strong on Asian art and antiquities.

## ACCOMMODATION                                                                    CHAPEL HILL

**Carolina Inn** 211 Pittsboro St ⓦ carolinainn.com. This popular, historic, university-owned inn with cosy rooms is near Franklin St, on the northwestern side of campus. Enjoy local Southern cuisine at *Crossroads Chapel Hill*. $$$$

**The Siena Hotel** 1505 E Franklin St ⓦ sienahotel.com.

Relax at this Italian-inspired hotel, which has spacious rooms with high ceilings, Juliet balconies and marble bathrooms. The *Il Palio* restaurant serves hearty Italian pastas and grilled meat and fish. $$$

## EATING, DRINKING AND NIGHTLIFE

**Cat's Cradle** 300 E Main St, Carrboro ⓦ catscradle.com. Legendary Triangle music venue that got its start in the folkie heyday of the 1960s, and has since hosted everyone from Iggy Pop to Lucinda Williams.

**Crook's Corner** 610 W Franklin St ⓦ crookscorner.com.

This classic joint is known as the "home of shrimp and grits" because founding chef Bill Neal made his name with the finest shrimp and grits in the South, if not the country. This signature dish is still served daily, along with other fun favourites such fried green tomatoes and the Southern

Vegetable Sampler, including collards and grilled corn. $\overline{\$\$\$}$ **Lantern** 423 W Franklin St ⓦlanternrestaurant.com. Though its menu is distinctly Pacific Rim, *Lantern* honours its roots by sourcing local ingredients. There's an upmarket dining room with a bordello-style bar with glowing red lanterns, and a leafy back garden. Try the salt-and-pepper shrimp, the crispy okra and the green curry stew with pumpkin, red onions and coconut milk. Reservations recommended. $\overline{\$\$}$

**Orange County Social Club** 108 E Main St, Carrboro ⓦorangecountysocialclub.net. Hip, laidback bar with vintage decor, a pool table, a top-notch jukebox and a garden. **Sunrise Biscuit Kitchen** 1305 E Franklin St, Chapel Hill, 2 miles east of downtown ⓦsunrisebiscuits. com. Buttery breakfast heaven: huge biscuit sandwiches crammed with golden-fried chicken and gooey cheddar cheese. Excellent cinnamon rolls too. Though you can order inside (it's mainly a drive-through), there's no seating.

# Winston-Salem

Though synonymous with the brand name of its cigarettes, **WINSTON-SALEM**, eighty miles west of Chapel Hill, owes its spot on the tourist itinerary to **Old Salem**, a well-preserved twenty-block area that honours the heritage of the city's first Moravian settlers. Escaping religious persecution in what is now the Czech Republic, the first Moravians settled in the Piedmont in the mid-eighteenth century. They soon established trading links with the frontier settlers and founded the town of Salem on a communal basis – they permitted only those of the same religious faith to live here. Demand for their crafts helped establish the adjacent community of Winston, which, accruing tremendous wealth from tobacco, soon outgrew the older town. The two merged in 1913 to form Winston-Salem.

## Old Salem Museums and Gardens

900 Old Salem Rd • Tues–Sat 9.30am–4.30pm, Sun 1–4.30pm • Charge • ⓦ oldsalem.org

**Old Salem** is a living history museum, with costumed craftspeople demonstrating nineteenth-century skills, including paper-cutting and pottery, in a number of **restored buildings** and seasonal gardens growing Moravian crops. Admission includes entrance to the far-reaching **Museum of Early Southern Decorative Arts**, which houses a dignified collection of folk art, paintings and textiles.

## ARRIVAL AND INFORMATION                                                WINSTON-SALEM

**By bus** Greyhound buses (☎ 336 724 1429) stop at 100 W 5th St.
**Visitor centre** 200 Brookstown Ave, three blocks from Old

Salem (Mon–Fri 8.30am–5pm, Sat 10am–4pm; Jan & Feb closed Sat; ☎ 336 728 4200, ⓦvisitwinstonsalem.com).

## ACCOMMODATION AND EATING

**Sweet Potatoes** 607 N Trade St ☎336 727 4844, ⓦsweetpotatoes.ws. Located in Winston-Salem's burgeoning Arts District, hospitable *Sweet Potatoes* dishes up top-notch Southern comfort food such as fried green tomatoes and okra, shrimp and grits, and of course, sweet potato pie. $\overline{\$\$}$

**The Zevely Inn** 803 S Main St ⓦzevelyinn.com. Restored to its nineteenth-century appearance, this handsome brick pile at the heart of Old Salem is named after Augustus T. Zevely, the Moravian doctor who lived here in 1845. The comfortable rooms, many with four-poster beds, have heated brick tile floors. Continental breakfast included. $\overline{\$\$\$}$

# Charlotte

The prosperous banking centre of **CHARLOTTE**, where I-77 and I-85 meet near the South Carolina border, is the largest city in the state. It's also a transport hub, with direct flights from Europe, and some fine museums to divert anyone in transit.

## The museums

Downtown (more commonly called "uptown" or "center city"), a mass of skyscrapers and commerce focused on **Tryon Street**, boasts the kids-oriented **Discovery Place**, 301 N Tryon St, with an aquarium and an IMAX theatre (Mon–Fri 9am–5pm, Sat

10am–6pm, Sun noon–5pm; charge; ⓦdiscoveryplace.org) and the **Bechtler Museum**, 420 S Tryon St (Mon & Wed–Sat 10am–5pm, Sun noon–5pm; charge; ⓦbechtler. org) whose quality collection of mid-twentieth-century art includes pieces by Picasso, Warhol and Miró. Arts, crafts and modern design are displayed at the stylish **Mint Museum Uptown**, 500 S Tryon St (Tues, Thurs & Sat 11am–6pm, Wed & Fri 11am–9pm, Sun 1–5pm; charge; ⓦmintmuseum.org). The same ticket covers admission to sister museum **Mint Museum Randolph** (same hours) in the Eastover neighbourhood, where exhibits include everything from ceramics to African art. The **Harvey B. Gantt Center**, 551 S Tryon St, focuses on African American art and photography (Tues–Fri & Sun noon–6pm, Sat 10am–6pm; charge; ⓦganttcenter.org). A few blocks away, the excellent **Levine Museum of the New South**, 200 E 7th St (Mon–Sat 10am–5pm, Sun noon–5pm; charge; ⓦmuseumofthenewsouth.org), looks at the growth of the region from Reconstruction onwards.

For a fascinating glimpse into the world of working contemporary artists, stop by the **McColl Center for Art & Innovation**, 721 N Tryon St, featuring the works of a wide variety of artists-in-residence (Thurs 10am–9pm; free; ⓦmccollcenter.org).

### ARRIVAL AND INFORMATION CHARLOTTE

**By plane** Charlotte/Douglas International Airport, 7 miles west of town, is a $25–30 taxi ride from uptown.

**By train or bus** Greyhound (☎704 375 3332) stops at 601 W Trade St, while Amtrak pulls in at 1914 N Tryon St. Destinations Atlanta, GA (6 daily; 4hr 15min); Wilmington, NC (2–3 daily; 8hr 25min); Winston Salem, NC (5 daily; 1hr 40min).

**Visitor centre** 329 S Tryon St (Mon & Thurs–Sun 11am–2pm; ☎800 231 4636, ⓦcharlottesgotalot.com); there are smaller branches in the Levine Museum of the New South and at the airport.

### ACCOMMODATION AND EATING

**Dunhill Hotel** 237 N Tryon St ⓦdunhillhotel.com. Uptown's 1929 *Dunhill* has an old-fashioned charm, with comfortable rooms with marble bathrooms. Perks include an evening turndown service and a smart restaurant. $$$$
**Kindred** 131 Main St, Davidson ⓦkindreddavidson. com. This award-winning restaurant, set in a reconstructed pharmacy 22 miles north of Charlotte, is well worth the drive for creative, contemporary Southern cuisine such as the signature milk bread, duck fat potatoes with dill, and squid ink pasta with local shrimp and sea urchin butter. $$$
**Mariposa** 500 S Tryon St, in the Mint Museum Uptown ☎704 910 0865, ⓦmariposaclt.com. Every bit as stylish as you'd hope for in an art museum restaurant, this "world-to-table" spot has impeccable design sense. Its sophisticated, eclectic menu ranges from sweetcorn fritters to Gullah paella and chipotle short ribs. $$$$

## Blue Ridge Parkway

The best way to see the **mountains** of North Carolina is from the exhilarating **Blue Ridge Parkway**, which runs across the northwest of the state from Virginia to the **Great Smoky Mountains National Park**. It's a delight to drive; the vast panoramic expanses of forested hillside, with barely a settlement in sight, may astonish travellers fresh from the crowded centres of the East Coast. This rural region has been a breeding ground since the early twentieth century for **bluegrass** music, which is still performed regularly; laidback, liberal **Asheville** is a good place to see the edgier stylings of "newgrass".

The peak tourist season for the **Blue Ridge Parkway** is October, when the leaves of the deciduous trees turn vivid shades of yellow, gold and red. Year-round, however, this twisting mountain road – largely built in the 1930s by President Roosevelt's Civilian Conservation Corps – is a worthwhile destination in itself, peppered with state-run campgrounds, short hiking trails and dramatic overlooks. Although the Parkway is closed to commercial vehicles, the constant curves make it hard to average anything approaching the 45mph speed limit.

### Boone

Friendly **BOONE** is the most obvious northern base for exploring the mountains. Just a few miles off the Parkway, it has the feel of a Western frontier town, spiced up with

## BLUE RIDGE PARKWAY MOUNTAIN ACTIVITIES

Organized **outdoor pursuits** available along the Blue Ridge Parkway include **whitewater rafting** and **canoeing**, most of it on the Nolichucky River near the Tennessee border, south of Johnson City, Tennessee, but also on the Watauga River and Wilson Creek. Companies running trips include Nantahala Outdoor Center (Ⓦnoc.com) and High Mountain Expeditions (Ⓦhighmountainexpeditions.com), who also offer biking, hiking and tubing trips. Expect to pay around $95 per person for a full day of rafting.

Winter sees **skiing** at a number of slopes and resorts, particularly around **Banner Elk**, sixteen miles southwest of Boone. Resort accommodation is expensive, ski passes less so. Appalachian Ski Mountain (Ⓦappskimtn.com) is near Blowing Rock, while Ski Beech (Ⓦbeechmountainresort.com), the highest ski area in the east, is at Beech Mountain. You can pick up full listings at visitor centres, or check Ⓦhighcountryhost.com.

a bit of Appalachian music heritage: guitarist Doc Watson traced his roots here, and other bluegrass musicians still ply their trade in the area. Main drag **King Street** is a picturesque stretch of nineteenth-century brick buildings, sharply framed by the forested mountains.

### ACCOMMODATION AND EATING  BOONE

**Hidden Valley Motel** 8275 Hwy-105, 8 miles west of town Ⓦhiddenvalleymotel.com. You'll get clean, comfortable rooms at this friendly motel, nestled at the base of the mountains and surrounded by a pretty garden. $\overline{\underline{\$\$}}$

★ **Vidalia** 831 W King St Ⓦvidaliaofboonenc.com. This lovely little restaurant with an open kitchen serves inventive New Southern food fired up with fresh local produce. Reservations recommended. $\overline{\underline{\$\$\$}}$

**Wild Craft Eatery** 506 W King St Ⓦwildcraftboone. com. The excellent, globally influenced menu – with a wide variety of vegetarian dishes – is organic and locally sourced. Standouts include the tacos with sautéed tempeh and gouda cheese, the venison burger topped with goat cheese and the Arroz con Pollo – a heaping plate of Mexican red rice with tender chicken breast. $\overline{\underline{\$\$}}$

### Blowing Rock and around

Hwy-321 • daily: April–Oct 8.30am–7pm; Nov–March 9am–5pm • Charge • Ⓦtheblowingrock.com

Eight miles south of Boone, **BLOWING ROCK** is a pleasant, if touristy, resort just south of the Blue Ridge Parkway. The "Blowing Rock" itself is a high cliff from which light objects thrown over the side will simply blow back up – it's a fun, if somewhat frivolous, diversion to observe.

### Grandfather Mountain

2050 Blowing Rock Hwy, in Linville • Daily: spring & fall 9am–6pm; summer 8am–7pm; rest of year 9am–5pm • Charge • Ⓦgrandfather.com

The privately owned nature preserve of **Grandfather Mountain** (5964ft), fifteen miles south of Blowing Rock, with access at milepost 305, offers nature trails, alpine hiking paths, ranger-led programmes and the **Mile High Swinging Bridge**, the highest suspension footbridge in the country. The price is high, but the owners make a genuine attempt to protect this unique environment.

## Asheville

Relaxed **ASHEVILLE** is both an outdoors sports hub and a vibrant arts community, with a strong student presence from UNC and superb restaurants, microbreweries, galleries, boutique stores and live music venues. Retaining an appealing 1920s downtown core, it's a nice place to walk around, with handsome **Art Deco** buildings and intriguing local crafts. Twentieth-century novelist Thomas Wolfe memorialized the town in his autobiographical novel, *Look Homeward, Angel*. **Wolfe's childhood home**, a yellow Victorian pile that also served as a boarding house called Old

**1**

---

### HIKING AROUND LINVILLE GORGE WILDERNESS

**Rough Ridge**, at milepost 302.8, is one of several access points to the 13.5-mile **Tanawha Trail**, which runs along the ridge above the Parkway from Beacon Heights to Julian Price Park, looking out over the dense forests. Another good hiking destination is the **Linville Gorge Wilderness**, at milepost 316.4, a couple of miles outside **Linville Falls village**. There are two main trails; one is a steep, 1.6-mile round-trip climb to the top of the high and spectacular **Linville Falls** themselves. Breathtaking views from either side of the gorge look down 2000ft to the **Linville River**. An easier walk leads to the base of the falls. You can also climb **Hawksbill** or **Table Rock** mountains from the nearest forest road, which leaves Hwy-181 south of the village of Jonas Ridge (signposted "Gingercake Acres", with a small, low sign to Table Rock).

**Linville Falls Campground** 717 Gurney Franklin Rd, via Hwy-221 ⓦ linvillefalls.com. This friendly campground in amiable Linville Falls village is shaded by mountain laurel and offers laundry facilities, grills and hot showers. Open May–Sept. ⸱S⸱

**Linville Falls Lodge & Cottages** 48 Hwy-183 ⓦ linvillefallslodge.com. Peaceful, family-owned mountain lodge with cosy rooms as well as cottages. ⸱SS⸱, cottages ⸱SSS⸱

---

Kentucky Home, has been preserved at 52 N Market St (tours Tues–Sat 9am–5pm; charge; ⓦwolfememorial.com).

## Biltmore Estate

1 Lodge St • Hours and prices vary: typically daily 8.30am–6.30pm • admission: charge; overnight stays $$$ at various on-site properties (includes admission, breakfast and other amenities) • ⓦ biltmore.com

Asheville's big attraction, two miles south of town, is the **Biltmore Estate**, the largest private mansion in the USA, with 250 rooms. Built in the late nineteenth century by George Vanderbilt – the youngest son of the wealthy industrialist family – and loosely modelled on a Loire chateau, it's a wild piece of nouveau-riche folly, from the Victorian chic of the indoor palm court to the gardens designed by Frederick Law Olmsted, he of New York's Central Park. Unless you're thrilled by displays of opulence, it may seem like an extraordinarily expensive place to visit, for relatively little reward. At the time Biltmore was built it took a week simply to travel the estate on horseback; today you can easily fill a day or more taking a tour, sampling tastings at the winery, renting a bike to explore the eight thousand acres of grounds, hopping on a river raft or a kayak and eating at its restaurants and lounges, from afternoon tea to Southern feasts; there are also a variety of accommodations for overnight stays, including the Biltmore Village Inn (see page 60).

### ARRIVAL, INFORMATION AND TOURS                                    ASHEVILLE

**By bus** Asheville's Greyhound terminal (☎ 828 253 8451) is 2 miles out of downtown at 2 Tunnel Rd, a highway lined with motels.

**Visitor centre** 36 Montford Ave, reached via exit 4C off I-240 (daily 9am–5pm; ☎ 828 258 6129, ⓦ exploreasheville.com).

**Bus tours** For a madcap, but informed, historical overview, join a comedy city bus tour with LaZoom (90 Biltmore Ave;

ⓦ lazoomtours.com), who also offer a Band and Beer Tour, a Haunted Comedy Tour and a Kids' Comedy Tour.

**Walking tours** Numerous walking tours explore the city, including the Asheville Insider by Asheville by Foot tours (1hr 30min, charge, ⓦ ashevillebyfoottours.com), departing from the heart of downtown at 1 North Pack Square, near the Vance Memorial.

### ACCOMMODATION

**Biltmore Village Inn** 119 Dodge St ⓦ biltmorevillageinn. com. Former residence of George Vanderbilt's lawyer, who helped the tycoon secure Biltmore, this spectacular 1892 Victorian offers the consummate B&B experience: posh rooms, caring staff, sweeping scenery and chef-driven meals. ⸱SSS⸱

**Campfire Lodgings** 116 Old Marshall Hwy, 7 miles north of town via Hwy-26 ⓦ campfirelodgings.com. Set in tranquil forest 10min north of Asheville, this friendly outfitter offers campgrounds, cabins and luxurious yurts. Tents ⸱S⸱, yurts ⸱SS⸱, cabins ⸱SSS⸱

**LEAF FESTIVAL**

Laidback **Black Mountain**, sixteen miles east of Asheville on I-40, hosts the hugely enjoyable **Leaf Festival** (ⓦtheleaf.org), a folk music and arts and crafts gathering, held in mid-May and October. Showcasing Appalachian and world folk music, it attracts major European and African musicians. There's little to do here otherwise, but the town has a few good **music** venues, restaurants and coffeeshops.

## EATING, DRINKING AND NIGHTLIFE

**12 Bones Smokehouse** 5 Foundy St ⓦ12bones.com. Queue up for the outrageously good barbecue, cornbread and jalapeno grits at this smokehouse. Order at the counter, sit under the covered deck and prepare to get messy with the home-made sauce. There's also a location in Arden (South Asheville), south of *Biltmore Estate*, which includes *12 Bones Brewing* (ⓦ12bonesbrewing.com). $$$

★ **Corner Kitchen** 3 Boston Way, 3 miles south of downtown ⓦthecornerkitchen.com. Exceptional New American cuisine in a century-old house close to the Biltmore Estate, with oodles of character. Though the menu rotates, at breakfast you might find pecan-crusted trout and eggs; at lunch, a salad of corn-fried oysters over arugula; and chilli-rubbed pork chop with Spanish tomato rice. $$$

**Cúrate** 13 Biltmore Ave ⓦcuratetapasbar.com. In a city of excellent restaurants, this tapas hot spot stands out with its pre-eminent Spanish cuisine, modern dining room with a huge marble bar and top-notch service. Sample small plates of *jamón ibérico*, served on pig-shaped cutting boards; potato and onion omelettes, lamb skewers and sangria

mixed tableside. Reservations highly recommended. $$$

**Jack of the Wood** 95 Patton Ave ⓦjackofthewood.com. Asheville has a lively nightlife scene, with lots of places to drink craft beer and listen to live music. This enjoyable Celtic bar has hand-brewed beer and regular bluegrass, folk and newgrass shows. $$$

**Tupelo Honey** 12 College St ⓦtupelohoneycafe.com. Landmark sidewalk café with great people-watching and a breakfast-all-day menu boasting delicious sweet potato pancakes, pecan pie French toast and Eggs Betty, with smoked ham and potato cracklins'; you'll also find salads, sandwiches and sophisticated dinner mains such as mountain trout with brown butter. Meals come with a basket of warm biscuits and home-made jam. $$$

**White Duck Taco Shop** 388 Riverside Drive, 1 mile west of downtown ⓦwhiteducktacoshop.com. Bright, cheerful *taqueria* with ingenious taco variations such as Thai peanut chicken with tropical salsa, Korean beef bulgogi and, of course, duck. There's often a queue, but it moves quickly. There's nice alfresco seating overlooking the river, too. $$

Chimney Rock

431 Main St, Chimney Rock • Daily: hours vary • Charge • ⓦchimneyrockpark.com

Twenty-five miles southeast of the Parkway on US-64/74A, the natural granite tower of **Chimney Rock** protrudes from the almost-sheer side of Hickory Nut Gorge. After taking the elevator 26 storeys up through the body of the mountain, you can walk along protected walkways above the impressive cliffs. Many of the climactic moments of *The Last of the Mohicans* were filmed here; you may recognize the mighty **Hickory Nut Falls**, which tumble 400ft from the western end of the gorge.

# South Carolina

The relatively small state of **SOUTH CAROLINA** remains, with Mississippi, one of the most rural in the USA. **Politics** in the first state to secede from the Union in 1860 have traditionally been conservative, particularly following the Civil War during the tumultuous period of **Reconstruction** and **Jim Crow** segregation. The region's main fascination lies in the subtropical coastline, also called the **Low Country**, and its **sea islands**. Wild beaches, swampy marshes and lush palmetto groves preserve traces of a virtually independent black culture (featuring the unique patois, "Gullah"), dating back to the start of the Civil War when enslaved Africans stayed put but area plantation owners fled the scene. There are no interstates along the coast, so journeys take longer than you might expect, the views are pretty and the pace of life definitely feels slower. Beyond the grand old peninsular port of **Charleston** –

1

one of the most elegant towns in the nation with its pastel-coloured old buildings, appealing waterfront and Caribbean ambience – restored plantations stretch as far north as **Georgetown**, en route toward tacky **Myrtle Beach**.

## Myrtle Beach

**MYRTLE BEACH** is an unmitigated stretch of commercial seaside development twenty miles down the coast from the North Carolina border. Predominantly a golf centre and family resort, it's packed during mid-term vacations with students drinking and partying themselves into a frenzy. Fans of elaborate water parks, factory outlet malls, funfairs and parasailing will be in heaven. The widest stretch of sand is at **North Myrtle Beach**, a chain of small communities centring on Ocean Boulevard. South of Myrtle Beach lies **Murrells Inlet**, a fishing port with lots of good seafood restaurants and **Pawleys Island**, a secluded resort once favoured by plantation owners and today retaining a slower pace than its neighbours.

## Georgetown and around

The peaceful waterfront community of **GEORGETOWN** – the first town in forty miles beyond Myrtle Beach that's anything more than a resort – makes a nice contrast to the northerly commercialism. It's hard to imagine today, but in the eighteenth century Georgetown was the centre of a thriving network of Low Country rice plantations; by the 1840s the area produced nearly half the rice grown in the United States. While Front Street, the main street, has a time-warped, late-1950s feel, Georgetown's 32-block **historic district** features many fine eighteenth-century and antebellum houses.

The **Rice Museum**, in the Clock Tower at 633 Front St (Mon–Sat 10am–4.30pm; charge; ⓦ ricemuseum.org), tells of the Low Country's long history of rice cultivation and its dependence on a constant supply of enslaved Africans brought over from the Windward coast for their expertise. There are also displays on local heroes such as Ruby Forsythe, who taught at the region's little one-room schoolhouse for 53 years.

### Hopsewee Plantation

494 Hopsewee Rd, 13 miles south of Georgetown on US-17 • Tours Tues–Fri 10am–3pm, Sat 11am–3pm • Charge • ⓦ hopsewee.com

The grand 1740 mansion home of Thomas Lynch, a signatory of the Declaration of Independence, **Hopsewee Plantation** is set in Spanish-moss-draped grounds. The estate was once a profitable rice-growing enterprise; in 1850 alone Hopsewee churned out 560,000lb of the crop. Nowadays, it's known for its gorgeous tearoom, set with gilded china and white tablecloths and pouring plenty of cuppas.

### Hampton Plantation State Historic Site

Two miles off US-17 on Hwy-857, 16 miles south of Georgetown • House tours Mon, Tues & Fri noon & 2pm, Sat & Sun 10am, noon & 2pm; grounds daily: April–Oct 9am–6pm; Nov–March 9am–5pm • Charge for house, grounds free • ⓦ southcarolinaparks.com/hampton

Tours of the **Hampton Plantation State Historic Site** concentrate on the history of slavery. The grounds are lovely, but the house is most impressive. An eighteenth-century Neoclassical monolith built by Huguenots, the inside is relatively bare. The plantation itself is isolated in the heart of the dense **Francis Marion National Forest**, a heavily African American area particularly known for its sweetgrass basket-weaving, which originated with enslaved peoples from West Africa.

### INFORMATION AND TOURS          GEORGETOWN AND AROUND

**Visitor centre** 531 Front St (Mon–Fri 9am–5pm, Sat 9am–3pm; ⓦ visitgeorge.com).

**Boat tours** Hop on the *Carolina Rover* (1 tour daily; 3hr;

$38, reservations recommended; ⓦ roverboattours.com) for a cruise of the coast, including a spell shelling on a nearby barrier island as well as wildlife-spotting.

## ACCOMMODATION AND EATING

**Mansfield Plantation** 1776 Mansfield Rd ⓦmansfieldplantation.com. One of the best places in the state to experience a plantation stay. Hauntingly authentic, *Mansfield* dates from 1718 and retains its original slave quarters, chapel, schoolhouse and plantation home. Guest rooms, spread amongst the historic structures, are tastefully done up, and the ground's thousand acres, dripping with Spanish moss, invite exploration on foot or by boat. $\overline{\underline{\$\$\$}}$

**Root** 919 Front St ☎843 461 9344. "American cuisine, local roots" is the apt slogan at this welcoming restaurant that serves homey, locavore fare like meatballs and grits with creamy burrata, lobster mac and cheese and blackened diver scallops with bacon and spring peas. $\overline{\underline{\$\$\$}}$

# Charleston and around

**CHARLESTON**, one of the finest-looking towns in the USA, is a compelling place, its **historic district** lined with tall, narrow houses of peeling, multicoloured stucco, adorned with wooden shutters and wide piazzas (porches). The palm trees and tropical climate give the place a Caribbean air, while the hidden gardens, leafy patios and ironwork balconies evoke the romance of New Orleans.

Charleston's **historic district** is a predominantly residential area of leaning lines, weathered colours and exquisite courtyards bounded by Calhoun Street to the north

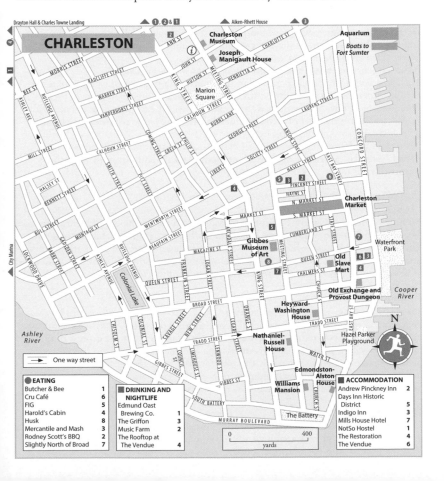

| EATING | | DRINKING AND NIGHTLIFE | | ACCOMMODATION | |
|---|---|---|---|---|---|
| Butcher & Bee | 1 | Edmund Oast Brewing Co. | 1 | Andrew Pinckney Inn | 2 |
| Cru Café | 6 | The Griffon | 3 | Days Inn Historic District | 5 |
| FIG | 5 | Music Farm | 2 | Indigo Inn | 3 |
| Harold's Cabin | 4 | The Rooftop at The Vendue | 4 | Mills House Hotel | 7 |
| Husk | 8 | | | NotSo Hostel | 1 |
| Mercantile and Mash | 3 | | | The Restoration | 4 |
| Rodney Scott's BBQ | 2 | | | The Vendue | 6 |
| Slightly North of Broad | 7 | | | | |

**1**

---

### CHARLESTON'S HISTORIC HOUSES

Many of the city's fine **houses** are available for **tours**. The late nineteenth-century **Williams Mansion**, 14–16 Meeting St, is fabulously over-the-top, with ornate plaster and woodwork, hand-painted porcelain ballroom chandeliers and a beautiful music room showered with light from a skylight (daily 11am–5pm, every 30min; charge; ⓦcalhounmansion.net). Nearby, the antebellum **Edmondston-Alston House**, one of the first houses built on the Battery (in 1825), overlooks the harbour at 21 E Battery St (Mon & Sun 1–4.30pm, Tues–Sat 10am–4.30pm; charge; ⓦedmonstonalston.org). The elegant Neoclassical **Nathaniel-Russell House**, 51 Meeting St (Mon–Sat 10am–5pm, Sun 2–5pm; charge; ⓦhistoriccharleston.org), is noted for its flying staircase, which soars unsupported for three floors. North of downtown, the antebellum urban plantation **Aiken-Rhett House**, 48 Elizabeth St, retains not only its original decor and furnishings but also the work yard and slave quarters (Mon–Sat 10am–5pm, Sun 2–5pm; charge; ⓦhistoriccharleston.org). For more historic homes, visit the Charleston Museum.

---

and East Bay Street by the river. The further south of Broad you head, the posher and more residential the streets become. The district is best taken in by strolling at your own pace – though that pace can get pretty slow in high summer, when the heat is intense. Attractive spots to pause in the shade include the elegantly landscaped **Waterfront Park**, a greenway with fountains and boardwalks leading out over the river and **White Point Garden**, by the Battery on the tip of the peninsula, where the breezy, flower-filled lawns have good views across the water.

The long-awaited **International African American Museum** (IAAM; ⓦafricanamericancharleston.com), a landmark institution intended to illuminate the African-American history of the South, was set to open as this book went to press. One of its most powerful features is the location: the museum rises over the historic Gadsden's Wharf, the port of arrival for nearly half of all enslaved Africans, who took their first steps on American soil here.

Around Charleston, the **river road**, Hwy-61, leads **west** from the city along the Ashley River past a series of opulent **plantations**. An easy jaunt from the city, these country estates make for a diverting afternoon's visit.

### The Old Exchange and Provost Dungeon

122 E Bay St • Daily 9am–5pm • Charge • ⓦ oldexchange.com

Built in 1771 as the Customs House and used as a prison during the Revolutionary War, the **Old Exchange and Provost Dungeon** is a hugely significant colonial structure. The upper floors feature exhibits on the history of the building and of Charleston; the tone changes in the dank confines below, however, where spotlit dummies recount tales of revolutionaries, gentlemen pirates and all manner of derring-do.

### The Old Slave Mart

6 Chalmers St • Mon–Sat 9am–5pm • Charge • ⓦ oldslavemart.org

Following Charleston's inception in 1670, one third of the nation's enslaved Africans passed through the city. The **Old Slave Mart** was built in 1856 for the express purpose of buying and selling enslaved African Americans. The detailed exhibits in this compact, haunting place document the reach and effects of the transatlantic slave trade, and include rare personal audio recordings from ex-slaves. Upstairs, the "Triumph over Slavery" exhibit delineates and celebrates African American history.

## The market area and around

Charleston's **market area** runs from Meeting Street to East Bay Street, focusing on a long, narrow line of enclosed, low-roofed, nineteenth-century sheds. Undeniably touristy, packed with hard-headed "basket ladies" weaving sweetgrass crafts, this is one of the liveliest spots in town, selling knick-knacks, spices, tacky T-shirts, jewellery and rugs.

### Gibbes Museum of Art

135 Meeting St • Tues & Thurs–Sat 10am–5pm, Wed 10am–8pm, Sun 1–5pm; free tours Tues 12.30pm, Wed 6pm, Thurs 2.30pm, Fri 12.30pm & 2.30pm, second Sun of the month 2.30pm • Charge • ⓦ gibbesmuseum.org

The intriguing **Gibbes Museum of Art** places a strong emphasis on Charleston itself, providing a quick history of the city through art. The first floor holds eighteenth- and nineteenth-century oil paintings, including an engaging collection of miniature portraits with frames of velvet, gold and pearls. The second and third floors display rotating and contemporary exhibits. Top off your visit by relaxing outdoors, in the sun-dappled Lenhardt Garden. The museum hosts an annual summer series, including the Art of Jazz, featuring music inspired by current exhibits.

### The Charleston Museum

360 Meeting St • Mon–Sat 9am–5pm, Sun 1–5pm • Charge • ⓦ charlestonmuseum.org

The vast **Charleston Museum**, opposite the visitor centre, is filled with a wealth of city memorabilia, videos on subjects from rice-growing to the Huguenots, and exhibits on historic weaponry, Native Americans and the natural history of the region, including an 18ft-long prehistoric crocodile. You can buy combo tickets that include the 1803 **Joseph Manigault House**, a lovely structure built by descendants of Huguenot settlers, and the 1772 **Heyward-Washington House**, at the south end of the peninsula at 87 Church St, which was built by Thomas Heyward, a rice baron and signatory of the Declaration of Independence.

### South Carolina Aquarium

100 Aquarium Wharf • Daily 9am–5pm • Charge • ⓦ scaquarium.org

At the end of Calhoun Street, overlooking the harbour, you'll find Charleston's splendid **Aquarium**. With a 40ft-deep tank at the core, its open, eye-level exhibits recreate South Carolina's various watery habitats – including the Piedmont, swamps, salt marshes and ocean – and their indigenous aquatic, plant and animal life. The porch-like terrace, with wide benches, is a nice place to catch the river breezes; watch out for schools of dolphins playing in the water below.

### Fort Sumter National Monument

**Monument** Five miles offshore • Accessed by boat tour; 2–3 daily • Charge • ⓦ fortsumtertours.com • **Visitor centre** 340 Concord St • Daily 8.30am–5pm • Free • ⓦ nps.gov/fosu

The first shots of the Civil War were fired on April 12, 1861, at **Fort Sumter**, a redoubtable federal garrison that occupied a small artificial island at the entrance to Charleston Harbor. After secession, the federal government had to decide whether to reprovision its forts in the south. When a relief expedition was sent to Fort Sumter, Confederate General Pierre Beauregard demanded its surrender. After a relentless barrage, the garrison gave in the next day.

Fort Sumter may only be seen on regular **boat tours** that leave from near the Aquarium at the eastern end of Calhoun Street. Just one of the fort's original three storeys is left, thanks not to the assault that started the war, but to its subsequent siege and bombardment by Union troops, who finally reoccupied it on Good Friday 1865, the very day Lincoln was assassinated. Exhibits in the mainland **visitor centre** cover not only the fort but also the history of Charleston and the build-up to the conflict.

### Drayton Hall

3380 Ashley River Rd, 15 miles northwest of Charleston • Mon & Wed–Sat 9am–5pm, Sun 11am–5pm • Charge • ⓦ draytonhall.org

**Drayton Hall** is an elegant Georgian mansion with handcarved wood and plasterwork; a variety of guided tours (various times) focus on the fine architecture as well as on

1

different themes, like **Connections: From Africa to America**, tracing the story of slavery and emancipation and how it relates to Drayton Hall. Tours also take in the fascinating African American **cemetery** here, one of the oldest still in use.

## Magnolia Plantation and Gardens

3550 Ashley River Rd, northwest of Drayton Hall • Daily 9am–5pm • Charge • ⓦ magnoliaplantation.com

The **Magnolia Plantation and Gardens** is famed for its stunning ornamental gardens, particularly in spring when the azaleas are blooming. Admission gives you access to the grounds, which include a tropical greenhouse, a petting zoo, a maze and a wildlife observation tower, but you have to pay extra for **house tours**, the "**Slavery to Freedom**" tour, a visit to the **Audubon Swamp**, complete with alligators and lush plant life, "nature train" tour of the grounds or a "nature boat" tour of the swamp.

## Charles Towne Landing

1500 Old Towne Rd • Daily 9am–5pm • Charge • ⓦ southcarolinaparks.com

West of the Ashley River bridge, **Charles Towne Landing** is a 663-acre state park on the site where in 1670 the English colonists established the first permanent settlement in the Carolinas. As well as the landing site itself, you can see a living history settlement, a replica of a seventeenth-century merchant ship and a zoo, home to creatures the colonists would have encountered when they landed here – pumas, bison, alligators, black bears and otters. The park is also crisscrossed with excellent hiking and biking trails.

## The beaches

East of Charleston, **beaches** such as **Isle of Palms** and **Sullivan's Island** are heavily used by locals on weekends. The further from town, the more likely you are to find a peaceful stretch. South of the city, the waves of **Folly Beach** are rated highly by surfers.

### ARRIVAL AND DEPARTURE                                    CHARLESTON AND AROUND

**By plane** Charleston International Airport is 12 miles north of downtown, off I-526 (ⓦ iflychs.com); a Charleston Green taxi (ⓣ 843 819 0846) into town costs around $30.
**By bus** The Greyhound station (ⓣ 843 744 4247) is at 3610 Dorchester Rd, a disreputable spot near I-26. There's a daily

service to Savannah, GA (2hr 10min).
**By train** The Amtrak station is in a dodgy area at 4465 Gaynor Ave, 8 miles north of downtown.
Destinations Atlanta, GA (2 daily; 4hr 40min); Savannah, GA (2 daily; 1hr 45min).

### GETTING AROUND, INFORMATION AND TOURS

**By bus or trolleybus** CARTA buses (ⓦ ridecarta.com) cover most areas, including nearby beaches, and there are three useful trolleybus routes, the Downtown Area Shuttles (DASH). One- two- and three-day passes are available, covering both.
**Visitor centre** 375 Meeting St (daily 8.30am–5pm; ⓣ 843 853 8000, ⓦ charlestoncvb.com).
**Horse and carriage rides** These provide a lively and

leisurely overview; Old South Carriage Co leaves regularly from 14 Anston St (1hr; charge; ⓦ oldsouthcarriage.com). They also offer a range of other tours, including evening carriage tours and haunted walking tours.
**Walking tours** Charleston is a lovely place to stroll around; the visitor centre has details of walking tours covering everything from pirates through architecture to black history, as well as discount coupons, maps and bus/tram passes.

### ACCOMMODATION                                                       SEE MAP PAGE 63

To enjoy the best of Charleston, plan to spend at least a few nights in the historic district, where many of the old-world mansions serve as elegant B&Bs. Further out, the usual **motels** cluster around US-17 and along I-26.
**Andrew Pinckney Inn** 40 Pinckney St ⓦ andrewpinckney inn.com. Stylish, Caribbean-style rooms in this boutique hotel beside the historic market. Continental breakfast served on the rooftop terrace. $$$
**Days Inn Historic District** 155 Meeting St ⓦ wyndham

hotels.com. This two-storey motel lacks the charm of the B&Bs, but rooms are spacious and comfortable, with attractive wrought-iron balconies and an unbeatable location. The pool and free onsite parking are a bonus. $$$
**Indigo Inn** 1 Maiden Lane ⓦ indigoinn.com. This straightforward but well-run inn checks off the important boxes: location, price, comfort. The cosy inn, so named because the first commercial crops of indigo – used for blue dye – were planted and harvested in Charleston, has

a touch of that Southern charm – patterned bedspreads, antique furnishings, a garden courtyard. $\overline{\$\$\$}$

**Mills House Hotel** 115 Meeting St ⓦ millshouse.com. Large, smart, very central hotel, in business since 1853. Guestrooms combine elegant period furnishings with modern comfort, with a variety of views, including of the historic centre or breezy pool. $\overline{\$\$\$\$}$

**NotSo Hostel** 156 Spring St ⓦ notsohostel.com. Appealing, very friendly, well-run hostel in a double-porched 1850 house on the northern edge of downtown. Rates include free parking and a full breakfast. An annexe a few blocks away has simple rooms. Dorms $\overline{\$}$, doubles $\overline{\$\$}$

**The Restoration** 75 Wentworth St ⓦ therestorationhotel. com. One of Charleston's premier boutique hotels is comprised of five historic buildings. Its 54 suite-like rooms have rustic brick walls, wood beams and designer toiletries. The hotel also abounds with on-trend amenities, such as the The *Rise Coffee Bar*, which pours small-batch brews, and *The Watch Rooftop and Spirits*, serving seasonal Low Country Cuisine. $\overline{\$\$\$\$}$

**The Vendue** 30 Vendue Range ⓦ thevendue.com. This lovely, superbly located boutique hotel, filled with local artwork, features classically elegant rooms plus all sorts of free goodies, like evening milk and cookies, daily art tours led by the hotel's art docent, complimentary bicycles to explore the city and more. $\overline{\$\$\$\$}$

## EATING

SEE MAP PAGE 63

Charleston has emerged as one of the culinary capitals of the South, playing host to a superb array of restaurants that are continually reinventing Low Country cuisine.

**Butcher & Bee** 1085 Morrison Drive ⓦ butcherandbee. com. Dine on artisanal, lovingly crafted cuisine in a sleek, industrial-style setting. For breakfast, try the brown rice bowl with poached egg and almond butter; lunch includes a creative array of sandwiches, including roast beef with smoked onion jam; and for dinner, lamb sausage and roast peppers. $\overline{\$\$}$

★ **Cru Café** 18 Pinckney St ☎ 843 534 2434. Cosy, pretty restaurant in an eighteenth-century house with a porch, dishing up satisfying, sophisticated food that puts a modern global twist on local staples. Try the tangy Thai seafood risotto, and the grilled salmon with a honey-ginger glaze. $\overline{\$\$\$}$

**FIG** 232 Meeting St ⓦ eatatfig.com. Minimalist neighbourhood bistro, open for dinner only, with a focus on fresh Low Country ingredients. Menus change seasonally, but the fish stews, and fig tart with pancetta are good bets, and the farm-fresh veggies are wonderful. $\overline{\$\$\$}$

**Harold's Cabin** 247 Congress St ⓦ haroldscabin.com. A former snowball (snowcone) shop, gourmet grocery store and local icon, *Harold's Cabin* was reborn in 2016 as a wonderfully eclectic restaurant, where the seasonal, foraged menu matches the whimsical and changing wall art – look for the rabbit with antlers. Try pickled shrimp, cornmeal-fried okra and beer-battered fried chicken. $\overline{\$\$}$

★ **Husk** 76 Queen St ⓦ huskrestaurant.com. This highly regarded restaurant marries scrupulously sourced local ingredients with culinary wizardry – oysters with peach mignonette and cornmeal-dusted catfish with sweet peppers. Though it's housed in a dignified 1893 Queen Anne, the ambience is markedly unfussy. $\overline{\$\$\$}$

**Mercantile and Mash** 701 E Bay St ⓦ mercandmash. com. A gourmet food hall housed in a former cigar factory, *Mercantile and Mash* offers a delicious grazing experience: from duck confit salad with artisanal greens to warm grits with cheddar, bacon and chives to a pulled rotisserie chicken sandwich on a hoagie roll. Top off the afternoon with a local beer or whiskey at *Bar Mash*, which also has bocce courts, shuffleboard and an Eighties arcade game. $\overline{\$\$}$

★ **Rodney Scott's BBQ** 1011 King St ⓦ rodneyscottsbbq. com. Award-winning pitmaster (barbecue-pit operator) Rodney Scott goes whole hog in Charleston, with his wildly popular BBQ joint. The ambiance is communal and casual – belly up to the counter or sink into a booth – and the BBQ is the stuff of legend. Feast on pulled pork, juicy ribs, chicken and turkey – or go for a combo platter and sample 'em all. The banana pudding for dessert is a must. $\overline{\$\$}$

**Slightly North of Broad** 192 E Bay St ⓦ snobcharleston. com. This buzzy bistro shows off the best of nouvelle Southern cuisine, with an inventive mix-and-match menu of small, medium and large plates, from grilled peach salad with goat cheese to quail with lemon and rosemary sausage to BBQ tuna with fried oysters. $\overline{\$\$\$\$}$

## DRINKING AND NIGHTLIFE

SEE MAP PAGE 63

Charleston has a lively nightlife, though downtown bars tend to be touristy. For **listings**, see the free weekly *City Paper* (ⓦ charlestoncitypaper.com), or *Eater Charleston* (ⓦ charleston.eater.com), which chronicles in full detail the rise (and fall) of the city's bars and restaurants. Chief among the city's many **festivals** is Spoleto (ⓦ spoletousa.org), an extraordinarily rich extravaganza of international arts held in late May/early June.

**Edmund's Oast Brewing Co.** 1505 King St ⓦ edmundsoast.com. Come for the craft beer, stay for the food. This welcoming, lively brew bar offers an immense array of craft beer, from tart concoctions like the Peach Fizz – wild ale, Champagne yeast, fresh peaches hops – to dark brews. The cocktails are also top-notch, including sake bombs and strawberry daiquiris. Soak up the drinks with pizza, pork-fried egg rolls, catfish and Italian sausage. Happy hour (daily 4.30–6.30pm) is the time to come by, with house beer and wine at low prices.

**The Griffon** 18 Vendue Range ⓦ griffoncharleston. com. Cosy tavern, serving craft ales as well as tasty English-

**1**

style fish and chips. Every inch of its bar, walls and ceiling beams is covered with scribbled-on dollar bills.

**Music Farm** 32 Ann St ⓦ musicfarm.com. This warehouse-like building alongside the visitor centre is the best place in Charleston to see regional and national touring bands.

**The Rooftop at The Vendue** 19 Vendue Range ⓦ thevendue.com. Enjoyable and stylish cocktail bar and restaurant with dramatic views over the harbour, the historic district and out to Fort Sumter.

## The sea islands

South of Charleston toward Savannah, the coastline dissolves into small, marshy **sea islands** peppered with oyster beds and prickly palmetto groves. Along this romantic strand, icy drinks are sipped on bayfront verandas, century-old oak trees take up whole streets, and a West African dialect that pre-dates America is spoken.

### Edisto Island

On pretty **Edisto Island**, south of US-17 on Hwy-174, live oaks festooned with drapes of Spanish moss form canopies over the roads, bright green marshes harbour rich birdlife and fine beaches line the seaward side. There are no motels, but **Edisto Beach State Park** (daily 8am–6pm; charge; ⓦ southcarolinaparks.com) has a **campground**.

| ACCOMMODATION | EDISTO ISLAND |
|---|---|
| **Edisto Beach State Park campground** 8377 State Cabin Rd ⓦ southcarolinaparks.com. Inviting campground near a beach lined with palmetto trees and | other semitropical plants. The park also maintains a/c cabins (sleeping four) which fill up months in advance and come with utensils, linens and TVs. Tents $\overline{\underline{5}}$, cabins $\overline{\underline{5}}$$\overline{\underline{5}}$ |

### Beaufort

The largest town in the area, **BEAUFORT** (pronounced "Byoofert") has a lovely historic district, brought to life in novels by writer and resident Pat Conroy, and in films such as *Forrest Gump* and *The Big Chill*. Despite being a vanguard of the secessionist movement, this tidal village was one of the first taken by Union troops at the start of the Civil War. Hoping to prevent the destruction of their homes, cotton and indigo planters fled town (in what was dubbed "The Great Skedaddle") at the beginning of the conflict. The thousands of West African slaves left behind – isolated on islands with no bridge to the mainland – thrived, and their community's language (known as "Gullah"), customs and culture remain preserved to this day.

| ARRIVAL, INFORMATION AND TOURS | BEAUFORT |
|---|---|
| **By bus** The Greyhound station (☎ 843 524 4646) is 2 miles north of town on US-21.<br>**Visitor centre** 713 Craven St (Mon–Sat 9am–5pm, Sun noon–5pm; ☎ 843 525 8500, ⓦ beaufortsc.org); offers | details of local tours and information on accommodation.<br>**Kayaking tours** Get out on the water by renting a kayak (from $25) with knowledgeable Lands End Tours (ⓦ beaufortlandsendpaddling.net), who also do guided trips. |

#### ACCOMMODATION AND EATING

| | |
|---|---|
| **Cuthbert House Inn** 1203 Bay St ⓦ cuthberthouseinn.com. General Sherman himself stayed at this esteemed B&B, where, inside the fireplace, Union soldiers etched their names. Overlooking the bay, the inn offers nine spacious guest rooms, free bike use and happy hour on a veranda filled with rocking chairs. $\overline{\underline{5}}$$\overline{\underline{5}}$$\overline{\underline{5}}$$\overline{\underline{5}}$<br>★ **Old Bull Tavern** 205 West St ⓦ oldbulltavern.com. | Central, arty gastropub that feels like it could have been airlifted from Manhattan, yet its setting – between tidal marshes and antebellum homes – only adds to its charm. Dimly lit by Edison bulbs, the bar mixes a mean cocktail, while the kitchen dishes up sophisticated fare such lamb shank braised in red wine and addictive rosemary cashews. Check out the witty, rotating sayings above the bar. $\overline{\underline{5}}$$\overline{\underline{5}}$ |

### St Helena Island

Across the bridge southeast of Beaufort, **ST HELENA ISLAND**, dotted with small shrimp- and oyster-fishing communities, is among the least spoiled of the eastern sea islands.

1

The further south you go the more gorgeous the **landscape** gets: amazing Spanish moss hangs from ancient oaks, while enormous, wide views stretch out across vibrant green marshes patterned with small salt creeks.

## The Penn Center

16 Penn Center Circle W, off US-21 • Tues–Sat 9am–4pm • Museum charge, grounds free • ⓦ penncenter.com

St Helena Island is a region of strong **black communities**, descended from slaves who acquired parcels of land after they were freed by the Union army; their Gullah dialect is an Afro-English patois with many West African words. The **Penn Center** houses the **school** started for freed slaves in 1862 by Laura Towne, a white teacher from Pennsylvania. During the 1960s, this remote campus was the only place in South Carolina where interracial groups could safely convene, and, as such, served as an important retreat for civil rights leaders.

Upon arrival, head into the well-curated **York W. Bailey Museum**, filled with historic photos and island artefacts. Also, don't miss the **Gantt Cottage**, a humble building with an astounding history – it was once home to Martin Luther King, Jr. and handwritten drafts of his "I Have a Dream" speech were uncovered here.

## Hunting Island State Park

2555 Sea Island Pkwy (US-21) • Daily: summer 6am–9pm; rest of year 6am–6pm • Charge • **Lighthouse** Daily: March–Oct 10am–4.45pm; Nov–Feb 10am–3.45pm • Charge • ⓦ southcarolinaparks.com

St Helena's main **beach**, at **Hunting Island State Park**, can get crowded, but it's ravishing: soft white sand, wide and gently shelving, scattered with shards of pearly shells and fringed with a mature maritime forest of palmettos, palm trees and sea oats. Pelicans come here to feed, particularly in the early morning; it's also a turtle-nesting site. Tackling the 175 steps of the little black-and-white **lighthouse**, you're rewarded with views that extend forty miles.

### ACCOMMODATION                                                     ST HELENA ISLAND

**Hunting Island State Park campground** 2555 Sea Island Pkwy ⓦ southcarolinaparks.com. Lodgings by the lighthouse in one weather-beaten cabin (sleeping six); reserve well in advance. There's also a large campground near the water. Tents $̶$, cabin $̶$$̶$$̶$

# Georgia

Compared to the rest of **GEORGIA**, the largest of the Southern states, the bright lights of its capital Atlanta are a wild aberration. Apart from some beaches and towns on the highly indented coastline, this rural state is composed of slow, easy-going settlements where the best, and sometimes the only, way to enjoy your time is to sip iced tea and have a chat on the porch.

Settlement in Georgia, the thirteenth British colony (named after King George II), started in 1733 at Savannah, intended as a haven of Christian principles for poor Britons, with both alcohol and slavery banned. However, under pressure from planters, **slavery** was introduced in 1752 and by the time of the **Civil War** almost half the population were African slaves. Little fighting took place on Georgia soil until Sherman's troops advanced from Tennessee, burned Atlanta to the ground, and, in the infamous "March to the Sea", laid waste to all property on the way to the coast.

Today, bustling **Atlanta** stands as the unofficial capital of the South. The city where **Martin Luther King, Jr.** was born, preached and is buried bears little relation to *Gone With the Wind* stereotypes and its forward-thinking energy is upheld as a role model for the "New South". The state's main tourist destination, though, is the **coast**, stretching south from beautiful old **Savannah** via the **sea islands** to the semitropical

**1**

**Okefenokee Swamp,** inland near Florida. In the **northeast,** the **Appalachian foothills** are fetching in the fall, while the college town of **Athens** is known for its offbeat rock heroes R.E.M. and the B-52s.

# Atlanta

At first glance, **ATLANTA** is a typical large American city, with an especially massive urban sprawl: the population of the entire metropolitan area exceeds 6 million. It is also undeniably upbeat and progressive, with little interest in lamenting a lost Southern past, and since electing the nation's first black mayor, the late Maynard Jackson, in 1974, it has remained the most conspicuously black-run city in the USA. As if to counterbalance the alienating sprawl, the city maintains plenty of active, prettily landscaped green spaces (most notably, the 22-mile BeltLine), and its neighbourhoods have distinct, recognizable identities; quaint Virginia Highlands is just a short drive away from trendy Inman Park and grungier, punky Little Five Points, for example, but the three have little in common. Once you accept the driving distances and the roaring freeways, dynamic Atlanta has plenty to offer, with must-see attractions from sites associated with Dr King to the fascinating National Center for Civil and Human Rights to cultural institutions including the High Museum of Art.

### The CNN Center

190 Marietta St NW • Tours daily 9am–5pm; VIP Tour Mon–Sat 9.30am–3.30pm • Charge; reservations recommended • ⓦ center.cnn.com

In the heart of downtown, the **CNN Center** is the headquarters of the largest news broadcaster in the world. Energetic guided tours of assorted lengths rush you past frazzled producers and toothy anchorpersons. You'll also learn some of the nitty-gritty of television production, such as how dialogue prompts get posted into cameras. One lucky tour-taker will get to don an invisible cloak via a "green screen" – used when reporting the weather forecast.

### Georgia Aquarium

225 Baker St NW • Summer: Sun–Fri 9am–9pm, Sat 8am–9pm; rest of year Mon–Fri 10am–8pm, Sat–Sun 9am–8pm • Charge; various passes and combo tickets available • ⓦ georgiaaquarium.org

On the north side of **Centennial Olympic Park**, the city's most beloved open space, the **Georgia Aquarium** is a state-of-the-art facility that is so popular you should book in advance. Highlights include the biggest tank in the world, filled with sharks and manta rays and recreations of Georgia habitats; and the Dolphin Celebration, featuring bottlenose dolphins leaping through the air.

### National Center for Civil and Human Rights

100 Ivan Allen Jr Blvd • Mon–Sat 10am–5pm, Sun noon–5pm • Charge • ⓦ civilandhumanrights.org

---

### ATLANTA ORIENTATION

Atlanta's layout is confusing, with its roads following old Native American trails rather than a logical grid. An unbelievable number of streets are named "Peachtree"; be sure to determine whether you're looking for Avenue, Road or Boulevard and pay special attention to whether it's "NW", "W" or so forth. The most important, **Peachtree Street**, cuts a long north–south swath through the city. Note also that the city is split into three urban centres: downtown (home to major attractions like the **World of Coca-Cola**), midtown (the arts district) and Buckhead (fancy suburbia). Sights are scattered, but relatively easy to reach by car or on the subway. Most neighbourhoods, including **downtown**, the Martin Luther King Jr Historic District along **Auburn Avenue** and trendy **Little Five Points**, are easy to explore on foot.

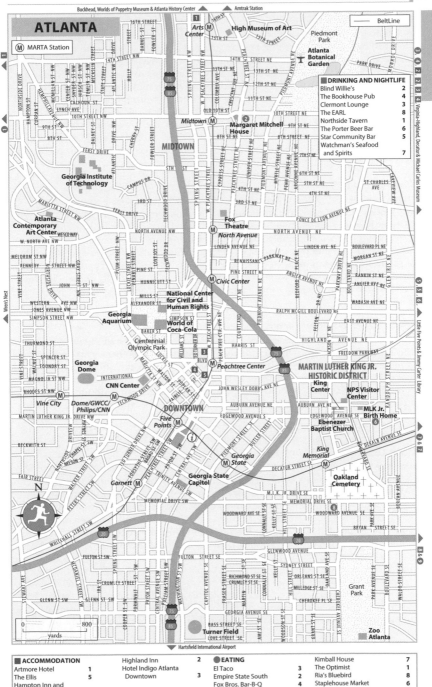

# ATLANTA

Ⓜ MARTA Station

⎯⎯ BeltLine

Virginia-Highland, Decatur & Michael Carlos Museum ▶

Little Five Points & Jimmy Carter Library

Wren's Nest ◀

**■ DRINKING AND NIGHTLIFE**

| Blind Willie's | 2 |
| The Bookhouse Pub | 4 |
| Clermont Lounge | 3 |
| The EARL | 8 |
| Northside Tavern | 1 |
| The Porter Beer Bar | 6 |
| Star Community Bar | 5 |
| Watchman's Seafood and Spirits | 7 |

Piedmont Park

High Museum of Art

Arts Center

Atlanta Botanical Garden

Georgia Institute of Technology

Atlanta Contemporary Art Center

Fox Theatre

North Avenue Ⓜ

MIDTOWN

Midtown Ⓜ

Margaret Mitchell House

Civic Center Ⓜ

National Center for Civil and Human Rights

Georgia Aquarium

World of Coca-Cola

Centennial Olympic Park

Georgia Dome

CNN Center

Dome/GWCC/ Philips/CNN Ⓜ

Vine City Ⓜ

Peachtree Center Ⓜ

MARTIN LUTHER KING JR. HISTORIC DISTRICT

King Center

NPS Visitor Center

MLK Jr. Birth Home

Ebenezer Baptist Church

DOWNTOWN

Five Points Ⓜ

ⓘ

Georgia State Ⓜ

Georgia State Capitol

Garnett Ⓜ

King Memorial Ⓜ

Oakland Cemetery

Turner Field

Grant Park

Zoo Atlanta

N

0 — 800
yards

Hartsfield International Airport

| **■ ACCOMMODATION** | | ● EATING | | Kimball House | 7 |
|---|---|---|---|---|---|
| Artmore Hotel | 1 | El Taco | 3 | The Optimist | 1 |
| The Ellis | 5 | Empire State South | 2 | Ria's Bluebird | 8 |
| Hampton Inn and | | Fox Bros. Bar-B-Q | 4 | Staplehouse Market | 6 |
| Suites Downtown | 4 | Gunshow | 9 | The Vortex | 5 |
| Highland Inn | 2 | | | | |
| Hotel Indigo Atlanta | | | | | |
| Downtown | 3 | | | | |

**1** Downtown Atlanta is awash in striking architecture, but the **National Center for Civil and Human Rights**, which opened in 2014, manages to eclipse everything around it. Designed by noted architect Phil Freelon, the stunning, grandly curving structure, which embraces soaring galleries, was inspired by the universal gesture of unity: the joining of hands. Within, the exhibits superbly bridge the past and present, linking Atlanta's civil rights history and the global human rights movement. The galleries feature permanent exhibits on everything from human rights history around the world to the 1963 March on Washington, as well as temporary shows such as *Rhythm, Blues, Resistance*, connecting music and social justice. There's also a Woolworth lunch-counter simulator that recreates a famous 1960 sit-in protest by four black students. Through it all, the Center's mission is front and centre: "to empower people to take the protection of every human's rights personally".

## World of Coca-Cola

121 Baker St NW • Mon–Thurs from 10am, Fri–Sun from 9am; closing times vary • Charge • ⓦ worldofcoca-cola.com

The **World of Coca-Cola** is a shiny, happy slice of modern Americana. Pushed by its relentlessly smiley guides as an "entertainment experience", it's stuffed with high-tech displays and hokey memorabilia illustrating the iconic brand's extraordinary journey from Atlanta soda fountain to world domination. Above all, it's an eye-opening study of genius marketing, peaking in the "Taste it" room, where kids and parents alike excitedly slurp Coke drinks from around the world – best avoid Italy's bitter "Beverly" – a hyper feeding frenzy that pumps visitors full of sugar before siphoning them off to the gift store.

## Atlanta Contemporary Art Center

535 Means St NW • Tues–Wed & Fri–Sat 11am–5pm, Thurs 11am–8pm, Sun noon–4pm • Free • ⓦ atlantacontemporary.org

This is the place to catch artists on the rise. The **Atlanta Contemporary Art Center** is one of the few art centres in the region that commissions new works, offering a glimpse into emerging artists of the Southeast. The museum presents over 100 local – as well as national and international – artists throughout the year, from sculpture and mixed media to photography and paintings. The events calendar is equally vibrant, including Contemporary Cocktails (Thurs 6–8pm), where creative cocktails are prepared by a monthly mixologist-in-residence.

## Martin Luther King, Jr. National Historic Site

**Visitor centre** 450 Auburn Ave NE • Daily 9am–5pm • Free • ⓦ nps.gov/malu

One and a half miles east of Centennial Park, **Auburn Avenue** stands as a monument to Atlanta's black history. During its heyday in the 1920s, "**Sweet Auburn**" was a prosperous, progressive area of black-owned businesses and jazz clubs, but it went into a decline with the Depression from which it has never truly recovered. Several blocks have been designated as the **Martin Luther King, Jr. National Historic Site**, in honour of Auburn's most cherished native son. This short stretch of road is the most visited attraction in all Georgia and it's a moving experience to watch the crowds of school kids waiting in turn to take photographs. Head first for the park service's **visitor centre** where an exhibition covers King's life and campaigns. If you're looking for a broader account of the civil rights years, the museum in Memphis is much more comprehensive (see page 98), but this provides a powerful summary, culminating with the mule-drawn wagon used in King's funeral procession in Atlanta on April 9, 1968.

## Birth Home

501 Auburn Ave NE • Daily 10am–4pm • Free • ⓦ nps.gov/malu

Check in at the visitor centre for a free tour of King's **Birth Home**, a short walk east. As only fifteen people can visit at a time and school groups often visit en masse, it can be

## REVEREND DR MARTIN LUTHER KING, JR. (1929–68)

**Martin Luther King, Jr.** was born at 501 Auburn Ave, Atlanta, on January 15, 1929. The house was then home to his parents and his grandparents; both his maternal grandfather, Rev A.D. Williams, and his father, Martin Luther King, Sr, served as pastor of **Ebenezer Baptist Church** nearby. Young Martin was ordained at 19 and became co-pastor at Ebenezer with his father, but continued his studies at Crozer Theological Seminary in Pennsylvania, where he was profoundly influenced by the ideas of Mahatma Gandhi, and at Boston University. Returning to the South, King became pastor of Dexter Avenue Baptist Church in **Montgomery**, Alabama, in 1954, where his leadership during the bus boycott a year later (see page 98) brought him to national prominence. A visit to India in 1959 further cemented his belief in nonviolent resistance as the means by which racial segregation could be eradicated. He returned to Atlanta in 1960, becoming co-pastor at Ebenezer once more, but also taking on the presidency of the **Southern Christian Leadership Conference**. As such, he became the figurehead for the civil rights struggle, planning strategy for future campaigns, flying into each new trouble spot, and commenting to the news media on every latest development. His apotheosis in that role came in August 1963, when he addressed the **March on Washington** with his "I Have a Dream" speech. He was awarded the **Nobel Peace Prize** in 1964. Despite King's passionate espousal of nonviolence, J. Edgar Hoover's **FBI** branded him "the most dangerous and effective Negro leader in the country", and persistently attempted to discredit him over his personal life. King himself became more overtly politicized in his final years. Challenged by the stridency of Malcolm X and the radicalism of urban black youth, he came to see the deprivation and poverty of the cities of the North as affecting black and white alike, and only solvable by tackling "the triple evils of racism, extreme materialism, and militarism". In the South, he had always been able to appeal to the federal government as an (albeit often reluctant) ally; now, having declared his opposition to the war in **Vietnam**, he faced a sterner and lonelier struggle. In the event, his **Poor People's Campaign** had barely got off the ground before King was assassinated (see page 98) in Memphis on April 4, 1968.

tough to get a spot – visit early in the week or on Sunday morning for the best chance. If you don't make it in, you can always do a "virtual tour", using the computers at the visitor centre. The house itself is a fourteen-room Queen Anne-style shotgun, restored to its prosperous 1930s appearance. Home to King until he was 12 (he was born in an upstairs bedroom), it remained in his family until 1971.

### King Center

449 Auburn Ave NE · Daily: summer 9am–6pm; rest of year 9am–5pm · Free · ⓦ thekingcenter.org

Across from the visitor centre, the **King Center** is privately run by King's family. Chiefly a research facility, it features artefacts such as his travelling case and the hotel key from the room at the *Lorraine Motel* where he was assassinated (see page 98), as well as tiny rooms devoted to Mahatma Gandhi and Rosa Parks. King's mortal remains, along with those of his wife, Coretta, who died in 2006, are held in a plain marble **tomb** inscribed with the words "Free at last, Free at last, thank God Almighty I'm Free at last", which stands, guarded by an eternal flame, in the shallow Reflecting Pool outside.

### Ebenezer Baptist Church

101 Jackson St · Daily 9am–5pm · Free · ⓦ nps.gov/malu

Next door to the King Center, the **Ebenezer Baptist Church**, where both King's baptism and funeral took place – and where his mother was assassinated while playing the organ in 1974 – has been carefully restored. During the 1960s, King worked as a pastor here with his father. Inside, you can listen to King's speeches (they're piped in on a loop) from the same pews where his congregants sat. It will give you chills.

**1**

### Fox Theatre

660 Peachtree St NE · Tours Mon, Thurs & Sat on the hour from 10am–1pm · Charge · ⓦ foxtheatre.org

Nestled among the glass skyscrapers, the flamboyant Art Deco **Fox Theatre**, with its strong Moorish theme, is a rare and gorgeous remnant of old Atlanta. If you're not attending one of its fairly mainstream shows, you can see the lovely interior on an organized tour.

### Margaret Mitchell House

990 Peachtree St NE · Mon–Sat 10am–5.30pm, Sun noon–5.30pm · Charge · ⓦ atlantahistorycenter.com

Three blocks north of the Fox Theatre, the only brick home left on Peachtree Street is the **Margaret Mitchell House**. Mitchell and her husband lived in the small apartment she called "the dump" during the ten years she took to write her best-selling novel, *Gone With the Wind*. Published in 1936, it took just six weeks to sell enough copies to form a tower fifty times higher than the Empire State Building; the 1939 movie scaled further peaks of popularity. Lively guided tours tell the fascinating tale.

### High Museum of Art

1280 Peachtree St NE · Tues–Thurs & Sat 10am–5pm, Fri 10am–9pm, Sun noon–5pm · Charge · ⓦ high.org

Part of the **Woodruff Arts Center**, an umbrella organization that houses the city's symphony orchestra and **Alliance Theatre**, Atlanta's splendid **High Museum of Art**, in stunning, airy premises designed by Renzo Piano and Richard Meier, is world-class. Permanent collections include idiosyncratic folk art by Howard Finster and Mose Tolliver, some fabulous mid-twentieth-century American furniture and extensive European galleries covering five centuries from Renaissance Italy to the French Impressionists.

### Worlds of Puppetry Museum

1404 Spring St · Tues–Fri 9am–5pm, Sat 10am–5pm, Sun noon–5pm · Charge · ⓦ puppet.org

The magical **Worlds of Puppetry Museum**, which opened in 2015, forms part of the Center for Puppetry Arts, the country's largest nonprofit organization dedicated to the art of puppet theatre. Explore the well-curated museum, which features puppets from throughout history, including all the Jim Henson characters – Kermit the Frog, Miss Piggy, Bert and Ernie – as well as global puppets, from Sicilian marionettes to Indonesian shadow puppets. The Center also features lively puppet shows and a hugely popular create-a-puppet workshop.

### Atlanta Botanical Garden

1345 Piedmont Ave NE · April–Oct Tues 9am–7pm, Wed–Sun 9am–5pm; Nov–March Tues–Sun 9am–5pm · Charge · ⓦ atlantabg.org

With its leafy trails, playgrounds, tennis courts, boardwalk and public pool, elegant **Piedmont Park** has provided a lot of pulse to Atlanta since its construction in 1904. The highlight of the park, however, is the wonderfully landscaped **Atlanta Botanical Garden**. In addition to its manicured gardens and vast conservatories of gorgeous orchids and tropical plants, the garden hosts summer-long sculpture exhibitions and big-name concerts.

### Atlanta History Center

130 W Paces Ferry Rd NW · Mon–Sat 10am–5pm, Sun noon–5.30pm · Charge · ⓦ atlantahistorycenter.com

---

## THE BELTLINE

An excellent way to sightsee in Atlanta is via the **BeltLine** (ⓦ beltline.org), a 22-mile train corridor that has been transformed into an appealing green space and massive bike loop. Encircling the city, the path skirts Piedmont Park, and comes quite close to Zoo Atlanta. With or without an itinerary, though, it's great for ambling, with plenty of entrance points and restaurants close at hand. The Atlanta Bicycle Barn (ⓦ atlbikebarn.com) has friendly staff and **rents bikes** by the hour or day.

## THE BURNING OF ATLANTA AND THE MARCH TO THE SEA

In summer 1864, following the comprehensive Confederate defeats of Spotsylvania and the Wilderness in May, Union General William Tecumseh Sherman invaded north Georgia. Outflanking the much smaller Confederate forces, he laid siege to Atlanta; the city eventually surrendered at the start of September.

Sherman announced that the entire population of the city must leave forthwith, and that he would **burn** their property as he deemed necessary. The Confederate commander, General Hood, powerless to resist, expostulated: "Sir, permit me to say that the unprecedented measure you propose transcends, in studied and ingenious cruelty, all acts ever before brought to my attention in the dark history of war. In the name of God and humanity, I protest." Sherman responded: "In the name of common sense, I ask you not to appeal to a just God in such a sacrilegious manner . . . Talk thus to the marines, but not to me." On November 16, Sherman put a torch to the city, and set out on his notorious "March to the Sea." As he later exulted, "Behind us lay Atlanta, smouldering in ruins, the black smoke rising high in the air, and hanging like a pall over the ruined city."

Sherman's March is seen as an early example of total war; some accuse him of inventing the methods later followed in the Nazi Blitzkrieg. His explicit intention was to "make Georgia howl," via the systematic destruction of agricultural and industrial resources and terrorizing of civilians. One Georgia woman recorded in her diary that "there was hardly a fence left standing all the way from Sparta to Gordon. The fields were trampled down and the road was lined with carcasses of horses, hogs and cattle that the invaders, unable either to consume or carry away with them, had wantonly shot down, to starve out the people . . . the dwellings that were standing all showed signs of pillage, and on every plantation we saw . . . charred remains."

It was the final blow to the Southern war effort; though the Confederate armies struggled on for a few more months after Sherman took Savannah, their fate was sealed.

Tucked away in the west, the **Atlanta History Center** offers a superb run-through of the factors that led to the city's relentless growth and is strong on African American and women's history. A Civil War exhibit features an extraordinary number of artefacts; even if the military minutiae don't captivate you, the human stories will, and the whole combines to provide a clear history of the war. You can also tour two houses on the pretty grounds: the 1920s mock-Classical mansion **Swan House** and the rustic **Tullie Smith Farm**.

In 2019, the museum unveiled the splendidly restored **Cyclorama: The Big Picture**. This huge circular painting – longer than a football field and weighing 10,000 pounds – was executed in 1885–86 and depicts the Battle of Atlanta. Viewing the Cyclorama is a full experience: enter the painting rotunda, and then ascend an escalator to a platform for 360-degree views and a 12-minute presentation that's projected onto the painting.

### The Wren's Nest

1050 Ralph David Abernathy Blvd SW • Tues–Sat 10am–2.30pm, storytelling Sat 1pm • Charge • ⓦ wrensnest.org

Historically an African American neighbourhood, the **West End**, southwest of downtown, remains so today: a more upbeat counterpoint to Sweet Auburn. The **Wren's Nest** is the former home of Joel Chandler Harris, the white author of *Br'er Rabbit*. The house remains much as Harris left it upon his death in 1908, while a short film explains that he first heard the Uncle Remus stories from slaves when he trained as a printer on a plantation newspaper. On Saturday afternoon, storytelling sessions take place in the peaceful, untamed garden.

### Zoo Atlanta

800 Cherokee Ave SE • Mon–Fri 9.30am–5.30pm, Sat & Sun 9.30am–6.30pm • Charge • ⓦ zooatlanta.org

**Zoo Atlanta** features a giant pandas from Chengdu, gorillas, kangaroos, otters and flamingos plus recreations of various habitats. It also puts on lots of lively shows and

1

lectures, such as Wild World Weekends, with dances and other cultural events that celebrate animal species from around the world.

### Oakland Cemetery
248 Oakland Ave SE • Daily dawn–dusk; tours offered at various times – check website • Free, charge for tours • ⓦ oaklandcemetery.com

The city's oldest and largest burial ground, **Oakland Cemetery** is the resting place of famous Atlanta citizens, including Margaret Mitchell; walking tours are available. Built in the "garden cemetery" tradition, its sweeping 88 acres are beautifully landscaped with dogwood trees, delicate magnolias and ornate headstones and mausoleums. Guided tours explore the history, art and architecture of the cemetery.

## Little Five Points and around

Northeast of Auburn Avenue, around Euclid and Moreland avenues, the youthful, if gentrifying, **Little Five Points** district is a tangle of thrift stores, hip restaurants, body-piercing parlours, bars and clubs. Home to some of the city's best nightlife, it's equally diverting when the sun is up – pop into a record store, or spend the afternoon with coffee and a book.

Northeast, beyond the upmarket **Virginia-Highland** restaurant district, the trek to **Emory University**'s campus is rewarded by the lovely **Michael C. Carlos Museum** (571 S Kilgo Circle; Tues–Fri 10am–4pm, Sat 10am–5pm, Sun noon–5pm; charge; ⓦ carlos. emory.edu), which hosts a splendid collection of fine art and antiquities from all six inhabited continents.

### Jimmy Carter Presidential Library and Museum
441 John Lewis Freedom Pkwy • Mon–Sat 9am–4.45pm, Sun noon–4.45pm • Charge • ⓦ jimmycarterlibrary.gov

On the hill where Sherman is said to have watched Atlanta burn, the **Jimmy Carter Presidential Library and Museum** is devoted to the peanut farmer who rose to become Georgia state governor and the 39th president of the USA. Look out for 12-year-old Jimmy's school essay on health, in which he earnestly urges readers to keep their teeth clean.

## ARRIVAL AND DEPARTURE                                      ATLANTA

**By plane** The huge Hartsfield-Jackson International Airport (ⓣ 800 897 1910, ⓦ atl.com), the busiest in the country if not the world, is 10 miles south of downtown Atlanta, just inside I-285 ("the perimeter"). It's the southern terminus of the north/south lines of the subway, a 15min trip from downtown, and is also served by shuttle services and taxis.
**By bus** Greyhound buses (ⓣ 404 584 1728) arrive south of downtown at 232 Forsyth St, near the Garnett subway station.

Destinations Birmingham, AL (5 daily; 2hr 50min); Chattanooga, TN (9 daily; 2hr 10min); Macon, GA (10 daily; 1hr 40min); Montgomery, AL (5 daily; 4hr); Nashville, TN (8 daily; 4hr 30min); Savannah, GA (4 daily; 4hr 35min).
**By train** Atlanta's Amtrak station, 1688 Peachtree St NW, is at the north end of Midtown, just under a mile north of the nearest subway station, Arts Center.
Destinations Birmingham, AL (1 daily; 4hr 15min); Savannah, GA (2 daily; 4hr 40min).

## GETTING AROUND, INFORMATION AND TOURS

**By subway** The useful MARTA subway system has four lines, two east/west and two north/south, which intersect downtown at Five Points (Mon–Fri 5am–1am, Sat & Sun 6am–1am; one- and seven-day passes available; ⓦ itsmarta.com).
**Visitor centre** Centennial Park (Mon–Sat 10am–6pm,

Sun noon–6pm; ⓣ 404 521 6569, ⓦ atlanta.net).
**Walking tours** The Atlanta Preservation Center leads lively historical walking tours of several different neighbourhoods, from downtown to Sweet Auburn (around 90min; charge; ⓦ atlantapreservationcenter.com).

## ACCOMMODATION                                    SEE MAP PAGE 71

Atlanta has a wide range of accommodation, from chain hotels to boutique inns. Downtown puts you near the top sights, while midtown can be a bit cheaper, and offers closer proximity to nightlife.
**Artmore Hotel** 1302 W Peachtree St ⓦ artmorehotel.

com. This cool hotel in a refurbished historic building, near the High Museum of Art, has a lovely Spanish Mediterranean facade, comfortable rooms filled with red accents, plus a pretty candlelit courtyard. $$$
**The Ellis** 176 Peachtree St NE ⓦ ellishotel.com. Central,

stylish hotel close to Centennial Park and the aquarium. The modern rooms have limestone bathrooms. For a healthy stay, ask for a Stay Well room, which has mattress toppers made with hypoallergenic natural fibres as well as air purifiers and special lamps that simulate natural sunlight. $$$

**Hampton Inn and Suites Downtown** 161 Ted Turner Drive NW Ⓦhamptoninn.hilton.com. Located in a handsome brick building that dates from 1927, this downtown chain has comfortable rooms and is within walking distance of many attractions, making it one of the best-value central options. Rates include breakfast. $$

**Highland Inn** 644 N Highland Ave Ⓦthehighlandinn.

com. Hipsters flock to this cool, slightly tatty, hotel near Little Five Points and Virginia Highlands. It's a lively place, with an adjacent café, and a fun historic setup – dating from 1927, it once held a bowling alley and swimming pool, now converted to a courtyard and lounge. $$

**Hotel Indigo Atlanta Downtown** 230 Peachtree St Ⓦihg.com. Part of the *230 Peachtree* complex, the sleek *Hotel Indigo* reflects Atlanta's design history throughout, including in the cool-toned rooms, where murals depict the nearby AmericasMart, one of the world's largest wholesale trade centres. $$$$

## EATING

SEE MAP PAGE 71

Atlanta has scores of great restaurants to suit all budgets and tastes. The most popular neighbourhoods (such as Inman Park and Virginia-Highland) each have their own local bistros helmed by up-and-coming chefs. Many Midtown options are upmarket, while **Southern soul food** is best around Auburn Avenue.

**El Taco** 1186 N Highland Ave NE, Virginia-Highland Ⓦeltaco-atlanta.com. Boisterous Tex-Mex place distinguished by its gorgeous mural depicting Frida Kahlo, tequila-swilling party-goers and a *lucha libre* wrestler. Underneath lanterns shaped like stars, a hip clientele enjoys frozen margaritas, fried chicken tacos with grilled corn, cod fritters and quesadillas stuffed with chipotle-stewed chicken. $$

**Empire State South** 999 Peachtree St NE, Midtown Ⓦempirestatesouth.com. A great midtown itinerary would begin with brunch at this sophisticated Southern bistro – try unique blends like the farm egg, crispy rice, corn and baby leek – and the grouper with eggplant and peanut romesco – and continue with a stroll beside the dogwood trees and oaks of nearby historic Piedmont Park. It's also fun for cocktails, bocce ball and charcuterie "jars" of egg salad, catfish mousse and pickles, savoured on the terrace. $$$

★ **Fox Bros. Bar-B-Q** 1238 Dekalb Ave, Little Five Points Ⓦfoxbrosbbq.com. Atlanta's best barbecue, a few blocks from the heart of Little Five Points. It makes little difference if you choose a plateful of Texas-style ribs, juicy pulled pork or tangy fried pickles – everything is delicious. Parking can be tricky, and there's often a queue to get in. $$

**Gunshow** 924 Garrett St Ⓦgunshowatl.com. No guns, but rather a weird and wonderful menu that changes weekly, if not daily, and is brought out on rolling carts, dim sum-style. At the helm is chef Kevin Gillespie, who concocts such flavourful small plates as beef tartare with local berries, scallops with smoked avocado and Creole shrimp beignets, plus desserts such as warm banana pudding. $$$

★ **Kimball House** 303 E Howard Ave, Decatur ☏ 404 378 3502, Ⓦkimball-house.com. Everything – the decor,

the cocktails, the cuisine – comes together beautifully at this handsome restaurant and bar housed in the former Decatur train depot. Crustacean fans: don't miss the raw bar, with succulent oysters that pair perfectly with a dry cocktail or three. Or go for heartier plates, from steak to sturgeon to shrimp. $$$$

**The Optimist** 914 Howell Mill Rd, West Midtown Ⓦtheoptimistrestaurant.com. For some of the finest seafood in Atlanta, head to this charming hideaway, with an airy white decor and the fine lines of a classy yacht. For a more casual meal, take a seat in the inviting oyster bar, which serves small plates and shucked oysters. Come by for happy hour (Mon–Fri 5–6pm and weekends 3–5pm), when oysters are one buck each. $$$

**Ria's Bluebird** 421 Memorial Drive SE, Grant Park Ⓦriasbluebird.com. Queues snake out of the door for Ria's hearty and healthy daily breakfast and lunch specials – peach pancakes, overfilled burritos, tempeh Reuben sandwiches– in this cosy, friendly diner opposite Oakland Cemetery. $$

★ **Staplehouse Market** 541 Edgewood Ave Ⓦstaplehouse.com. Atlanta's renowned, high-end but always convivial *Staplehouse* restaurant, in the Old Fourth Ward district, has transformed itself into a welcoming neighbourhood grocery store and market, while still serving its trademark innovative New American cuisine to diners on its outdoor patio. Drop in for a snack or a full meal. $$

**The Vortex** 438 Moreland Ave, Little Five Points Ⓦthevortexatl.com. Stepping into this riotous bar and grill is like entering He-Man's castle – the property is fronted by an enormous 20ft skull with spinning neon eyes. An Atlanta legend, famed for its gut-busting burgers (try the "Elvis", stacked with bacon, peanut butter and fried bananas) and gluttonous appetizers like "Big-Ass Buffalo Wings". The interior is a wild display of shark and alligator heads, memorabilia and flying skeletons. Patrons must be 18 or older. $$

## DRINKING AND NIGHTLIFE

SEE MAP PAGE 71

The main nightlife areas are Virginia-Highland, Little Five Points and Midtown, the centre of Atlanta's thriving LGBTQ

1

scene. For **listings**, check the free weekly *Creative Loafing* (ⓦ clatl.com).

**Blind Willie's** 828 N Highland Ave NE, Virginia Highland ⓦ blindwilliesblues.com. One of the more casual joints in Virginia-Highland, this laidback blues bar has live music, strong drinks and a small dance floor. Occasional big-name acts. Cover charge.

**The Bookhouse Pub** 736 Ponce de Leon Ave, Virginia Highland ☎ 404 254 1176. Cosy up at this wood-lined lodge-style bar – and yes, there are plenty of books, as befits the name – which serves a wonderfully diverse array of drinks, from strong ales and frothy brews to small-batch bourbon and scotch to classic cocktails. The snacks are a serious cut above the usual bar food, including braised beef poutine.

**Clermont Lounge** 789 Ponce de Leon Ave NE, Poncey-Highland ⓦ clermontlounge.net. The oldest strip club in the city, the *Clermont* is at once a ramshackle dive bar, a jolting and unusual attraction, a source of community and an Atlanta institution. Charismatic women, some in their 60s, strut their stuff on a tiny bar to a melting pot of nervous tourists, enthusiastic regulars and celebrities. You must be 21 or older to enter.

**The EARL** 488 Flat Shoals Ave SE, East Atlanta ⓦ badearl.com. Part welcoming dive bar, part top-notch rock venue, the *EARL* cooks up great pub food and pulls a nice crowd of devotees. All shows are 21-up. Occasional cover charge.

**Northside Tavern** 1058 Howell Mill Rd NW, Westside ⓦ northsidetavern.com. In business since 1972, this wonderful, scruffy dive blues bar with cheap drinks gets the locals swinging with its soulful live-music performances. Cover charge Fri & Sat.

★ **The Porter Beer Bar** 1156 Euclid Ave NE, Little Five Points ⓦ theporterbeerbar.com. Stocking an international line-up of more than eight hundred beers, this buzzing bar turns out fantastic gastro-pub food such as goat's cheese fritters with cracked black pepper and honey, steamed mussels and divine salt-and-vinegar popcorn. Great location at the centre of Little Five Points.

**Star Community Bar** 437 Moreland Ave NE, Little Five Points ☎ 404 681 9018, ⓦ starbaratl.bar. Enjoyable, hip Little Five Points bar, in a former bank bursting with Elvis memorabilia, offering live Americana, funk, country and rockabilly. Many shows are free.

★ **Watchman's Seafood and Spirits** 99 Krog St ⓦ watchmansatl.com. Slurp oysters and sip cocktails at this breezy restaurant with rustic coastal flourishes – soothing pastels and aquamarine hues, hanging plants and wooden floors. Seasonal cocktails include the fresh Island Stream (white rum, mango, pineapple), while the seafood menu encompasses casual bites, from grilled oysters to sautéed clams to tangy ceviche.

# Dahlonega

**DAHLONEGA**, in the Appalachian foothills 65 miles northeast of Atlanta on US-19, owes its origins to the first-ever **Gold Rush** in the USA. Benjamin Parks discovered gold at Hall County, three miles south, in 1828; Dahlonega was established five years later as the seat of Lumpkin County. Soon enough gold had been excavated for Dahlonega to acquire its own outpost of the US Mint, which, by the time production was terminated by the Civil War, had produced over $6 million of gold coin. The story is recounted in the lively **Gold Museum** on the main square (Mon–Sat 9am–5pm, Sun 10am–5pm; charge; ⓦ gastateparks.org). From May to October, Saturday afternoons see bluegrass jams on the museum grounds; the town also hosts **Gold Rush Days**, a down-home hoedown, in October.

## ACCOMMODATION AND EATING | DAHLONEGA

**Barefoot Hills** 7693 US-19 ⓦ barefoothills.com. Previously a backpackers' hostel, this attractive log-cabin hotel has been upgraded to offer a wide range of accommodation, from comfortable hotel rooms and cosy cabin to individual eco-cabins in former shipping containers, while still retaining a four-bunk dorm room – there's truly something for everyone, even a shuttle service for hikers on the Appalachian Trail. Dorms $̄, rooms $̄$̄, cabins $̄$̄$̄

**Wolf Mountain Vineyards** 180 Wolf Mountain Trail ⓦ wolfmountainvineyards.com. Wine buffs, foodies and nature lovers alike will enjoy a visit to this gorgeous family-owned vineyard and café, tucked between grapevines and the Southern Appalachian Mountains. Lunch and brunch only; pizza and sandwiches; reservations required. Charge for wine tastings.

### Amicalola Falls State Park

Daily 7am–10pm • Charge • ⓦ amicalolafallslodge.com

Twenty miles west of Dahlonega on Hwy-52, **Amicalola Falls State Park** centres on a dramatic waterfall that cascades down a steep hillside. After driving to the overlook, continue another half-mile to the park's modern **lodge**, which has comfortable rooms and a restaurant with panoramic views. For even more seclusion, hike five miles toward the start of the **Appalachian Trail**, to reach the *Hike Inn*, accessible only on foot.

### ACCOMMODATION | AMICALOLA FALLS STATE PARK

**Amicalola Falls Lodge** 418 Amicalola Falls Lodge Rd Ⓦ amicalolafallslodge.com. Though the decor is a bit outdated, you're coming to this scenic mountain lodge for tranquillity, not style. A quick walk from the falls in the heart of the forest, and hiking opportunities abound. $\overline{S}\overline{S}$

**Hike Inn** The 5-mile hike to the inn begins atop Amicalola Falls Ⓦ hike-inn.com. Reached only by a mixed-terrain walk through the woods, this place has bunk beds, a lovely games room with a wood-burning stove and a porch for socializing. Blankets, towels, breakfast and lunch are included in the rate. Reservations essential. $\overline{S}\overline{S}$

# Athens

Appealing **ATHENS**, almost seventy miles east of Atlanta, is home to the 30,000-plus students of the University of Georgia and has a liberal feel. Its compact downtown, north of campus, is alive with clubs, bars, restaurants, galleries and – of course – record stores; **Broad Street** in particular is lined with arty shops. Probably best known as the home of rock groups such as R.E.M., the B-52s and Widespread Panic, it remains one of the top college music towns in the nation.

## The University of Georgia

405 College Station Rd • Ⓦ uga.edu

Established in 1785, the **University of Georgia** was the first state-chartered school in the nation and is now famed for its tailgate parties and Georgia Bulldogs football team. It's well worth meandering about the north end of campus, peppered with oak trees and stately columned buildings. Toward the southeast side, the marvellous **Georgia Museum of Art**, 90 Carlton St (Tues, Wed, Fri & Sat 10am–5pm, Thurs 10am–9pm, Sun 1–5pm; free; Ⓦ georgiamuseum.org) has a rich collection of modern works depicting American life.

## State Botanical Garden of Georgia

2450 S Milledge Ave • Daily: April–Sept 8am–8pm; Oct–March 8am–6pm • Free • Ⓦ botgarden.uga.edu

South of the university, the **State Botanical Garden of Georgia** is a peaceful retreat. Five miles of nature trails loop around winsome flower beds, medicinal herbs and horticulture greenhouses. There's a nice alfresco coffeeshop, too, with drinks sipped in the company of tropical palm fronds.

### ARRIVAL, INFORMATION AND TOURS | ATHENS

**By bus** Greyhound (☎ 706 549 2255, Ⓦ greyhound.com) arrives at 4020 Atlanta Hwy (US-78), 6 miles west of town.

**Visitor centre** 280 E Dougherty St (Mon–Sat 10am–5pm, Sun noon–5pm; ☎ 706 353 1820, Ⓦ athenswelcomecenter.com).

**Tours** The visitor centre has details of tours covering everything from historic buildings to music heritage.

**Listings** For full what's-on listings, check the free weekly *Flagpole* (Ⓦ flagpole.com).

### ACCOMMODATION

**Graduate Athens** 295 E Dougherty St Ⓦ graduateathens. com. This inviting boutique hotel lives in what was once a nineteenth-century ironworks foundry (the university's iconic entry arch was cast here). The rooms are stylish, with plump beds, and there are plenty of great amenities, including a soothing spa, the restaurant and music venue *The Foundry* (see page 80) and the café *Poindexter Coffee*. $\overline{S}\overline{S}\overline{S}$

**Hotel Indigo** 500 College Ave Ⓦ indigoathens.com. Restorative, hip hotel within walking distance of all the shops and restaurants of downtown. The contemporary guestrooms are decked out with picture windows, pale wood furniture and local Jittery Joe's coffee. Good restaurant, bar and café onsite, too. $\overline{S}\overline{S}\overline{S}$

### EATING, DRINKING AND NIGHTLIFE

**40 Watt Club** 285 W Washington St Ⓦ 40watt.com. It's well worth catching some live music in Athens. R.E.M. started out at this eclectic, now legendary rock venue, though it has moved from its original location.

**1**

★ **Five & Ten** 1073 S Milledge Ave ⓦ fiveandten.com. The wildly popular chef Hugh Acheson – of *Top Chef* fame – turns out stunning dish after dish at this Southern lair. The airy, elegant dining room is the perfect setting for the farm-fresh, changing menu, which might include smoked catfish tartine and pan-roasted grouper with shishito peppers. For a great sampling, try the prix-fixe menu – a great deal for three courses. The original restaurant opened just down the street in a five-and-dime store, hence the name. $$$

**The Foundry Bar & Mill** 295 E Dougherty St ⓦ thefoundryathens.com. Located in the handsome nineteenth-century *Graduate Athens* (see page 79), this lively bar and restaurant serves hearty seasonal fare. It also features a multi-tiered concert venue for Americana and roots bands. $$

**Georgia Theatre** 215 N Lumpkin St ⓦ georgiatheatre. com. Rebuilt after a 2009 fire, this lovely old cinema is one of Athens's top music venues, and also sports a great rooftop bar.

**The Grit** 199 Prince Ave ⓦ thegrit.com. One of the best vegetarian restaurants in town. Fill up on a grilled seitan steak sandwich heaped with sautéed onions and peppers and home-made vegan ice cream. The decor is as earthy as the cuisine, with chalkboard menus and wooden furnishings. $

**Mama's Boy** 197 Oak St, a mile east of downtown ☏ 706 548 6249, ⓦ eatatmamasboy.com. The plain, unpromising exterior of this tiny breakfast-all-day favourite belies an interior of black and turquoise wall-paper and eye-catching chandeliers, one made out of mismatched mason jars. Head here for strawberry lemonade, Georgia peach French toast and biscuits topped with sausage-thyme gravy. $

**The National** 232 W Hancock St ⓦ thenationalrestaurant. com. Athens's foodie concourse, reborn from an old tyre plant (of all things) as a stylish Mediterranean restaurant – try roast bass with squash and country ham, and warm salad of spiced ground lamb, okra and chickpeas – with pressed tin ceilings and whitewashed walls. $$$

**Trappeze Pub** 269 N Hull St, Suite #6 ⓦ trappezepub.com. Athens has a great beer scene, best experienced at this artisanal bar and restaurant which stocks a huge range of stouts, lagers, ales and ciders. Grab a barstool and order one of the excellent pints produced by Terrapin, the city's local brewery.

**Weaver D's** 1016 E Broad St ☏ 706 353 7797. R.E.M. fans head straight for this soul food café, whose motto, "Automatic for the People", inspired the band's 1992 album. A short walk east of downtown, it serves delicious fried chicken and veggies. $$

**The World Famous** 351 N Hull St ☏ 706 543 4002. Just down the block from *Trappeze*. Start your night at the latter, then mosey on down to catch a show at this retro bar with great live music, fun cocktails, pinball machines and delicious comfort food such as chicken and waffle sandwiches.

## Macon

**MACON** (rhymes with bacon), set along the **Ocmulgee River** eighty miles southeast of Atlanta, makes an attractive stop en route to Savannah, especially when its 300,000 **cherry trees** erupt with frothy blossoms, celebrated by a ten-day festival in March (ⓦ cherryblossom.com). Founded in 1823, and once a major cotton port, this sleepy place is permeated with music history: home to **Little Richard**, **Otis Redding** and the **Allman Brothers**, it was also where **James Brown** recorded his first smash, the epoch-making *Please Please Please*, in an unlikely-looking antebellum mansion at 830 Mulberry St. Otis is commemorated by a bronze statue beside the unremarkable Otis Redding Memorial Bridge. Duane Allman and Berry Oakley, killed here in motorcycle smashes in 1971 and 1972 respectively, are buried in **Rose Hill Cemetery** on Riverside Drive, the inspiration for several of the band's songs.

**Cherry Street**, which looks little changed since Otis Redding's day, is downtown's main commercial strip.

### Tubman African American Museum

310 Cherry St • Tues–Sat 9am–5pm • Charge • ⓦ tubmanmuseum.com

The **Tubman African American Museum**, named for Underground Railroad leader Harriet Tubman, is dedicated to African American arts, culture and history. Exhibits range from African drums and textiles through to intricate quilts and dazzling avant-garde work. The museum also hosts an excellent series of regular lectures and concerts, from jazz to funk; check website for times.

### Ocmulgee National Monument

1207 Emery Hwy • Daily 9am–5pm • Free • ⓦ nps.gov/ocmu

1

Between 900 and 1100 AD, a Native American group migrated from the Mississippi Valley to a spot overlooking the Ocmulgee River a couple of miles east of modern downtown Macon, where they levelled the site that is now **Ocmulgee National Monument**. Their settlement of thatched huts has vanished, though two grassy mounds, each thought to have been topped by a temple, still rise from the plateau. Near the visitor centre, you can enter the underground chamber of a ceremonial **earthlodge**, the clay floor of which holds a ring of moulded seats and a striking bird-shaped altar.

### ARRIVAL, INFORMATION AND TOURS                                                      MACON

**By bus** Greyhound (☎ 478 743 5411) is at 65 Spring St.
**Visitor centre** 450 Martin Luther King Jr Blvd (Mon–Sat 10am–5pm; ☎ 478 743 1074, ⓦ maconga.org).
**Rock Candy Tours** Created by a confectioner and the

daughter of one of Capricorn Records' co-founders (the masterminds behind the Allman Brothers), this tour outfit offers music history walks imbued with incredible personal stories (ⓦ rockcandytours.com).

### ACCOMMODATION, EATING AND DRINKING

**1842 Inn** 353 College St ⓦ 1842inn.com. This luxurious antebellum inn offers lovely rooms with four-poster beds and a full Southern breakfast in the courtyard. $$$
★ **Dovetail** 543 Cherry St ⓦ dovetailmacon.com. For a superb farm-to-table meal, head up a flight of stairs to this voguish gem, where you can eat in a barn-like dining room strung with Edison bulbs. Try unique dishes like Coca-Cola-brined fried quail, and shrimp and grits with Manchego cheese and chorizo. $$$
**Grant's Lounge** 576 Poplar St ⓦ historicgrants.com. For a living, breathing, whiskey-swilling piece of Southern rock history, head to this downtown dive bar and live music venue where the Allman Brothers and Lynyrd Skynyrd got their start.

**The Rookery** 543 Cherry St ⓦ rookerymacon.com. Dimly lit burger joint where the walls are covered in patrons' scribbles and meals are served in ancient wooden booths. Try the Jimmy Carter burger, topped with peanut butter and bacon and wash it down with a pineapple upside-down shake. Top-notch beer selection, too. $$
**Whistle Stop Café** 443 McCrackin St in Juliette, 20 miles north of Macon ⓦ thewhistlestopcafe.com. This weathered clapboard restaurant, by the old railroad tracks, dishes up the (delicious) Fried Green Tomatoes of book and film fame to a friendly Southern crowd straight out of Central Casting. $$

# Savannah

American towns don't come much more beautiful than **SAVANNAH**, seventeen miles up the Savannah River from the ocean. The ravishing **historic district**, arranged around Spanish-moss-swathed garden squares, formed the core of the original city and boasts examples of just about every architectural style of the eighteenth and nineteenth centuries, while the cobbled **waterfront** on the Savannah River is edged by towering old cotton warehouses. Savannah's **historic district** is flanked by the river to the north, Martin Luther King Jr Boulevard to the west, Gaston Street to the south and Broad Street – long since replaced by the appealingly retro Broughton Street as downtown's main commercial thoroughfare – to the east. The main draw here is in wandering the side streets and admiring the shuttered Federal, Regency and antebellum houses, embellished with intricate iron balconies. More than twenty residential **squares**, shaded by canopies of ancient live oaks and ablaze with dogwood trees, azaleas and creamy magnolias, offer peaceful respite from the blistering summer heat, while subtropical **greenery** creeps its way through the ornate railings, cracks open the streets, casts cool shadows and fills the air with its warm, sensual fragrance.

### Brief history

Savannah was founded in 1733 by **James Oglethorpe** as the first settlement of the new British colony of Georgia. His intention was to establish a haven for debtors, with no Catholics, lawyers or hard liquor – and, above all, no slaves. However, with the arrival of North Carolina settlers in the 1750s, plantation agriculture, based on slave labour, thrived. The town became a major export centre, at the end of important railroad lines by which **cotton** was funnelled from far away in the South. Sherman arrived here in December 1864 at the end of his March to the Sea; he offered the town to Abraham Lincoln as a Christmas gift, but at Lincoln's urging left it intact and set to work apportioning land to freed slaves. This was the first recognition of the need for "reconstruction", though such concrete economic provision for ex-slaves was rarely to occur again. After the Civil War, the plantations floundered, cotton prices slumped and Savannah went into decline. Not until the 1960s did local citizens start to organize what has been the successful restoration of their town. In the last three decades, the private **Savannah College of Art and Design** (SCAD) has injected even more vitality, attracting young artists and regenerating downtown by buying up a number of wonderful old buildings. Today it's a prosperous, relaxed place, more raffish than Charleston, less rowdy than New Orleans, but sharing their faded, melancholy beauty. Savannah acquired notoriety in the mid-1990s thanks to its starring role in John Berendt's best-selling *Midnight in the Garden of Good and Evil*; a compelling mix of cross-dressing, voodoo and murder that sums up this rather louche, very lovable place to a tee.

## Cathedral of St John the Baptist

222 E Harris St • Daily 9–11.45am & 12.45–5pm • Free (donations welcome) • ⓦ savannahcathedral.org

The **Cathedral of St John the Baptist** is Savannah's pride and joy. Inside, 66ft-high ceilings soar dramatically, framing the organ's medallion-shaped stained-glass window and accenting the structure's exquisite ceiling murals. The towers of the French Gothic exterior, which dates from 1873, hold a mighty 4000lb steeple bell.

## House Museums

Most visitors take in a few **mansion tours**. The **Green-Meldrim House**, on Madison Square (Tues & Fri 10am–4pm, Sat 10am–12.30pm; charge; ⓦstjohnssav.org), is the Gothic Revival mansion that General Sherman used as his headquarters. Its ironwork is a rare example of pre-Civil War craftsmanship; most iron in Savannah was melted down during the conflict. Literature fans will appreciate the **Flannery O'Connor Childhood Home** at 207 E Charlton St (Fri–Sun 10am–1pm; charge; ☏912 233 6014, ⓦflanneryoconnorhome.org), where the legendary Southern Gothic writer lived from her birth in 1925 until 1938.

## Massie Heritage Center

207 E Gordon St • Mon–Sat 10am–4pm, Sun noon–4pm • Charge • ⓦ massieschool.com

At the southern edge of the historic district, on Calhoun Square, the **Massie Heritage Center** is housed in Savannah's first public school. Today it's a simple, effective museum, illuminating Savannah's architecture with displays on its city plan, its neighbourhoods and its growth, and tracing influences from as far away as London and Egypt.

## Telfair Museum of Art

Three sites: Telfair Academy at 121 Barnard St; Jepson Centre at 207 W York St; Owens-Thomas House at 124 Abercorn St • All three sites: Mon & Sun noon–5pm, Tues–Sat 10am–5pm • Charge • ⓦ telfair.org

The **Telfair Academy**, a Regency mansion designed by English architect William Jay, forms the original core of the venerable **Telfair Museum of Art**, which now spreads across three sites. Its collection of nineteenth- and twentieth-century American and European art is missable (though it is nice to catch a glimpse of the wistful *Bird Girl*, moved here from Bonaventure Cemetery after being depicted on the cover of *Midnight in the Garden of Good and Evil*). More interesting are the Telfair's **Jepson Centre**, also on Telfair Square – a deliciously cool, light and airy modern structure that hosts changing contemporary exhibitions from photography to sculpture – and the **Owens-Thomas House** – designed by Jay when he was just 23. Tours here tell the history of

| ■ ACCOMMODATION | | ● EATING | | | | ■ DRINKING AND NIGHTLIFE | |
|---|---|---|---|---|---|---|---|
| Azalea Inn | 6 | Back in the Day Bakery | 10 | Leopold's Ice Cream | 3 | El-Rocko Lounge | 2 |
| Hamilton-Turner Inn | 5 | Gallery Espresso | 6 | Local 11 Ten | 9 | Jazz'd Tapas Bar | 1 |
| Marshall House | 2 | Green Truck Pub | 11 | Mrs Wilkes' | 8 | Pinkie Masters | 3 |
| Perry Lane | 4 | The Grey | 4 | The Olde Pink House | 2 | | |
| Planters Inn | 1 | Gryphon Tea Room | 7 | Wiley's Championship BBQ | 1 | ● SHOPPING | |
| Thunderbird Inn | 3 | Husk Savannah | 5 | | | Savannah Bee Company | 1 |

the town through the history of the building, which, rather than being all gussied up, reveals fascinating glimpses of its structure and workings.

## The waterfront

Though the city squares are redolent of the Old South, Savannah's **waterfront**, at the foot of a steep little bluff below Bay Street and reached by assorted stone staircases and alleyways, resembles more an eighteenth-century European port and offers a rare evocation of early America. The main thoroughfare, River Street, loomed over by five-storey brick cotton warehouses, is cobbled with the ballast carried by long-vanished sailing ships. It's now a touristy stretch, lined with seafood restaurants and salty bars filled with partying crowds, but well worth a stroll.

### First African Baptist Church

23 Montgomery St • Tues–Sat 11am, 2pm & 4pm, Sun 1pm • Charge • ⓦ firstafricanbc.com

The 1775 **First African Baptist Church** is one of the oldest black churches in North America, built by slaves. The superbly informative tours point out the tribal carvings on the sides of the pews upstairs, and, downstairs, the diamond shapes made by holes in the floor – ventilation for slaves hiding in the 4ft subterranean crawl spaces while waiting to escape to safe havens via the Underground Railroad.

### Ships of the Sea Maritime Museum

41 Martin Luther King Jr Blvd • Tues–Sun 10am–5pm • Charge • ⓦ shipsofthesea.org

Savannah's diverting little **Ships of the Sea Maritime Museum**, on the northwestern edge of the historic district, features painstakingly constructed ship models, beautifully displayed in glass and mahogany cases, scrimshaw, figureheads and other maritime art, all housed in a stunning 1819 Greek Revival mansion.

### SCAD Museum of Art

601 Turner Blvd • Mon, Wed, Fri & Sat 10am–5pm, Thurs 10am–8pm, Sun noon–5pm • Charge • ⓦ scadmoa.org

Though less compelling than the Telfair museums (see page 82), the contemporary works at **SCAD Museum of Art**, administered by the Savannah College of Art and Design, are worth a look, particularly the vibrant pieces of the African American collection and the glittery designs in the fashion gallery, named after *Vogue* icon André Leon Talley.

## ARRIVAL AND DEPARTURE                                             SAVANNAH

**By plane** Savannah's airport (ⓦ savannahairport.com) is 9 miles west of the city; a taxi to downtown costs around $30.
**By bus** The Greyhound bus station (☎ 912 232 2135) is on the western edge of downtown at 610 W Oglethorpe Ave.
**By train** Amtrak trains pull in about 3 miles southwest of downtown, at 2611 Seaboard Coastline Drive.

## GETTING AROUND, INFORMATION AND TOURS

**By shuttle bus** The historic district is best explored on foot, though Chatham Area Transit (CAT; ⓦ catchacat.org) operates the free CAT Shuttle service between downtown, the visitor centre, the waterfront and City Market, and a number of fare-charging buses for destinations further afield.
**Visitor centre** 301 Martin Luther King Jr Blvd (Daily 9am–4pm; ☎ 912 944 0455, ⓦ visitsavannah.com). There's another small information office at River St on the waterfront (daily: Jan & Feb 9am–6pm; March–Dec 9am–8pm; ☎ 912 651 6662).
**Tours** The visitor centre has details of numerous walking tours, and serves as the starting point for several different trolley tours (from around $20). Relaxing horse-and-carriage tours set off from the *Hyatt Regency*, next to City Hall on W Bay St (ⓦ savannahcarriage.com), while Savannah Riverboat Cruises (9 E River St; ⓦ savannahriverboat.com). offers a range of lazy cruises, with fancier options including a Gospel Dinner Cruise (Mon 7pm) and Sunset Cruises (Sun–Fri 7pm). Savannah Dan (ⓦ savannahdan.com) sports full Southern regalia – seersucker suit, Panama hat and bow tie – when giving his superlative, no-nonsense walking tours of the historic district.

## ACCOMMODATION                                             SEE MAP PAGE 84

Ideally, you should budget to stay in the **historic district**, which is packed with gorgeous B&Bs and a few nice hotels. The usual chain **motels** can be found near the Greyhound station and further out on Ogeechee Road (US-17).
★ **Azalea Inn** 217 E Huntingdon St ⓦ azaleainn.com. Charming, laidback B&B in a nineteenth-century mansion at the edge of the historic district near Forsyth Park, complete with adorable Yorkies, bright, delightfully furnished rooms and complimentary evening wine and snacks. Superb Southern breakfasts are served daily, too. $$$
★ **Hamilton-Turner Inn** 330 Abercorn St ⓦ hamilton-turnerinn.com. This beautifully maintained inn was originally built in 1873 as Samuel Pugh Hamilton's family mansion and in 1883 became the first residence in Savannah to have electricity. Today, the mansion welcomes visitors with beautiful suites, many with high ceilings and fireplaces, as well as clawfoot tubs in the bathrooms. Generous complimentary goodies, like a daily Southern

**1**

breakfast and wine and nibbles in the evening. $$$$
**Marshall House** 123 E Broughton St w marshallhouse. com. Savannah's oldest hotel, dating from 1851, is located on one of its hippest streets. It was once a hospital for Civil War soldiers, but its rooms are decidedly plusher nowadays, with traditional decor, soft robes and a breakfast buffet. $$$
**Perry Lane** 266 E Perry St w perrylanehotel.com. Rising over the downtown historic district, this stylish hotel, which opened in 2018, captures the elegant charm of Savannah. The plush interior recalls a grand manor house, with eclectic local artwork, a collection of historic maps and spacious rooms with comfortable beds piled with Italian Frette linens. Food and drink options abound, including in the Emporium Kitchen and

Wine Market with a tasty seasonal menu, and the Peregrin rooftop bar, with sweeping views of the city. $$$$
**Planters Inn** 29 Abercorn St w plantersinnsavannah. com. A formal, welcoming, hotel rather than a B&B, in a lovely position in the historic district. Added perks include a nightly turndown service, wine and cheese hour and hand-delivered breakfasts. The excellent *Olde Pink House* restaurant (see page 86) is next door. $$
**Thunderbird Inn** 611 W Oglethorpe w thethunderbirdinn. com. Quirky vintage motel with retro fittings, opposite the Greyhound station. Free popcorn, Krispy Kremes, MoonPies and RC Cola included. Very pet-friendly (they even have their own dog run). $$

## EATING
SEE MAP PAGE 84

Savannah abounds with excellent restaurants. **City Market** – four blocks of restored grain warehouses a few blocks back from the river – is downtown's prime dining and nightlife district; restaurants on the historic district squares are a little classier. Bustling **Broughton Street** also has a number of options, many of them in lovely restored Deco buildings.
**Back in the Day Bakery** 2403 Bull St, 2 miles south of downtown w backinthedaybakery.com. Baby-blue, artisanal bakery with tempting trays of moist red velvet cupcakes and coconut macaroons, plus light lunches and espresso drinks. $
**Gallery Espresso** 234 Bull St w galleryespresso.com. Overlooking verdant Chippewa Square, this coffeeshop is a Savannah fixture, with a lively cast of artist regulars, a thrift-store decor, stout mugs of coffee and generous pours of wine. $
**Green Truck Pub** 2430 Habersham St, 3 miles south of downtown w greentruckpub.com. There are always queues for this venerable burger and fries joint that locally sources all its ingredients and makes everything – down to the delectable ketchup – from scratch. $$
★**The Grey** 109 Martin Luther King Jr Blvd w thegreyrestaurant.com. Savannah's Art Deco Greyhound bus terminal, originally built in 1938, has been impeccably restored, down to every stainless steel curve. It's now *The Grey* restaurant, where chef Mashama Bailey has crafted a menu that's one part Southern and two parts wholly her own: try duck liver tart with onion jelly and smoked lamb with green tomato. $$$$
**Gryphon Tea Room** 337 Bull St w scadgryphon.com. Enjoy high tea at this modish tearoom that's housed in an old pharmacy with its original counter and a stunning stained-glass ceiling. Hundreds of special teas, genteel gourmet lunches and mouthwatering cakes. $$
**Husk Savannah** 12 W Oglethorpe Ave w husksavannah.

com. Set in a fine old mansion in the heart of historic Savannah, this sumptuous restaurant sets out to put a contemporary twist on authentic, traditional Southern flavours. The precise menu changes daily, but you can expect plenty of pork, catfish and barbecue, along with Japanese-style miso and pickles, and there's also a raw bar. $$$$
**Leopold's Ice Cream** 212 E Broughton St w leopoldsice cream.com. Hollywood producer Stratton Leopold has revamped his family's traditional ice-cream parlour, originally opened in 1919, and serves home-made ices, plus a full menu of sandwiches, salads and burgers. $
**Local 11 Ten** 1110 Bull St w local11ten.com. A hip, buzzy interpretation of Low Country, French and Italian food (pastas are made from scratch), with a small, seasonal menu using the freshest local ingredients and a thorough wine list. $$$
**Mrs Wilkes'** 107 W Jones St ☎ 912 232 5997, w mrswilkes. com. This local institution offers a real Southern experience, serving all-you-can-eat lunches for a fixed and great-value price. Diners sit around communal tables helping themselves to delicious mounds of fried chicken, sweet potatoes, spinach, beans and pickled beets. There's no sign and no reservations; arrive early and join the line. Cash only. $$$
**The Olde Pink House** 23 Abercorn St w theoldepinkhouse restaurant.com. With its pink Regency facade and effortlessly elegant upstairs dining room, the romantic *Pink House* is perfect for relaxed, special-occasion dining. You can also order its delicious Low Country food in the cheery, high-spirited tavern downstairs. Highlights include she-crab soup and almond-crusted tilapia. $$$
**Wiley's Championship BBQ** 4700 Hwy-80, 7 miles east of downtown w wileyschampionshipbbq.com. On the way to Tybee Island, this tiny barbecue hut serves succulent ribs and pulled pork with devilishly good sides like sweet potato casserole and mac and cheese. $$

## DRINKING AND NIGHTLIFE
SEE MAP PAGE 84

Savannah's nightlife is decidedly laidback, given energy by its large student population. Almost uniquely in the USA

(New Orleans is another exception) you can drink **alcohol** on the streets in open cups. For **listings**, pick up the free weekly *Connect* newspaper (ⓦconnectsavannah.com). **St Patrick's Day** (March 17) is a big deal in Savannah, with its large Irish population. Around a million visitors descend here to guzzle copious amounts of Guinness; many residents choose this weekend to leave town.

**El-Rocko Lounge** 117 Whitaker St ⓦelrockolounge. com. Hip but very friendly downtown bar, with killer cocktails and local brews, and DJs in action most evenings.

**Jazz'd Tapas Bar** 52 Barnard St ⓦjazzdtapasbar.com.

Industrialist decor meets splashy folk art cheer at this buzzy basement martini bar/restaurant, which has live music (Tues–Sun). The tasty "tapas" are Southern-style appetizers.

**Pinkie Masters** 318 Drayton St ⓦtheoriginalpinkies. com. With its throwback jukebox and dartboards, Savannah's best dive bar is a great place to hang out with locals; it's also where Jimmy Carter first announced he was running for president.

## SHOPPING SEE MAP PAGE 84

**Savannah Bee Company** 104 W Broughton St ⓦsavannahbee.com. No visit to Savannah would be complete without a trip to this honey purveyor's flagship store. There's a buffet of free samples and great gifts for lucky friends back home.

# Brunswick

**BRUNSWICK**, the one sizeable settlement south of Savannah, is a hop-off point for the offshore **Golden Isles**. The town in itself is industrial, though there's a lovely old-fashioned downtown, and the shrimp docks can be quite interesting when the catch is brought in. To get a taste of local fishing culture, head out on a two-hour cruise with the *Lady Jane* (ⓦshrimpcruise.com), a commercial shrimp trawler that's been outfitted for educational tours. Winding lazily among the creeks, you'll spot oyster beds and watch fiddler crabs skittering onshore. Up on deck, the crew catches and releases rays, horseshoe crabs, even rare sea turtles, while a biologist interprets everything to passengers. The best part, however, is when a trove of shrimp is hauled in and cooked right in front of you – some of the freshest crustaceans you'll ever lay your hands on. The whole experience is a Georgia coast must-do, especially if you're travelling with kids.

## ACCOMMODATION AND EATING                                                  BRUNSWICK

★ **Hostel in the Forest** Hwy-82, 10 miles west of Brunswick ⓦforesthostel.com. At this alternative hostel in the forest, guests can spend up to three nights in a rustic room in one of nine treehouses, with rates including a communal vegetarian dinner. The hostel is a membership organization, so on your first visit, you must become a member and pay a one-time $10 fee. Guests are expected to perform a small daily chore. $

**Indigo Coastal Shanty** 1402 Reynolds St ⓦindigocoastalshanty.com. The worldly menu of this unassuming local café riffs on everything from Southern classics to Caribbean curries and Mexican sandwiches; try the plantains with guacamole or the black bean burger topped with a juicy slice of green tomato. $$

# The Golden Isles

Patterned with briny marshes, massive oak trees and perfect beaches, the **Golden Isles** make an appealing seashore break destination for inlanders. Comprised of a string of barrier islands linked by causeways, this idyllic retreat has great restaurants and a mellow pace.

## Jekyll Island

A few miles south of Brunswick, **Jekyll Island** (reached by a toll road) was originally bought in 1887 for use as an exclusive "club" by a group of millionaires including the Rockefellers, the Pulitzers, the Macys and the Vanderbilts. Their opulent residences, known as "cottages", are still standing, surrounded by natural habitats that are legislated to remain forever wild. A small **Welcome Center** stands on the causeway (Mon–Sat 9am–6pm, Sun 10am–5pm;ⓦjekyllisland.com); the renovated **Jekyll Island Museum**, in the old club stables on Stable Road  daily 9am–5pm, tours 11am, 1pm & 3pm; charge) provides a good overview of the island's history and runs seasonally

**1**

changing tours. The island's tiny historic district centres on the rambling old original club building, which, as the *Jekyll Island Club Hotel*, now offers elegant **accommodation** (see page 88).

More than half of Jekyll Island is undeveloped, and activities including biking, swimming and horseback riding abound.

## St Simons Island

Most of **St Simons Island**, reached via a causeway across a green marsh inhabited by wading birds, is still an evocative landscape of palms and live oaks covered with Spanish moss. The village is pleasantly quiet and the nearby beach is nice for **swimming** and strolling. Southeast Adventure Outfitters, 313 Mallory St (⊛southeastadventure. com), rents **kayaks** and runs bird- and dolphin-watching tours. **Fort Frederica National Monument**, five miles north of the causeway (daily 9am–5pm; free; ⊛nps.gov/fofr), was built by General Oglethorpe in 1736 as the largest British fort in North America; it's now an atmospheric ruin.

## Cumberland Island

To the south of St Simons Island, **Cumberland Island** (⊛nps.gov/cuis) is a stunning wildlife refuge of marshes, beaches and semitropical forest roamed by wild horses, with the odd deserted planter's mansion. You can get here by ferry from the village of **St Mary's**, back on the mainland near the Florida border.

### ARRIVAL AND DEPARTURE        THE GOLDEN ISLES

**By car** Jekyll and St Simons islands are easily reached by causeways; Jekyll Island charges an entrance fee, while St Simons is free to visit.

**By ferry** Cumberland Island is only accessible by a 45min ferry, which docks in the town of St Mary's (⊛stmaryswelcome.com).

### ACCOMMODATION AND EATING

**Crabdaddy's** 1217 Ocean Blvd, St Simons ⊛crabdaddysgrill.com. Upmarket seafood restaurant with a casual ambience. Steak lovers will be well pleased with the Angus in coriander cream sauce; shrimp and grits are another favourite. $$$

**Jekyll Island Club Hotel** 371 Riverview Drive, Jekyll Island ⊛jekyllclub.com. Dating from 1888, this historic hotel, once the summer stomping ground of the country's elite, is now an expansive waterfront resort with rooms set in dignified old mansions and a huge turreted Victorian. $$$$

★**Southern Soul Barbeque** 2020 Demere Rd, St Simons ⊛southernsoulbbq.com. Certainly the island's

– and arguably the state's – best barbecue, fired up by hip, tattooed servers in a refurbished vintage gas station. Seating is limited, but it's fun combining parties at the communal picnic tables. $$

**Village Inn & Pub** 500 Mallery St, St Simons ⊛villageinnandpub.com. In the heart of St Simons, this 28-room inn has the welcoming ambience of a B&B but the quiet and seclusion of a boutique hotel. Densely shaded by towering live oaks, with a lovely pool and flower-filled courtyard, the property was endearingly constructed so that not one branch of these century-old trees would be broken or damaged. $$

### Okefenokee Swamp

Hwy-177 off US-23/1 • Daily 9am–5.30pm • Charge • ⊛okeswamp.com

The dense **Okefenokee Swamp** stretches 684 square miles from a point roughly thirty miles southwest of Brunswick. Tucked away in its astonishing profusion of luxuriant plants and trees are some twenty thousand alligators and more than thirty species of snake, as well as bears and pumas. You can enter at the **Okefenokee Swamp Park**, a private charity-owned concession at the northeast tip (Fargo and Folkston are the reserve's other access points). Admission grants access to a wildlife interpretive centre, observation tower and reconstructed pioneer buildings; paying an additional fee will buy you a **boat tour** through the swamp (slick yourself with bug repellent).

# Kentucky

Both of the rival presidents during the Civil War, Abraham Lincoln and Jefferson Davis, were born in **KENTUCKY**, where acute divisions existed between slave-owning farmers and the merchants who depended on trade with the nearby cities of the industrial North. While the state remained officially neutral, more Kentuckians joined the Union army than the Confederates; after the war, however, Kentucky sided with the South in its hostility to Reconstruction and has tended to follow southern political trends ever since.

Kentucky's rugged beauty is at its most appealing in the mountainous **east**, which suffers from acute rural poverty but boasts the fine scenery of the **Natural Bridge** and **Cumberland Gap** regions. Perhaps the most iconic area of the state is the **Bluegrass Downs**, home to bluegrass, bourbon and thoroughbred horses. The name comes from the unique steel-blue sheen of the buds in the meadows, only visible in early morning during April and May. The area centres on the reserved state capital **Lexington**, a major horse-breeding market, and holds some of the oldest towns west of the Alleghenies.

Hipper **Louisville**, however, home of the **Kentucky Derby**, lies eighty miles west and offers more reasons to linger. It is also a good access point to the bourbon country around **Bardstown**. Rural western Kentucky, where the Ohio River meets the Mississippi, is flat, heavily forested and generally less attractive. Meanwhile, in the **southern** hinterland, numerous small towns retain their tree-shaded squares and nineteenth-century townhouses – and their strict Baptist beliefs – while the endless caverns of **Mammoth Cave National Park** attract spelunkers and hikers in the thousands.

## Lexington

Although the lack of a navigable river has always made its traders vulnerable to competition from Louisville, the productivity of the **bluegrass** fields has kept **LEXINGTON**'s economy ticking over since 1775, especially after its emergence as the world's largest **burley tobacco** market following World War I. However, its most conspicuous activity these days is the **horse** trade, with an estimated 450 farms in the vicinity. The glass office blocks and shopping malls of Lexington's city centre, set in a dip on the Bluegrass Downs, crowd in on fountain-filled **Triangle Park**, juxtaposed against some older Victorian-era streets.

### University of Kentucky Art Museum

405 Rose St • Tues–Sun noon–5pm, Fri until 8pm • Free • ⓦ finearts.uky.edu/art-museum

One of Lexington's few non-equine-related attractions is the **University of Kentucky Art Museum**, in the Singletary Center for the Arts, which has a good permanent collection of contemporary American art and Native American artefacts. There are also frequent special exhibitions of international works, for which there is usually a charge.

---

### ARRIVAL AND INFORMATION                                    LEXINGTON

**By plane** Lexington's airport is 6 miles west of town on US-60 W.

**By bus** Greyhound drops off about a mile northeast from downtown at 477 New Circle Rd, opposite the local bus station (bus #3 goes downtown).

**Destinations** Cincinnati (3 daily; 1hr 25min); Louisville (4

daily; 1hr 20min–1hr 40min); Nashville (4–5 daily; 5hr 10min–9hr 30min).

**Visitor centre** 215 W Main St (Mon–Fri 9am–5pm, Sat 10am–5pm, plus Sun April–Oct noon–5pm; ☏ 859 233 7299, ⓦ visitlex.com). Another useful resource is the free *ACE Weekly* (ⓦ aceweekly.com).

---

### ACCOMMODATION

**Clarion Hotel** 1950 Newtown Pike ⓦ clarionhotellex. com. Chain franchise northeast of downtown, with smart

rooms, an indoor swimming pool and gym plus bars and restaurants. $\overline{\underline{\$\$}}$

1

## LEXINGTON'S HORSES

Along **Paris** and **Ironworks pikes**, northeast of Lexington in an idyllic Kentucky landscape, sleek thoroughbred horses cavort in bluegrass meadows, often penned in by immaculate white-plank fences. To the west, you can watch the horses' early-morning workouts at **Keeneland** racetrack, 4201 Versailles Rd (April–Oct daily dawn–10am; free; ⓦkeeneland. com) or take a guided tour (Tues, Thurs, Fri & Sat 8.30am; charge). Dark-green grandstands emphasize the crisp white rails around the one-mile oval track, where **meetings** are held for three weeks in both April (Wed–Sun 7.30pm) and Oct (Wed–Sun 1pm). A small fee grants general admission, and seats cost extra. There is a great canteen too.

The easiest way to see a farm is to take a guided bus tour out of Lexington; **Blue Grass Tours** (April–Oct daily 9am & 1.30pm; charge; ⓦbluegrasstours.com) offer a three-hour, fifty-mile itinerary that includes a stop to see retired steeds at **Old Friends Farm** (ⓦoldfriendsequine.org), plus a visit to Keeneland. Alternatively, hop on the pricier five-hour entertaining **Horses, Hooch and History Tour** (April–Oct 1 daily 10am, hours vary), where you'll visit a bourbon distillery and thoroughbred horse farm. Another farm conducting its own tours is **Three Chimneys** (Tues–Sat by appointment; charge; ⓦthreechimneys.com) on Old Frankfort Pike, about fifteen minutes west of downtown. The **Thoroughbred Center**, 3380 Paris Pike (9am: April–Oct Mon–Sat; Nov–March Mon–Fri; charge; ⓦthethoroughbredcenter.com), allows you to watch trainers at work. The enjoyable 1032-acre **Kentucky Horse Park**, a little further along at 4089 Ironworks Pkwy (Wed–Sun 9am–5pm; charge; ⓦkyhorsepark.com), features more than thirty different equine breeds, a working farm and guided **horseback rides**; its fascinating **International Museum of the Horse** traces the use of horses throughout history. In nearby Georgetown, at **Whispering Woods**, experienced equestrians can canter unsupervised, while novices ride with a guide (ⓦwhisperingwoodstrails.com).

**Eighth Pole Inn B&B** 3463 Rosalie Lane ⓦeighthpoleinn.com. An appealing rural retreat, offering six comfortable guest suites in a stately colonnaded mansion on a thoroughbred farm with expansive grounds. $\overline{\underline{\$\$\$}}$

**Horse Park** 4089 Ironworks Pkwy ⓦkyhorsepark.com. The best and nearest campground to downtown, which has fine shared facilities and offers campers discounts to the Horse Park itself. $\overline{\underline{\$}}$

**La Quinta** 1919 Stanton Way, junction I-64 & I-75, exit 115 ⓦwyndhamhotels.com. Handily placed motel with a pool, compact but comfortable rooms and free continental breakfast. $\overline{\underline{\$\$}}$

**The Sire** 120 W 2nd St ☎859 231 1777, ⓦhilton.com. Formerly *Grantz Park Inn* – downtown's oldest hotel – the fully renovated Sire features a grand nineteenth-century style throughout, including spruced-up rooms with luxe bedding and a soothing palette of tan woods and creams and whites. Enjoy seasonal fare and top-shelf bourbon at *Distilled*. $\overline{\underline{\$\$}}$

### EATING AND DRINKING

Lexington's large student population means it has a fair selection of places to eat besides the **steakhouses** catering to the horse crowd and conventioneers. The streets around the junction of Broadway and Main Street hold a few lively bars.

**Coles** 735 E Main St ⓦcoles735main.com. It's the attention to detail that has made Coles Lexington's favourite special-occasion restaurant. Expect classic meat and fish entrees prepared to perfection, along with vegetarian-friendly dishes like the jackfruit "crabcakes". Outdoor seating available. $\overline{\underline{\$\$\$\$}}$

**Le Deauville** 199 N Limestone St ⓦledeauvillebistro.com. Enjoy a touch of Paris at this delightful bistro with pavement seating, which specializes in dishes such as *bouillabaisse Marseillaise*, duck leg confit or filet mignon. $\overline{\underline{\$\$\$\$}}$

**Lexington Diner** 841 Lane Allen Rd ⓦlexingtondiner. com. This popular, atmospheric diner serves up great range of filling breakfasts – like The King (waffles topped with peanut butter mousse, bananas, bacon and chocolate sauce) – as well as hearty lunch and dinners, including open-face roast beef sandwiches and Kentucky nachos, topped with chilli and cheddar. $\overline{\underline{\$\$}}$

**Saul Good** 3801 Mall Rd ⓦsaulgoodpub.com. Sleek modern gastropub in the Fayette Mall, serving sandwiches, pizza, burgers and main courses such as sesame crusted *mahi-mahi*. $\overline{\underline{\$\$}}$

**West Sixth Brewing** 501 W 6th St ⓦwestsixth.com. Lexington's best brewery and taproom, where you can sample fine ales such as Heller Heaven Double IPA and munch on light snacks.

## Around Lexington: Bluegrass Country

Other than the horse farms directly to the north, most places of interest near Lexington lie southwards, including the fine old towns of Danville and Harrodsburg, the restored **Shaker Village of Pleasant Hill** and **Berea College**. After about forty miles, the meadows give way to the striking **Knobs** – random lumpy outcrops, shrouded in trees and wispy low-hanging clouds, that are the eroded remnants of the Pennyrile Plateau.

### The Shaker Village of Pleasant Hill

The utopian settlement of the **Shaker Village of Pleasant Hill**, hidden among the bluegrass hillocks near Harrodsburg, 26 miles southwest of Lexington, was established by **Shaker missionaries** from New England around 1805. Within twenty years, nearly five hundred villagers here were producing seeds, tools and cloth for sale as far away as New Orleans. During the Civil War, the pacifist Shakers were obliged to billet Union and Confederate troops alike. Numbers declined until the last member died in 1923, but a nonprofit organization has since returned the village to its nineteenth-century appearance.

The Shaker values of celibacy (they maintained their numbers through conversion and adoption of orphans), hygiene, simplicity and communal ownership have left their mark on the 34 grey and pastel-coloured dwellings, which women and men entered via different doors. Visitors can watch demonstrations of traditional handicrafts including broom-making and weaving (Mon–Thurs & Sun 10am–5pm, Fri & Sat 10am–8pm; charge).

**ACCOMMODATION AND EATING**      **THE SHAKER VILLAGE OF PLEASANT HILL**

★ **The Inn at Shaker Village** 3501 Lexington Rd, Harrodsburg ⓦshakervillageky.org. The delightfully restored on-site inn offers good-value rustic rooms and also houses a superb restaurant specializing in boiled ham, lemon pie and other Kentucky favourites. $\overline{\underline{\$\$}}$

### Berea

**BEREA**, thirty miles south of Lexington, just off I-75 in the foothills where Bluegrass Country meets Appalachia, is home to unique **Berea College**, which gives its 1500 mainly local students free tuition in return for work in crafts ranging from needlework to wrought ironwork. It was founded in 1855 by abolitionists as a vocational college for the young people of East Kentucky – both white and black, making it for forty years the only integrated college in the South. **Tours** of the campus and student craft workshops leave from the sumptuous *Boone Tavern Inn* (see page 91).

The college's reputation has also attracted many private art and craft galleries to little Berea; for details on these and a chance to buy local goods, visit the **Kentucky Artisan Center** at 200 Artisan Way, off I-75 (daily 9am–6pm; free; ⓦkentuckyartisancenter.ky.gov).

**ACCOMMODATION AND EATING**      **BEREA**

**Boone Tavern Inn** 100 Main St N ⓦboonetavernhotel. com. You can get a taste of college life at this student-run inn, which offers neat, colourful rooms and a high-quality restaurant. $\overline{\underline{\$\$}}$

## Daniel Boone National Forest

Almost the entire length of Kentucky east of Lexington is taken up by the steep slopes, narrow valleys and sandstone cliffs of the unspoiled **Daniel Boone National Forest**. Few Americans can have been so mythologized as **Daniel Boone**, who first explored the region in 1767 and thus ranks as one of Kentucky's earliest fur-trapping pioneers. Sadly, Boone failed to legalize his land claims and was forced to press further west to Missouri, where he died in 1820 at the age of 86.

**ACCOMMODATION**      **DANIEL BOONE NATIONAL FOREST**

**Twin Knobs** 5195 Twin Knobs Campground Rd, Salt Lick ⓦreserveamerica.com. At the north end of the forest, this is a good campground, with decent facilities and a great setting near Cave Run Lake. Open mid-March to Nov. $\overline{\underline{\$}}$

**1**

Natural Bridge State Resort Park

2135 Natural Bridge Rd, Slade · Open access · Free, charge for chairlift · Ⓦ parks.ky.gov

The geological extravaganza of the **Red River Gorge**, sixty miles east of Lexington via the Mountain Parkway, is best seen by driving a thirty-mile loop from the **Natural Bridge State Resort Park** on Hwy-77, near the village of Slade. Natural Bridge itself is a large sandstone arch surrounded by steep hollows and exposed clifflines; for those reluctant to negotiate the half-mile climb, there is a chairlift. The park also offers hiking trails, canoeing, fishing, horseback riding, birding and rock climbing.

**ACCOMMODATION**                        **NATURAL BRIDGE STATE RESORT PARK**

**Hemlock Lodge** Natural Bridge State Resort Park Ⓦ parks.ky.gov. Weekends can be reserved a year in advance at this excellent rustic lodge with comfortable rooms and great views, not far from the bridge itself. Info on the park's two campgrounds is also available. $$$

## Cumberland Gap National Historic Park

On the tri-state border of Kentucky, Tennessee and Virginia, the **Cumberland Gap National Historic Park**, a natural passageway used by migrating deer and bison, served as a gateway to the West for Boone and other pioneers. **Pinnacle Overlook**, a 1000ft lookout over the three states, is the finest spot to admire the extensive vista.

## Louisville

**LOUISVILLE**, just south of Indiana across the Ohio River, is firmly embedded in the American national consciousness for its multimillion-dollar **Kentucky Derby**. Each May, the horse race attracts more than half a million fans to this cosmopolitan industrial city, which still bears the traces of the early French settlers who came upriver from New Orleans. The Louisville region also produces a third of the country's **bourbon**.

Besides a vibrant arts and festivals scene, the city boasts an excellent network of public parks. One native son who took advantage of the recreation facilities was three-times world heavyweight boxing champion **Muhammad Ali**, who would do his early-morning training in the scenic environs of Chickasaw Park.

Downtown Louisville rolls gently toward Main Street, then abruptly lunges to the river. **Riverfront Plaza**, between Fifth and Sixth streets, is a prime observation point for the natural **Falls of the Ohio** on the opposite side of the river. The modern Big Four Bridge, accessed via the Louisville Waterfront Park a mile or so further east allows pedestrian and cycle access to Indiana. Away from the river, the **Historic District** around Central Park, which straddles Fourth Street, contains the highest concentration of Victorian houses in the country.

Muhammad Ali Center

144 N 6th St · Tues–Sat 9.30am–5pm, Sun noon–5pm · Charge · Ⓦ alicenter.org

Louisville's star attraction is the excellent **Muhammad Ali Center**, beside the river, which, apart from chronicling the local hero's boxing career with entertaining

---

### THE ORIGINAL FRIED CHICKEN

In 1940, "Colonel" Harland Sanders, so titled as a member of the Honorable Order of Kentucky Colonels, opened a small clapboard diner, the *Sanders Café*, alongside his motel and petrol station in tiny **Corbin**, ninety miles south of Lexington on I-75. His **Kentucky Fried Chicken** empire has since spread all over the world. The original hundred-seat restaurant, at 688 US-25 W (☎ 606 528 2163), has been restored with 1940s decor and an immense amount of memorabilia. The food served is the usual *KFC*, but it's an atmospheric little spot.

## THE KENTUCKY DERBY

The **Kentucky Derby** is one of the world's premier horse races; it's also, as Hunter S. Thompson put it, "decadent and depraved". Derby Day itself is the first Saturday in May, at the end of the two-week **Kentucky Derby Festival**. Since 1875, the leading lights of Southern society have gathered at **Churchill Downs**, three miles south of downtown Louisville, for an orgy of betting, haute cuisine and mint juleps in the plush grandstand, while tens of thousands of the beer-guzzling proletariat cram into the infield. Apart from the infield tickets, available in advance or on the day – which offer virtually no chance of a decent view – all seats are sold out months ahead. The actual race, traditionally preceded by a mass drunken rendition of *My Old Kentucky Home*, is run over a distance of one and a quarter miles, lasts barely two minutes and offers around a million dollars in prize money.

multimedia displays, provides insight into his political activism and Muslim faith, refreshingly presented in a positive light. Visits have become all the more poignant since Ali's passing in 2016.

### Louisville Slugger Museum

800 W Main St • Mon–Sat 9am–5pm, Sun 10am–4pm • Charge • Ⓦ sluggermuseum.com

Even non-baseball fans will be impressed by the **Louisville Slugger Museum**, which is actually the factory of the country's prime baseball bat manufacturer. The revamped guided tour, which kicks off with a film about the forests and mills from which Louisville bats come, is full of information on the history and process of bat making. All visitors receive a souvenir miniature bat at the end. You can also try your batting skills by facing ten pitches for an extra dollar. The museum also hosts an array of daily events, including the interactive Babe Ruth trivia game (11.30am & 2.30pm).

### Frazier History Museum

829 W Main St • Mon–Sat 9am–5pm, Sun noon–5pm • Charge • Ⓦ fraziermuseum.org

Spread over three mildly diverting floors, the permanent collection of the **Frazier History Museum** – no connection with Muhammad Ali's arch-rival Joe Frazier – includes a surprising wealth of treasure from the UK armouries and lots of displays on US history, while another section houses rotating special exhibitions.

### Speed Art Museum

2025 S 3rd St • Tues–Sat 10am–5pm, Sun noon–5pm • Charge • Ⓦ speedmuseum.org

The **Speed Art Museum**, located on the university campus, contains art spanning millennia, from ancient Asian artefacts through the Renaissance period and artists such as Rembrandt to contemporary works in the new wing. There is also an art **cinema**, with a superb array of films, from documentaries to indie shorts.

### Kentucky Derby Museum

Next to Churchill Downs at 704 Central Ave • Mid-March to Nov Mon–Sat 8am–5pm, Sun 11–5pm; Dec to mid-March Mon–Sat 9am–5pm, Sun 11am–5pm • Charge • Ⓦ derbymuseum.org

The excellent hands-on **Kentucky Derby Museum** will appeal to horseracing enthusiasts and neophytes alike. Admission includes a magnificent audiovisual display that captures the Derby Day atmosphere on a 360° screen. For additional fees, you can take a wide variety of tours, including a Behind the Scenes tour of the stables and racecourse, a Twilight Tour, and a Horses & Haunts Tour, where you'll see the Kentucky Derby Museum cemetery and the racetrack.

## ARRIVAL AND GETTING AROUND                                                    LOUISVILLE

**By plane** Most major US airlines fly into Louisville International Airport, 5 miles south on I-65; it's around a

1

$20 cab fare into town.

**By bus** The Greyhound terminus is fairly central at 720 W Muhammad Ali Blvd.

Destinations Cincinnati (5 daily; 1hr 45min); Indianapolis (5 daily; 2hr 10min–3hr 30min); Lexington (3 daily; 1hr 40min); Memphis (5 daily; 8–10hr); Nashville (9 daily; 3hr).

**By tram (trolley)** Ride around downtown for free on the all-electric TARC LouLift routes (Mon–Fri 6am–-8pm, Sat 10am–6pm; ☎ 502 585 1234, ⓦ ridetarc.org).

## INFORMATION AND TOURS

**Visitor centre** 401 W Main St (Mon–Sat 10am–6pm, Sun noon–5pm; ☎ 888 568 4784, ⓦ gotolouisville.com).

**Boat tours** In summer, two sternwheelers, the *Belle* *of Louisville* and the *Mary M. Miller*, conduct various cruises from the wharf at 401 W River Rd (schedules vary; ⓦ belleoflouisville.org).

## ACCOMMODATION

**21C Museum Hotel** 700 W Main St ⓦ 21cmuseumhotels. com. This boutique hotel has luxuriously classy rooms and also houses an art museum and top-notch restaurant. Look out for the colourful penguin statues dotted around the property. **$$$**

**Central Park B&B** 1353 S 4th St ⓦ centralparkbandb. com. Opulent Victorian B&B in the heart of the Historic District with six quaintly decorated rooms in the main building and a converted carriage house. **$$**

**Econo Lodge** 401 S 2nd St ⓦ choicehotels.com. About as cheap as you'll find right downtown. Most rooms are simple but perfectly adequate, while the priciest have hot tubs. **$$**

**Galt House** 140 N 4th St ⓦ galthouse.com. The official hotel of the Kentucky Derby is a massive high-rise right on the riverfront, with spacious and well-appointed rooms and a range of top facilities. **$$$**

**Hampton Inn Downtown Louisville** 101 E Jefferson St ⓦ hilton.com. Comfortable standard chain rooms plus free buffet breakfast, indoor pool and fitness centre. **$$**

## EATING AND DRINKING

★ **Mayan Café** 813 E Market St ☎ 502 566 0651, ⓦ themayancafe.com. Traditional Maya dishes, such as oven-roasted rabbit with pumpkin seed mole, are served in a bright dining room. **$$**

**Ramsi's Café on the World** 1293 Bardstown Rd ⓦ ramsiscafe.com. Atmospheric café offering eclectic, tasty selections from around the world such as Moroccan lamb chops with bourbon tomato jam and pumpkin mint sauce. **$$$**

**Toast On Market** 620 E Market St ☎ 502 569 4099, ⓦ toastonmarket.com. Heaps of eggs and pancakes for breakfast or filling sandwiches and grilled cheese plus trimmings all go for bargain prices here. **$**

## DRINKING, NIGHTLIFE AND ENTERTAINMENT

The two-mile strip around Bardstown Road and Baxter Avenue is punctuated by fun bars, while the best LGBTQ+ clubs are on the eastern edge of downtown. Check **listings** in the free *LEO* (Louisville Eccentric Observer; ⓦ leoweekly. com).

### BARS, CLUBS AND LIVE MUSIC VENUES

**Great Flood Brewing Co** 2120 Bardstown Rd ⓦ greatfloodbrewing.com. Splendid micro-brewery that makes fine ales, including the hoppy Tomahawk IPA and the Oaked Scotch Ale.

**Headliners Music Hall** 1386 Lexington Rd ⓦ headlinerslouisville.com. Lively club that showcases local, national and even international indie bands, as well as cabaret acts.

**Holy Grale** 1034 Bardstown Road ⓦ the grales.com. One-of-a-kind bar, housed in a converted former church and serving great pub food like Belgian-style mussels and chips along with a seductive array of beers.

**Stevie Ray's Blues Bar** 230 E Main St ⓦ stevieraysbluesbar.com. One of the best places in the area to catch an intimate gig, this is a loud, rocking blues bar, with live acts most nights.

★ **Whiskey Dry** 412 S Fourth St ☎ 502 749 7933. As the name implies, whiskey is celebrated here, as is bourbon, scotch and other stellar cocktails made with the amber liquid, like The Commonwealth; bourbon, sorghum coffee, peppercorns and sassafras. The playful comfort food ranges from fat burgers – try the patty melt, heaped with whiskey onions, melted Swiss cheese and mushrooms – to tater tots and boozy milkshakes.

### PERFORMANCE VENUES

**Actors' Theatre of Louisville** 316 W Main St ⓦ actorstheatre.org. The company that performs here has gained a national reputation for its new productions over fifty years of existence.

**Kentucky Center for the Arts** 501 W Main St ⓦ kentuckyperformingarts.org. Fronted by several outlandish sculptures, this place offers everything from dance lessons through rock and jazz to more highbrow stage shows.

# Bourbon Country

Kentucky's much-vaunted **Bourbon Country**, centred on attractive **Bardstown**, forty miles south of Louisville on US-150, is the place to get acquainted with **bourbon whiskey**. The now world-famous tipple was created in early pioneer days, so the story goes, when Elijah Craig, a baptist minister, added corn to the usual rye and barley. Named after Bourbon County near Lexington, Kentucky's whiskey soon gained a national reputation, thanks to crisp limestone water, strict laws concerning ingredients and the skills of small-scale distillers. Ironically, you can't drink the stuff in many counties, as they are **dry**. A good starting point is Bardstown's **Oscar Getz Museum of Whiskey History** in Spalding Hall, 114 N Fifth St (May–Oct Mon–Fri 10am–5pm, Sat 10am–4pm, Sun noon–4pm; Nov–April Tues–Sat 10am–4pm, Sun noon–4pm; free; ⓦwhiskeymuseum.com).

## The distilleries

Fourteen miles northwest of Bardstown at **Clermont**, the **Jim Beam's American Stillhouse** (526 Happy Hollow Rd; Mon–Sat 9am–5.30pm, Sun noon–4.30pm; charge; ⓦjimbeam.com) has an informative tour of the distillery and home, followed by a tasting. At **Maker's Mark Distillery**, twenty miles south of Bardstown on Hwy-49 near **Loretto**, whiskey is still hand-crafted in an out-of-the-way collection of beautifully restored black, red and grey plankhouses (3350 Burkes Spring Rd; Mon–Sat 9.30am–3.30pm; March–Dec also Sun 11.30am–3.30pm; charge; ⓦmakersmark.com).

# Abraham Lincoln National Historic Site

Three miles south of Hodgenville, on US-31 E · Daily: summer 8am–6.45pm; rest of year closes 4.45pm · Free · ⓦ nps.gov/abli

On February 12, 1809, **Abraham Lincoln**, the sixteenth president of the USA, was born in a one-room log cabin in the frontier wilds, son of a wandering farmer and, if some accounts are to be believed, an illiterate and illegitimate mother. The **National Historic Site** has a symbolic cabin of his birth, enclosed in a granite and marble Memorial Building with 56 steps, one for each year of Lincoln's life.

The family moved ten miles northeast in 1811 to the **Knob Creek** area, where Lincoln's earliest memory was of slaves being forcefully driven along the road. Here you can visit another re-creation of his boyhood home (April–Oct daily, varying hours; free).

| ACCOMMODATION | ABRAHAM LINCOLN NATIONAL HISTORIC SITE |
|---|---|
| **Nancy Lincoln Inn** Abraham Lincoln National Historic Site ⓦlaruecounty.org/lodging.shtml. Staying in one of the three log cabins in the woods right next to old | Abe's birthplace is a fairly spartan but highly atmospheric experience. $$ |

# Mammoth Cave National Park

The 365 miles of labyrinthine passages (with an average of five new miles discovered each year) and domed caverns of **MAMMOTH CAVE NATIONAL PARK** lie around ninety miles south of Louisville. Its amazing geological formations, carved by acidic water trickling through limestone, include a bewildering display of stalagmites and stalactites, a huge cascade of flowstone known as **Frozen Niagara** and **Echo River**, 365ft below ground, populated by a unique species of colourless and sightless fish. Among traces of human occupation are Native American artefacts, a former saltpetre mine and the remains of an experimental tuberculosis hospital, built in 1843 in the belief that the cool atmosphere of the cave would help clear patients' lungs. You can take a limited-access self-guided tour, but by far the best way to appreciate the caves is to join one of the lengthy **ranger-guided tours** – keep in mind that the temperature in the caves is a constantly cool 54°F.

The park's attractions are by no means all subterranean. You can explore the scenic **Green River**, as it cuts through densely forested hillsides and jagged limestone

**1**

cliffs, by following hiking trails or renting a canoe from Green River Canoeing (ⓦgreenrivercanoeing.com). The privately owned caves all around and the "attractions" in nearby Cave City and Park City are best ignored.

## INFORMATION AND TOURS                    MAMMOTH CAVE NATIONAL PARK

**Visitor centre** The on-site visitor centre is open daily (mid-April to Nov 8am–6.15pm; Dec to mid-April 9am–5pm; ⓦ nps.gov/maca).

**Tours** Various tours (30min–6hr; charge) are available from the visitor centre. You can check availability (ⓦ recreation. gov) in advance.

## ACCOMMODATION

**Mammoth Cave Hotel** Mammoth Cave National Park ⓦ mammothcavehotel.com. Spread across multiple units, the hotel contains motel-style rooms and good-value cottages. Camping is free in the backcountry, though you'll need a permit from the visitor centre. $\overline{\underline{\mathsf{SS}}}$

# Tennessee

A shallow rectangle, just one hundred miles from north to south, **TENNESSEE** stretches 450 miles from the Mississippi to the Appalachians. The marshy **western** third of the state occupies a low plateau edging down toward the Mississippi. Only in the far southwest corner do the bluffs rise high enough to permit a sizeable riverside settlement – the exhilarating port of **Memphis**, the birthplace of urban **blues** and longtime home of **Elvis**. The plantation homes and dull, tidy towns of **middle Tennessee's** rolling farmland reflect the comfortable lifestyle of its pioneers; smack in the heart of it sprawls hip **Nashville**, synonymous with **country music**. The mountainous **east** shares its top attraction with North Carolina – the peaks, streams and meadows of **Great Smoky Mountains National Park**.

## Memphis

Perched above the Mississippi River, **MEMPHIS** is perhaps the single most exciting destination in the South – especially for music-lovers. Visitors flock to celebrate the city that gave the world **blues**, **soul** and **rock'n'roll**, and to chow down in the unrivalled **barbecue** capital of the nation. Memphis is both deeply atmospheric – with its faded downtown streets dotted with retro stores and diners and the sun setting nightly across the broad Mississippi – and invigorating, with a cluster of superb museums and fantastic restaurants. If it's the **Elvis** connection that appeals, you won't leave disappointed – let alone empty-handed – but even the King represents just one small part of the rich musical heritage of the home of Sun and Stax studios.

Laidback and oddball, melancholy and determinedly nostalgic, Memphis has a friendly scale. **Downtown** still retains a healthy ensemble of buildings from the cotton era – best admired either along the riverfront or from the trolley down **Main Street** – along with a number of places that look unchanged since Elvis's day. Four miles southeast of downtown, the **Cooper-Young** intersection boasts a handful of hip restaurants and vintage stores.

### Beale Street

Now a fabled blues corridor, **Beale Street** began life in the mid-nineteenth century as one of Memphis's most exclusive enclaves; within fifty years its elite residents had been driven out by yellow fever epidemics and the ravages of the Civil War to be replaced by a diverse mix of blacks, Greeks, Jews, Chinese and Italians. But it was **black culture** that gave the street its fame. Beale Street was where black roustabouts and travellers passing through Memphis immediately headed. In the Jim Crow era, it served as the centre for black businesses, financiers and professionals, and in its Twenties' heyday it was jammed with vaudeville theatres, concert halls, bars and juke joints (mostly white-owned). Although Beale still drew huge crowds in the Forties, the drift to the suburbs and, ironically, the success of the **civil rights** years in opening the rest of Memphis to black businesses, almost killed it off. The **bulldozers** of the late Sixties spared only the grand Orpheum Theatre, at 203 S Main St, and a few commercial buildings between Second and Fourth streets.

Beale Street has now been restored as a touristy **Historic District**. Its souvenir shops, music clubs, bars and cafés are bedecked with retro facades and neon signs, while a

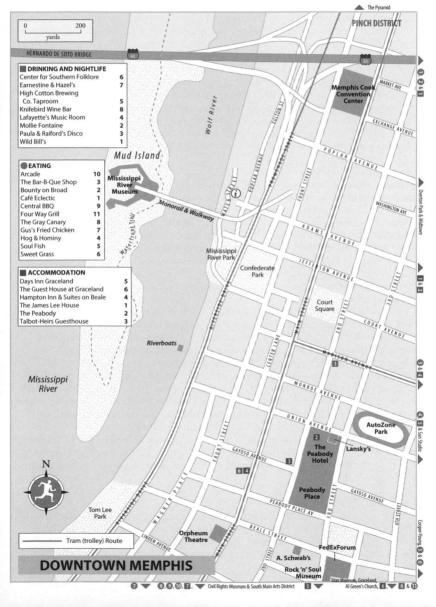

The Pyramid

**PINCH DISTRICT**

0    200
yards

HERNANDO DE SOTO BRIDGE

**Memphis Cook Convention Center**

MARKET AVE

EXCHANGE AVENUE

POPLAR   AVENUE

WASHINGTON AVE

■ **DRINKING AND NIGHTLIFE**
| | |
|---|---|
| Center for Southern Folklore | 6 |
| Earnestine & Hazel's | 7 |
| High Cotton Brewing | |
| Co. Taproom | 5 |
| Knifebird Wine Bar | 8 |
| Lafayette's Music Room | 4 |
| Mollie Fontaine | 2 |
| Paula & Raiford's Disco | 3 |
| Wild Bill's | 1 |

*Mud Island*

Wolf River

TALLON ST

FRONT STREET

BEALE STREET

POPLAR AVENUE

A D A M S   A V E N U E

● **EATING**
| | |
|---|---|
| Arcade | 10 |
| The Bar-B-Que Shop | 3 |
| Bounty on Broad | 2 |
| Café Eclectic | 1 |
| Central BBQ | 9 |
| Four Way Grill | 11 |
| The Gray Canary | 8 |
| Gus's Fried Chicken | 7 |
| Hog & Hominy | 4 |
| Soul Fish | 5 |
| Sweet Grass | 6 |

**Mississippi River Museum**

Monorail & Walkway

Mississippi River Park

Confederate Park

JEFFERSON AVENUE

3RD STREET

■ **ACCOMMODATION**
| | |
|---|---|
| Days Inn Graceland | 5 |
| The Guest House at Graceland | 6 |
| Hampton Inn & Suites on Beale | 4 |
| The James Lee House | 1 |
| The Peabody | 2 |
| Talbot-Heirs Guesthouse | 3 |

Court Square

COURT AVENUE

Waterfront Trail

*Riverboats*

CENTER LANE

M A D I S O N   A V E N U E

3

*Mississippi River*

MONROE AVENUE

U N I O N   A V E N U E

**AutoZone Park**

2

**The Peabody Hotel**

**Lansky's**

FRONT STREET

GAYOSO AVENUE

3

6 4

GAYOSO AVENUE

4TH STREET

**Peabody Place**

PEABODY PLACE AV

3RD STREET

**N**

Tom Lee Park

WAGNER PLACE

LINDEN AVENUE

**Orpheum Theatre**

B E A L E   S T R E E T

2ND STREET

**FedExForum**

**A. Schwab's**

**Rock 'n' Soul Museum**

Stax Museum, Graceland,

——— Tram (trolley) Route

**DOWNTOWN MEMPHIS**

7 ▼   8, 9, 10, 7, ▼   Civil Rights Museum & South Main Arts District   5 ▼   Al Green's Church, 6, ▼ 8 & 13

Overton Park & Midtown

1 & 2

9 & 4

4, 5 & Sun Studio

Cooper-Young, 5 & 6

**1**

Walk of Fame honours musical greats such as B.B. King and Howlin' Wolf. Blues fans in particular will be drawn to its music venues, which showcase top regional talent. At Beale's western end, no. 126 – the former home of the iconic **Lansky's**, tailor to the Memphis stars – is now home to a *Hard Rock Cafe*; if you're looking to buy any of their gorgeous rock'n'roll threads, including Elvis's blue cable-knit "*Jailhouse Rock*" sweater, Lansky's continues to thrive in the historic *Peabody* hotel (see page 103).

**A. Schwab's Dry Goods Store**, at 163 Beale St (Ⓦa-schwab.com) looks much as it must have done when it opened in 1876, with an incredible array of voodoo paraphernalia – best-sellers include Mojo Hands and High John the Conqueror lucky roots – as well as 99¢ neckties and Sunday School badges. As the cheeky store tagline says, "If you can't find it at Schwab's, you're better off without it".

### Rock'n'Soul Museum

191 Beale St • Summer daily 9.30am–7pm, winter Wed–Sun 10am–5pm • Charge • Ⓦ memphisrocknsoul.org

In the plaza of the enormous FedEx Forum, the lively and fascinating **Rock'n'Soul Museum**, created by the Smithsonian Institution, presents the story of the city's musical heritage scrapbook-style, making connections between migration, racism, civil rights and youth culture, with artefacts ranging from Elvis's stage gear and one of B.B. King's "Lucille" guitars to Isaac Hayes' diamond-encrusted "piano" watch.

### The National Civil Rights Museum

450 Mulberry St • Mon & Wed–Sun 9am–6pm • Charge • Ⓦ civilrightsmuseum.org

The **National Civil Rights Museum** provides the most rewarding and comprehensive history of the long and tumultuous struggle for civil rights to be had anywhere in the South. It's built around the shell of the former *Lorraine Motel*, where **Martin Luther King, Jr.** was assassinated by James Earl Ray on April 4, 1968. Dr King was killed by a single bullet as he stood on the balcony, the evening before he was due to lead a march in Memphis in support of a strike by black sanitation workers.

The *Lorraine* itself was one of the few places where blacks and whites could meet in Memphis during the segregation era; thus black singer Eddie Floyd and white guitarist Steve Cropper wrote soul classics such as *Knock on Wood* here, and Dr King was a regular guest. The facade of the motel is still all too recognizable from images of King's death, but once inside visitors are faced with a succession of galleries that recount the major milestones of the movement, from A. Philip Randolph of the Brotherhood of Sleeping Car Porters, who originally called for a march on Washington in 1941, through to the Nation of Islam and the Black Panthers. There is some horrifying and very emotional footage, but by far the most affecting moment comes when you reach King's actual room, Room 306, still laid out as he left it, and see the spot where his life was cut short. Another wing, across from the motel, completes the story by incorporating the boarding house from which the fatal shot was fired. The bedroom rented that same day by James Earl Ray, and the sordid little bathroom that served as his sniper's nest, can be inspected behind glass, with the death site clearly visible beyond. King's own family remain highly sceptical as to whether Ray acted alone, and detailed panels lay out all sorts of conspiracy theories.

### The South Main Arts District

A block west of the National Civil Rights Museum, the once flyblown South Main Street has been given a new lease of life. Spanning the nine or so blocks along Main between Vance and St Paul avenues, the **South Main Arts District** is a burgeoning stretch of galleries, stores and restaurants, complete with a crop of condos and lofts. It's particularly buzzing on the last Friday of the month, when the free "Art Trolley" (6–9pm) runs along Main and stores offer complimentary snacks and drinks.

1

## THE SOUND OF MEMPHIS

Since the start of the twentieth century, Memphis has been a meeting place for black musicians from the Delta and beyond. During the Twenties, its downtown pubs, clubs and street corners were alive with the sound of the blues. After World War II, young musicians and radio DJs such as Bobby Bland and B.B. King experimented by blending the traditional blues sound with jazz, adding electrical amplification to create rhythm'n'blues. White promoter Sam Phillips started **Sun Records** in 1953, employing Ike Turner as a scout to comb the Beale Street clubs for new talent. Among those whom Turner helped introduce to vinyl were his own girlfriend, Annie Mae Bullock (later **Tina Turner**), Howlin' Wolf and Little Junior Parker, whose *Mystery Train* was Sun's first great recording. In 1953, the 18-year-old **Elvis Presley** hired the studio to record *My Happiness*, supposedly as a gift for his mother, and something prompted Phillips' assistant Marion Keisker to file away his recording. The next summer, Phillips called Elvis back to the studio to cut *That's All Right*, and thereby set out towards proving his much-quoted conviction that "If I could find a white man who had the Negro sound and the Negro feel, I could make a billion dollars". Phillips swiftly dropped his black artists and signed other white rockabilly singers like Carl Perkins and **Jerry Lee Lewis** to make classics such as *Blue Suede Shoes* and *Great Balls of Fire*. Elvis was soon sold on to RCA (for just $35,000), and didn't record in Memphis again until 1969, when at Chips Moman's American Studios he produced the best material of his later career, including *Suspicious Minds*.

In the Sixties and early Seventies, Memphis's **Stax Records** provided a rootsy alternative to the poppier sounds of Motown. This hard-edged Southern soul was created by a multiracial mix of musicians, Steve Cropper's fluid guitar complementing the blaring Memphis Horns. The label's first real success was *Green Onions* by studio band Booker T and the MGs; further hits followed from Otis Redding (*Try a Little Tenderness*), Wilson Pickett (*Midnight Hour*), Sam and Dave (*Soul Man*) and Isaac Hayes (*Shaft*). The label eventually foundered in acrimony; the last straw for many of its veteran soulmen was the signing of the British child star Lena Zavaroni for a six-figure sum.

### Sun Studio

706 Union Ave • Daily 10am–6pm; tours (40min) depart on the half-hour • Charge • ⦿ sunstudio.com

Second only to Graceland, Memphis's principal shrine to the memory of Elvis is the hip little **Sun Studio**. This is where, in 1953, the shy 18-year-old trucker from Tupelo turned up with his guitar, claiming, "I don't sound like nobody". The studio then went on to introduce rock'n'roll to the world via not only the King but also artists like Jerry Lee Lewis, Johnny Cash and Roy Orbison. Though Sun Records moved out of the building in 1960, the soundproofing remained in place through a variety of incarnations – including a brief, unlikely period as a scuba-diving store – making possible its restoration as a functioning studio in 1985 and retaining the eerie, almost spiritual atmosphere of the place. Tours start in an upstairs room where you can see B.B. King's chair and Elvis's high school diploma, before heading down into the studio. Measuring just 18 by 30ft, the shabby room fills with music as enthusiastic rockabilly guides play wild rock'n'roll recordings and tell choice anecdotes. Few visitors leave unmoved – or without posing for a photo with Elvis's original mic stand.

### The Stax Museum of American Soul Music

926 E McLemore Ave • Tues–Sun 1–5pm • Charge • ⦿ staxmuseum.com

In 1960, one of Memphis's most famous addresses, 926 E McLemore Ave, was occupied by the Capitol Theatre, a landmark in a neighbourhood where blacks had just started to outnumber whites. The theatre became the headquarters of the **Stax** record label, a veritable powerhouse of funky soul where over the next fourteen years artists such as Otis Redding, Isaac Hayes, Albert King and the Staples Singers cut fifteen US

**1**

number-one hits and achieved 237 entries in the top 100. By the early 2000s, however, with Stax long since defunct, 926 E McLemore was just a derelict lot in a dodgy neighbourhood.

Since then, Stax has resurfaced, reconstructed larger than ever, with a music academy sitting next to the fabulous **Stax Museum of American Soul Music**, or **Soulsville**. Visits start with a film history of the label, using stunning footage to illuminate the triumphs and the tensions that arose from its all-but-unique status as a joint black-white enterprise in the segregated South. The first exhibit beyond, emphasizing soul music's gospel roots, is an entire African Methodist Episcopal Church, transported here from Mississippi. Among the wealth of footage and recordings, showpiece artefacts include Isaac Hayes's peacock-blue-and-gold Cadillac. The studio has been re-created in detail, featuring the two-track tape recorder used by Otis Redding to record *Mr Pitiful* and *Respect*.

## The Pyramid

The northern boundary of downtown Memphis is marked by the astonishing 32-storey, 321ft **Pyramid** glinting in the sun over the mighty river. Completed in 1991, at two-thirds the size of Egypt's Great Pyramid, it was created to make a symbolic link with Egypt's Nile Delta. After years hosting major exhibitions and shows, it has since been overshadowed by downtown's FedEx Forum. A marvellous folly, it's now an outdoor retailer – the Bass Pro Shops at the Pyramid.

### Mud Island River Park

125 N Front St • Daily 6am–7pm • Park free, Charge for museum • ⓦ mudisland.com

From Riverside Drive, which runs south from the Pyramid, a walkway heads across the Mississippi's Wolf Channel to **Mud Island River Park**; you can walk or bike across the walkway. Highlights of the island's slightly old-fashioned but enjoyable **Mississippi River Museum** include a full-sized reconstructed steamboat, a morbidly fascinating "Theater of Disasters", and salty tales of characters like keelboatman Mike Fink, who in 1830 styled himself "half horse, half alligator". **River Walk**, which runs to the southern tip of the island, is a scale replica of the lower Mississippi River; at the end, you can rent canoes and kayaks for a leisurely paddle around the nearby "Gulf of Mexico".

Mud Island hosts a variety of concerts and events: in summer, you can even bring a sleeping bag and join a mass camp-out where the tent, dinner, breakfast and entertainment is laid on.

## Tom Lee Park

On the mainland, a walk via the waterfront Confederate and Mississippi River parks brings you to **Tom Lee Park**, a venue for major outdoor events including **Memphis in May** (see page 104). Stretching a mile along the river, it commemorates a black boatman who rescued 32 people from a sinking boat in 1925 – despite not being able to swim.

### Graceland

3734 Elvis Presley Blvd, 10 miles south of downtown • Generally Mon–Sat 9am–4pm, but hours fluctuate wildly • Tour charges vary enormously according to degree of access; reservations recommended • ⓦ graceland.com

In itself, Elvis Presley's **Graceland** was a surprisingly modest home for the world's most successful entertainer – it's certainly not the "mansion" you may have imagined. And while Elvis was clearly a man who indulged his tastes to the fullest, Graceland has none of the pomposity that characterizes so many other showpiece Southern residences. Visits are affectionate celebrations of the man; never exactly tongue-in-cheek, but not cloyingly reverential either.

Elvis was just 22 when he paid $100,000 for Graceland in 1957. Built in 1939, the stone-clad house was then considered one of the most desirable properties in Memphis, though today the neighbourhood is distinctly less exclusive, its main thoroughfare – **Elvis Presley Boulevard** – slightly dodgy and lined with discount liquor stores, ancient beauty parlours, used car lots and surprisingly few Elvis-related souvenir shops. Tours start opposite the house in **Graceland Plaza**; excited visitors, kitted out with headphones, are ferried across the road in minibuses, which depart every few minutes and sweep through the house's famous "musical gate", etched with musical notes and Elvis's silhouette.

### Inside the house

Audio tours, peppered with spoken memories from Priscilla Presley and Elvis's daughter, Lisa Marie, and rousing choruses from the King himself, allow you to spend as long as you wish, although upstairs is out of bounds. The interior is a jubilant tribute to the taste of the Seventies, each room reflecting Elvis's personal passions. Highlights include the Hawaiian-themed **Jungle Room**, with its waterfall, tiki ornaments and green shag-carpeted ceiling, where Elvis recorded *Moody Blue* and other gems from his latter years; the **Pool Room**, whose walls and ceiling are covered in heavily pleated, paisley fabric suggesting a little-documented psychedelic phase; and the navy-and-lemon **TV Room**, mirrored and fitted with three screens that now show classic 1970s TV shows and Elvis's favourite movies.

### Other buildings and memorial

In the **trophy building**, you parade past Elvis's platinum, gold and silver records, some of his wilder Vegas stage costumes and cases of intriguing clippings, photos and memorabilia; footage of early TV performances offers breathtaking reminders of just how charismatic the young Elvis was. The tour of the interior ends with the **racquetball building**, where he played on the morning he died. In the attached lounge, the piano where he sang for the last time (apparently *Unchained Melody*) stands eerily silent, while in the court itself his resplendent, bejewelled capes and jumpsuits stand sentinel beneath a huge monitor showing a late performance of *American Trilogy*. Here, perhaps more than anywhere else, you can feel the huge presence of the man who changed the face of music forever. Elvis (Jan 8, 1935–Aug 16, 1977), his mother, Gladys, his father, Vernon, and his grandmother, Minnie Mae, lie buried in the **meditation garden** outside, their graves strewn with flowers and soft toys sent from fans. Elvis's body was moved here two months after his death, when security problems at the local cemetery became unmanageable. There's often a log-jam here, as visitors crane to read the messages sent by fans, take moments to offer their own prayers and snap photos of the bronze memorial plaques. Graceland Plaza, resounding with nonstop Elvis hits, holds several extra attractions. Since 2016, **The Guest House at Graceland** (see page 102) has offered the chance to stay in the Graceland grounds.

### The King's toys

Don't miss Elvis's personal **aeroplanes**, including the *Lisa Marie*, customized with a 24-carat-gold washroom sink and velvet furnishings. Quite apart from his many cars – among them a Harley-Davidson golf cart and super-sleek powder-pink 1955 Cadillac – the enjoyable **Elvis Presley Automobile Museum** shows a wittily edited film of action-packed and vaguely car-related clips from his movies. Finally, Graceland Plaza's many **gift stores** will keep you occupied for hours, whether you're after an Elvis toothbrush or a pair of blue suede shoes.

## Overton Park

The centrepiece of wooded **Overton Park**, three miles or so east of downtown on Poplar Avenue, is the **Memphis Zoo** (daily: March to mid-Oct 9am–5pm; mid-Oct to Feb 9am–4pm; grounds stay open 1hr after closing; charge; ⓦmemphiszoo.org). If the usual array of gorillas, orangutans and giraffes doesn't satisfy you, you can visit a pair of giant pandas.

1

The park also holds the impressive **Memphis Brooks Museum of Art** (Wed 10am–8pm, Thurs & Fri 10am–4pm, Sat 10am–5pm, Sun 11am–5pm; charge; ⓦbrooksmuseum. org), whose holdings feature a strong collection of medieval and Renaissance works.

Pink Palace

3050 Central Ave • Mon–Sat 9am–5pm, Sun noon–5pm • Charge • ⓦ memphismuseums.org

A couple of miles southeast of Overton Park, the **Pink Palace** centres on the marble mansion of Clarence Saunders, who founded America's first chain of self-service **supermarkets**, Piggly-Wiggly, in 1916. Saunders went bankrupt in 1923 and never actually lived here; instead, the building became an appealingly old-fashioned and quirky museum of Memphis history, with an adjacent IMAX theatre, planetarium and Lichterman Nature Center.

## ARRIVAL AND DEPARTURE                                            MEMPHIS

**By plane** Memphis International Airport (ⓦmscaa.com) is 12 miles south of downtown – about 15min by taxi ($30).

**By car** Memphis is on I-40 as it runs east–west and I-55 from the south. Both join I-240, which loops around the city, and cross the Mississippi River.

**By bus** Greyhound buses (☎901 395 8770) stop at 3033 Airways Blvd, about 2 miles from the airport, with

connections to local transport (ⓦmatatransit.com). Destinations Birmingham, AL (2–3 daily; 4hr 30min); Jackson, MS (1 daily; 4hr); Little Rock, AR (7 daily; 2hr 25min); Nashville, TN (5 daily; 4hr).

**By train** The Amtrak station, 545 S Main St, is on the southern edge of downtown. There's a daily service to Jackson (4hr 22min).

## GETTING AROUND

**By tram (trolley)** The Memphis Area Transit Authority (ⓦmatatransit.com) runs a useful downtown trolley along Main St and Riverside Drive, connecting Beale St, the Civil Rights Museum and the South Main Arts District (one- and

three-day passes available on board).

**By tour bus** Memphis Hop runs a hop-on, hop-off shuttle between the city's major attractions (charge; ⓦmemphishop.com).

## INFORMATION AND TOURS

**Visitor centres** The spacious Tennessee Welcome Center is just off I-40 downtown at 119 N Riverside and Adams, facing Mud Island at river level (daily 9am–3pm; ⓦmemphistravel.com). There's another visitor centre at 3205 Elvis Presley Blvd, on the way to Graceland.

**Carriage tours** Horse-drawn carriage tours (ⓦcarriagetoursofmemphis.com) abound downtown –

prices vary but you're looking at around $50 for a 30min ride.

**River cruises** A great way to see Memphis is to float along the mighty Mississippi: sternwheelers leave from the foot of Beale St (charge; ☎ 901 527 2628, ⓦmemphisriverboats. net), with options including a Sunday Jazz Brunch and midnight booze cruises.

## ACCOMMODATION                                          SEE MAP PAGE 97

The most convenient place to stay is **downtown**, with a good choice of historic hotels and upscale chains. There are cheaper options near **Graceland**, on Elvis Presley Boulevard, to the south, though note that this area gets a bit dodgy at night. Wherever you stay, it's best to **book in advance** at busy times, such as the anniversary of Elvis's death in mid-August and during the Memphis in May festival (see page 104).

**Days Inn Graceland** 3839 Elvis Presley Blvd ⓦwyndhamhotels.com. Good option within walking distance of Graceland, with lots of Elvis memorabilia and music, along with – bliss! – a guitar-shaped pool. Rates include continental breakfast. $\overline{\$\$}$

**The Guest House at Graceland** 3734 Elvis Presley Blvd, 10 miles south of Memphis ⓦgraceland.com. The only thing better than visiting Graceland? Sleeping at Graceland.

The *Guest House at Graceland* features 450 elegant rooms (many with design consulting from Priscilla Presley herself), making it the largest hotel project in Memphis in nearly a century. This property is a lot more than its "guest house" tag suggests. It also includes multiple restaurants and bars, a 464-seat theatre, a swimming pool, complimentary airport shuttle and more – all, of course, imbued with the spirit and aesthetic of the rock'n'roll legend. $\overline{\$\$\$}$

**Hampton Inn & Suites on Beale** 175 Peabody Place ⓦhilton.com/en/hampton. In an unbeatable location just half a block from Beale St, with modern, immaculate rooms at reasonable prices, a pool and complimentary breakfast. Note that the building does get a bit of street noise. $\overline{\$\$\$}$

★**The James Lee House** 690 Adams Ave ⓦjamesleehouse.com. Originally a two-storey farmhouse from 1848, this historic structure, not far east of downtown, has had many lives, including as an art school, until it re-opened as a luxury B&B. The lovingly restored suites offer a gorgeous mix of old and new, with wood floors, exposed-brick chimneys and four-poster beds. Wake up to a gourmet breakfast (included). $$$$

**The Peabody** 149 Union Ave ⓦ peabodymemphis.com. This opulent historic hotel – which celebrated its 150th anniversary in 2019 – is famed for its legendary mascot ducks, who waddle from the elevator promptly at 11am, spend the day in the lobby fountain and then return to their penthouse at 5pm. Rooms are comfortably elegant, while the glorious lobby is an attraction in itself, with a friendly, relaxed bar and Lansky's boutique (see page 98), where you can pick up a pair of genuine blue suede shoes and other designs favoured by the King. $$$$

**Talbot-Heirs Guesthouse** 99 S 2nd St ⓦ talbotheirs. com. Characterful and friendly family-run place near Beale St. Each of the eight themed suites has a full kitchen, Bluetooth speakers and access to laundry facilities. Continental breakfast included. $$$

## EATING

SEE MAP PAGE 97

Memphians love their food and justly proclaim their city to be the **pork barbecue** capital of the world. Fans should head for the **Memphis in May** festival (see page 104), when hundreds of teams compete in the World Championship Barbecue Contest. Soul food lovers, too, will be delighted at the choice and quality on offer. You'll have no problem finding somewhere good to eat downtown, from dives to sophisticated bistros, along **South Main**, or in the eclectic restaurants of **Cooper-Young**.

**Arcade** 540 S Main St, South Main Arts District ⓦ arcaderestaurant.com. Open since 1919, this landmark vintage diner – Elvis ate here! – was featured in Jim Jarmusch's movie *Mystery Train*, among many others. Come for big Southern breakfasts, pizzas and home cooking and heaps of atmosphere. $$

**The Bar-B-Que Shop** 1782 Madison Ave, midtown ⓦ dancingpigs.com. Past the door painted with dancing pigs, this atmospheric barbecue hut reels in locals and tourists alike and serves up succulent ribs, pulled pork on Texas toast (a thick slice of garlicky bread) and sweet, smoky BBQ spaghetti. $$

★ **Bounty on Broad** 2519 Broad Ave ⓦ bountyonbroad.com. This innovative restaurant is the embodiment of Broad Avenue, in East Memphis, which has transformed from disused storefronts to a vibrant arts and cultural district over the last decade. The farm-to-fork restaurant, in the restored Hanover pharmacy building, features creative seasonal dishes such as sweet tea-brined pork chop and seared scallops with white truffle oil. $$$$

★ **Café Eclectic** 603 N McLean Blvd, midtown ⓦ cafeeclectic.net. Delicious around-the-clock restaurant satisfying a nice range of appetites: wonderful for breakfast – try the French toast stuffed with Nutella or "The Kitchen Sink", an omelette with the works, including sausage, ham, bacon, spinach, mushroom, onions, bell peppers and more. They also do a mean cinnamon roll and blueberry pie, a top-notch latte and an excellent array of vegetarian and vegan dishes. $$

**Central BBQ** 147 E Butler Ave, South Main Arts District ⓦ eatcbq.com. Just around the corner from the Civil Rights Museum, this is one of the city's best barbecue purveyors, with huge, lip-smacking plates of pulled pork and spiced beef brisket. Its popularity has caused several locations to open up around town (the original restaurant is in Cooper-Young). $$

**Four Way Grill** 998 Mississippi Blvd, South Memphis ⓦ fourwaymemphis.com. Convenient for the Stax museum, this spotless little soul food joint – a favourite haunt of Martin Luther King, Jr. – dishes up unbeatable blue-plate specials, including catfish, smothered chicken, green tomatoes and the like at low prices. $$

★ **The Gray Canary** 301 S Front St ⓦ thegraycanary. com. This boisterous, spacious restaurant, in a renovated warehouse at the Old Dominick Distillery, turns out vibrant American fare – with plenty of twists. The lively open kitchen sets the tone – feast on broccoli with black garlic vinaigrette and pancetta, and the splendid signature burger with onion bacon sofrito on a brioche bun. The inventive cocktails also pack a punch. $$$

★ **Gus's Fried Chicken** 310 S Front St, downtown ⓦ gusfriedchicken.com. This tiny place near the South Main Arts District has caught the attention of the national press for its delicious, crackling-crisp and spicy chicken. Queues generally snake out the door, but it's worth the wait. $

**Hog & Hominy** 707 W Brookhaven Circle, East Memphis ⓦ hogandhominy.com. Hidden in a sea of chain development, this buzzed-about foodie delight marries exquisite Italian training with distinctively Southern flavours and whimsy. Coal-fired pizzas, short ribs with Meyer lemon, cabbage and fennel and collards with pepper vinegar are doled out in a cool, pared-down dining room with chartreuse seating and a patio with bocce ball. There's a fun outdoor bar, too. $$$

**Soul Fish** 862 S Cooper Ave, Cooper-Young ⓦ soulfishcafe.com. This big, stylishly bare-bones hot spot effortlessly combines trad and contemporary, dishing up phenomenal catfish and Southern sides (try the Cajun cabbage) to a fun, friendly crowd. $$

**Sweet Grass** 937 S Cooper Ave, Cooper-Young ⓦ sweetgrassmemphis.com. Half sophisticated bistro, half let-your-hair-down neighbourhood bar, Sweet Grass is the kind of place where you can spend the evening savouring high-class seafood – especially the rich coastal flavours of the Low Country – or drop in late to fill up on quality comfort food. $$$

## DRINKING AND NIGHTLIFE

SEE MAP PAGE 97

Memphis's thriving **music** scene can be tasted during the city's many **festivals**, especially **Memphis in May** (ⓦmemphisinmay.org), where big-name performances share space with barbecue contests, August's **Elvis Week** (ⓦelvisweek.com), and the free **Memphis Music and Heritage festival**, staged downtown over Labor Day weekend. While the best **blues clubs** are beyond downtown and usually open at weekends only, at other times even touristy **Beale Street** has things to offer. At the other end of the spectrum, the city's vibrant alternative scene sees garage **bands** playing holes-in-the-wall; head **midtown** for the hippest underground happenings. In Overton Park, the **Levitt Shell** (ⓦlevittshell.org) puts on more than fifty free, family-friendly concerts a year. On a Sunday, the **Rev Al Green's** gospel service is unmissable. The best source of **listings** is the free weekly *Memphis Flyer* (ⓦmemphisflyer.com). For all the latest on Memphis's music scene and oddball attractions, head on down to the wonderful Shangri-La Records, a treasure trove of Memphis music, midtown at 1916 Madison Ave (ⓦshangri.com).

### BARS AND CLUBS

★ **Earnestine and Hazel's** 531 S Main St, South Main Arts District ⓦearnestineandhazel.com. A legendary brothel-turned-juke joint, this spot was the haunt of everyone from Elvis to the Stax musicians. It's especially good late at night, when the Memphis jukebox blasts and the famed burgers start sizzling.

**High Cotton Brewing Co. Taproom** 598 Monroe Ave ⓦhighcottonbrewing.com. Come for the beer; stay for the good times. This high-ceilinged, wood-lined beer palace – made with salvaged materials – pours the namesake brews of this hugely popular Southern microbrewery, and also host events, music and more.

**Knifebird Wine Bar** 2155 Central Ave ⓦknifebirdwinebar.com. This charming spot, with mod furnishings and rustic woods, exudes both a classy and casual feel. Sample from the impeccable international wine list or try inventive cocktails like Pickled (vodka, cornichon brine and a prosciutto-wrapped olive).

**Mollie Fontaine** 679 Adams Ave, Victorian Village ⓦmolliefontainelounge.com. This rambling old Victorian house has been given an arty makeover, transforming it into the coolest nightspot in town. Order a muddled cocktail and drift through the enchanting rooms, dimly lit and decked out with bright pink furniture, zebra-print rugs and haunting black-and-white photographs.

**Paula & Raiford's Disco** 14 S 2nd St, downtown ⓦpaularaifords.com. Most definitely a disco and not a club, this old-school downtown hot spot – with a light-up dance floor, dry ice, disco-balls, 40oz beers and a free limo service – is a Memphis institution, where hipsters of all persuasions get down after hours to the funkiest jams. Cover charge.

### LIVE MUSIC VENUES

**Center for Southern Folklore** 119 S Main St, downtown ⓦsouthernfolklore.com. A few blocks north of Beale St, this tiny venue celebrates the culture of the South, with a café, a store full of books, folk art and CDs and a stage for live performances.

**Lafayette's Music Room** 2119 Madison Ave, Midtown ⓦlafayettes.com. This midsize, Midtown music hall, with two floors of seating, hosts local and national touring acts, and serves a decent menu of pizzas and burgers.

**Wild Bill's** 1580 Vollintine Ave, Vollintine ⓦwildbillsmemphis.com. Juke joint 3 miles northeast of downtown where in-the-know tourists join locals at the long tables for live blues and soul at weekends. Cover charge.

## Shiloh National Military Park

Approximately 110 miles east of Memphis and twelve south of Savannah, Tennessee, via US-64 and Hwy-22, **SHILOH NATIONAL MILITARY PARK** (daily 8am–5pm; free; ⓦnps.gov/shil) commemorates one of the most crucial battles of the Civil War. After victories at Fort Henry and Fort Donelson, General Grant's confident Union forces

---

### MEMPHIS GOSPEL: AL GREEN'S CHURCH

Memphis has been renowned for its **gospel** music since the Thirties, when Rev W. Herbert Brewster wrote **Mahalia Jackson**'s *Move On Up a Little Higher*. Following a religious revelation, the consummate soul stylist **Al Green**, who achieved chart success for **Hi Records** with hits including *Let's Stay Together* and *Tired of Being Alone*, has since the early 1980s ministered at his own **Full Gospel Tabernacle**, at 787 Hale Rd in the leafy suburb of Whitehaven. Visitors are welcome at the 11.30am Sunday services; continue a mile south of Graceland, then turn west (phone ahead to check he's in town; ☎901 396 9192). While they're very much church services rather than concerts, Green remains a charismatic performer and he does sing, backed by a smoking soul band.

were all but defeated by a surprise early-morning Confederate attack on April 6, 1862. A stubborn rump of resistance held on until around 5pm, and the Confederates elected to finish the task off the next morning rather than launching a twilight assault. However, Grant's decimated regiments were bolstered by the overnight arrival of new troops, and instead it was their dawn initiative that forced the tired and demoralized Confederates to retreat.

Shiloh was the first encounter on a scale that became common as the war continued, putting an abrupt end to the romantic innocence of many a raw volunteer soldier. Over 20,000 men in all were killed. Even the war-toughened General Sherman spoke of "piles of dead soldiers' mangled bodies . . . without heads and legs . . . the scenes on this field would have cured anyone of war."

The visitor centre displays artefacts recovered from the battlefield, while a self-guided ten-mile driving tour takes in the National Cemetery, whose moss-covered walls contain thousands of unidentified graves.

## Nashville

Set on a bluff by the Cumberland River amid the gentle hills and farmlands of central Tennessee, big-hearted **NASHVILLE** attracts millions of visitors each year. The majority come for the **country music**, whether at mainstream showcases like the **Country Music Hall of Fame** and the **Grand Ole Opry**, or in the hipper honky-tonks and other live music venues found not only downtown but also in Nashville's many characterful neighbourhoods.

Behind the rhinestone glitter and showbiz exists a conservative, hard-working city. Nashville has been the leading settlement in middle Tennessee since **Fort Nashborough** was established in 1779, and state capital since 1843. It is now a major **financial** and **insurance** centre and a notably **religious** place: there are more churches per head here than anywhere else in the nation.

---

### NASHVILLE COUNTRY

**Country music** is generally reckoned to have resulted from the interaction of British and Irish folk music, as brought by Tennessee's first Anglo settlers, with other ethnic music, including the spirituals and gospel hymns sung by African American slaves and their descendants. It first acquired its current form during the 1920s. As radios and record players became widely available, the **recording industry** took off and Nashville became the base for musicians of the mid-South. Local radio station **WSM** – "We Shield Millions", the slogan of its insurance-company sponsor – first broadcast on October 5, 1925, swiftly established itself as a champion of the country sound. Two years later, at the start of his *Barn Dance* show, compere George D. Hay announced "for the past hour we have been listening to music taken largely from Grand Opera, but from now on we will present **The Grand Ole Opry**". This piece of slang became the name of America's longest-running radio show, still broadcast live out to millions two to three nights per week on WSM-AM (650). Soon outgrowing the WSM studios, the show moved in 1943 to a former tabernacle – the **Ryman Auditorium**. There it acquired a make-or-break reputation; up-and-coming singers could only claim to have made it if they had gone down well at the Opry. Among thousands of hopefuls who tried to get on the show was Elvis Presley, advised by an Opry official in 1954 to stick to truck-driving.

The decade of prosperity after World War II witnessed country's first commercial boom. Recording studios, publishing companies and artists' agencies proliferated in Nashville and the major labels recognized that a large slice of the (white) record-buying public wanted something less edgy than rockabilly. The easy-listening **Nashville Sound** they came up with, pioneered by Patsy Cline and Jim Reeves, is kept alive today by million-selling artists like Taylor Swift, Carrie Underwood and Lady Antebellum.

1

## DOWNTOWN NASHVILLE

N

| 0 | | 200 |
|---|---|---|
| | yards | |

**● EATING**

| | |
|---|---|
| 5th & Taylor | 2 |
| Arnold's | 7 |
| Catbird Seat | 8 |
| Josephine | 10 |
| Loveless Café | 9 |
| Margot Café & Bar | 4 |
| Mas Tacos Por Favor | 3 |
| Monell's | 1 |
| Prince's Hot Chicken Shack | 6 |
| The Southern Steak & Oyster | 5 |

**■ ACCOMMODATION**

| | |
|---|---|
| The 404 Hotel | 4 |
| Homewood Suites | 1 |
| Kimpton Aerston | 5 |
| Omni Nashville Hotel | 2 |
| Thompson Nashville | 3 |
| Timothy Demonbreun House | 6 |

**■ DRINKING AND NIGHTLIFE**

| | |
|---|---|
| The Basement | 8 |
| Basement East | 1 |
| Bluebird Café | 7 |
| Exit/In | 6 |
| Patterson House | 5 |
| Robert's Western World | 2 |
| Station Inn | 4 |
| Tootsie's Orchid Lounge | 3 |

State Library
State Capitol
Fort Nashborough
Cumberland River
Riverfront Park
State Supreme Court
Tennessee State Museum
Ryman Auditorium
Patsy Cline Museum
Nashville Convention Center
Johnny Cash Museum
Schermerhorn Symphony Center
Country Music Hall of Fame
Hatch Show Print
Frist Center for the Visual Arts
THE GULCH
Third Man Records
MUSIC ROW

**Downtown Nashville** is spread along the Cumberland River, and while it looks much like any other regional business centre, "Lower Broad", along **Broadway** between Second and Fifth avenues, is prime **country music** territory, lined with honky-tonks, bars, restaurants and gift stores. In addition to the venerable structures you'd expect in a state capital, downtown boasts many of the city's premier attractions, including the **Country Music Hall of Fame**, the **Ryman Auditorium** and the **Johnny Cash Museum**. Downtown is also home to the ever-expanding **Riverfront Park** (ⓦnashvilleriverfront. org) with rolling lawns, greenway trails and the Ascend Amphitheater (see page 110).

Further afield, **Music Row**, which centres on Demonbreun Street a mile southwest of downtown, forms the heart of Nashville's recording industry, with companies including

1

Warner Bros., Mercury and Sony operating out of plush office blocks. The city has a number of hip little neighbourhoods ripe for discovery, including its newest cool corner, **The Gulch**, which unfolds between downtown and Music Row. Another spirited neighbourhood is **East Nashville**, located across the river. It's a left-leaning place made up of aspiring musicians and young families, where quirky galleries rub elbows with thrift stores and stylish restaurants. East of Centennial Park, across West End Avenue, the campus of **Vanderbilt University** abuts the colourful **Hillsboro Village**, a four-block radius sliced through by 21st Avenue South and abounding in cafés and arty boutiques. Most visitors will enjoy themselves immensely by launching full-tilt into what "Nash Vegas" is best known for: the flash and fun of country music. If you're hankering for more local flavour, venture out of downtown to swill regional beer, browse oddball music stores and hunt for the perfect pair of cowboy boots.

### Country Music Hall of Fame

**Museum** 222 Rep. John Lewis Hwy S • Daily 9am–5pm Charge • ⓦ countrymusichalloffame.org • **Hatch Show Print** 224 Rep. John Lewis Hwy S • Mon–Wed & Sun 9.30am–6pm, Thurs–Sat 9.30am–8pm • Free, charge for 75min guided tours • ⓦ hatchshowprint.com

Everyone's first stop should be the superb **Country Music Hall of Fame**. A wealth of paraphernalia from countless stars, including all manner of gowns, guitars and battered leather boots, not to mention Elvis's gold Cadillac – combine with video footage, photos and, of course, lots and lots of music, to create a hugely enjoyable account of the genre from its earliest days. Songwriters and musicians give regular live performances and masterclasses.

The Hall of Fame also offers short **bus tours** (daily 10.30am–2.30pm) of RCA's legendary **Studio B** on Music Row. Between 1957 and 1977, forty gold records were cut here, including Dolly Parton's *Jolene*, but it's probably most famous for a thirteen-year run of Elvis hits. Restored and rewired, it's open for business again, and is very much a hot ticket – book online to guarantee a time-slot.

In 2013, after more than a century in their original Broadway store, the music publicity wizards who make up **Hatch Show Print** found a new home here at the museum. Established in 1879, this atmospheric workshop prints and sells posters from the early days of country and rock'n'roll, using the original blocks, and continues to produce new work.

### Johnny Cash Museum

119 3rd Ave S • Daily 9am–7pm • Charge • ⓦ johnnycashmuseum.com

Set in a handsome brick building in the heart of downtown, the **Johnny Cash Museum** pays homage to one of the best-selling musicians (100 million records and counting) and most beloved country stars of all time. Born to cotton farmers in 1932, Cash signed with Memphis's Sun Studios (see page 99) in 1955, then went on to become a phenomenal crossover artist, appealing to gospel, bluegrass and rock fans alike over the course of his nearly fifty-year career. The museum is packed with appealing ephemera, much of it detailed in Cash's own handwriting ("my first 'professional' guitar. On loan from Marshall Grant, then and now"). Fans can listen to original recordings, view the Man in Black's high-school yearbook photo and his marriage certificate to June Carter, and gawk at rows of gold and platinum records. There's also a fun, campy gallery devoted to Cash's acting stints, including a clip where he appears on *The Simpsons* as a coyote – Homer's spirit animal.

### Patsy Cline Museum

113 3rd Ave S • Daily 9am–7pm • Charge • ⓦ patsymuseum.com

Certain names have become synonymous with country music – **Patsy Cline** is one of them. It's a testament to the power of her voice – and stage presence – that Cline's legacy lives on, despite her tragic death at the age of 30 in a 1963 plane crash. This vibrant museum, located above the Johnny Cash Museum, celebrates the songstress with an extensive array of artefacts, personal belongings, photographs, videos and more. Patsy Cline's hits are highlighted throughout the museum, including the 1962 Crazy, written by Willie Nelson, which changed the sound of country music, and is one of the most-played jukebox songs in the U.S.

## Ryman Auditorium

116 Rep. John Lewis Hwy N• Daily 9am–4pm • Charge, guided backstage tour extra • Ⓦ ryman.com

Near the Johnny Cash Museum, the **Ryman Auditorium**, the original home of the Grand Ole Opry, was built as a religious revival house. A church-like space, its wooden pews illuminated by stained glass, it beautifully evokes the heyday of traditional country, with small exhibits on everything from Johnny and June to Hatch Show Print (see page 107). It's also a great venue for live gigs and musicals.

## Frist Center for the Visual Arts

919 Broadway • Mon–Wed & Sat 10am–5.30pm, Thurs & Fri 10am–9pm, Sun 1–5.30pm • Charge • Ⓦ fristartmuseum.org

Downtown has some non-music-related diversions. Housed in a gorgeous Art Deco building (and one-time post office), the **Frist Center for the Visual Arts** features everything from sculpture and photography to ancient art. If you have little ones in tow, don't miss the **Martin ArtQuest Gallery**, where young Picassos can scribble, paint and sculpt to their hearts' delight.

## Tennessee State Museum

505 Deaderick St • Tues–Sat 10am–5pm, Sun 1–5pm • Free • Ⓦ tnmuseum.org

A few blocks northeast of the Frist Center, the **Tennessee State Museum** is strongest on Civil War history, highlighting the hardships suffered by soldiers on both sides, of whom 23,000 out of 77,000 died at Shiloh. One of the country's biggest museums, it has exhibits documenting regional life from prehistoric times through to the twentieth century.

## Third Man Records

623 7th Ave S • Daily 10am–6pm • Free, charge for tour, Fri–Sat 2pm • Ⓦ thirdmanrecords.com

Rock fans, particularly White Stripes aficionados, will enjoy a pilgrimage to Jack White's label and recording studio, **Third Man Records**, just south of downtown. A vibrant black, crimson and yellow brick pile, the studio also holds a tiny record shop and fun games such as the "voice-o-graph", where you can cut your very own vinyl record and mail it home in a specially made envelope.

## The Parthenon

2500 West End Ave • **Museum** Tues–Sat 9am–4.30pm; Sun 12.30–4.30pm • Charge • Ⓦ nashvilleparthenon.com

In 1897, Tennessee celebrated its Centennial Exposition in **Centennial Park**, two miles southwest of downtown at West End and 25th avenues. Nashville honoured its nickname as the "Athens of the South" by constructing a full-sized wood-and-plaster replica of the **Parthenon**. That proved so popular that it was replaced by a permanent structure in 1931, which is now home to a minor **museum** of nineteenth-century American art. The upper hall is dominated by a gilded 42ft replica of Pheidias's statue of the goddess Athena – said to be the largest indoor statue in the Western hemisphere.

## Cheekwood Botanical Garden and Museum of Art

1200 Forrest Park Drive, 8 miles south of downtown off Hwy-1 • Tues–Sun 9am–5pm • Charge • Ⓦ cheekwood.org

Set on 55 stunning acres of wildflowers, rustling hickory trees and lawns dotted with art installations, **Cheekwood** is the meandering former estate of a Maxwell House Coffee scion. The 1932 Georgian mansion at its centre holds a dignified museum of American paintings and decorative objects.

## ARRIVAL AND DEPARTURE

**By plane** Nashville International Airport (Ⓦflynashville. com) is 8 miles – around a $25 taxi ride – southeast of downtown. Numerous shuttles offer services into town, including InShuttle (Ⓦinshuttle.com). You can also hop on a WeGo bus (hourly; Ⓦwegotransit.com).

**By bus** The Greyhound station is downtown at 709 Rep. John Lewis Hwy S (Ⓣ615 255 3556).
Destinations Asheville, NC (2 daily; 6hr); Atlanta, GA (8 daily; 4hr 30min); Birmingham, AL (5 daily; 3hr 50min); Memphis, TN (5 daily; 4hr).

## INFORMATION AND TOURS

**Visitor centre** Rep. John Lewis Hwy S and Broadway, downtown (Mon–Sat 8am–5.30pm, Sun 10am–5pm; Ⓣ866 830 4440, Ⓦvisitmusiccity.com), In addition to its superb pre-planning website, the huge visitor centre has free wi-fi and features live music.

**Country music tours** If you like your country music laid on with lots of campy fun, hop aboard the "Big Pink Bus" and let the singing Jugg Sisters of Nash-Trash Tours dish the dirt on all your favourite stars (90min; charge; adults only; reservations essential, as far in advance as possible; Ⓦnashtrash.com).

## ACCOMMODATION

**SEE MAP PAGE 106**

The downtown Nashville skyline is changing, with a building boom that has resulted in many new hotels, including in the trendy neighbourhood of The Gulch, near downtown. Note that hotel rates increase during the **CMA Music Festival** in June (Ⓦcmafest.com).

**The 404 Hotel** 404 12th Ave S Ⓦthe404hotel.com. This unique boutique hotel captures the spirit of the artsy neighbourhood The Gulch. The five loft-style rooms feature vintage furnishings and changing local artwork. The *404 Kitchen* serves vibrant seasonal cuisine, as well as a superb whiskey line-up. $$$$

**Homewood Suites** 706 Church St Ⓦhilton.com/en/ homewood. Set in a genteel, Renaissance-style building that dates from 1910, this central hotel is an all-suiter with a fridge, microwave, dishwasher and pull-out couch in every room. $$$

★ **Kimpton Aerston** 2021 Broadway Ⓦaerstonhotel. com. This artful hotel in Midtown is named after Jan Aerston, a Dutch immigrant whose descendant was Cornelius Vanderbilt, who donated the initial funds to develop Vanderbilt University. Appropriately, the hotel rises near the Vanderbilt campus, and is also within easy saunter distance to Music Row. The lobby is an inviting blend of industrial and natural details and Southern

warmth, including unique, textured artwork and installations. The light-filled rooms, with leather headboards and wood elements, each feature a print from the legendary Hatch Show Print (see page 107). Refuel at Henley, which serves Southern cuisine and cocktails. $$$$

**Omni Nashville Hotel** 250 Rep. John Lewis Hwy S Ⓦomnihotels.com. This posh outpost of the *Omni* brand has become one of Nashville's signature hotels. Connected by walkway to the Country Music Hall of Fame, its litany of perks includes a rooftop pool with skyline views, myriad on-site restaurants, a spa and flashy guest rooms with picture windows. $$$$

**Thompson Nashville** 401 11th Ave Ⓦthompsonhotels. com. This inviting, trendy hotel has industrial-chic rooms, with hardwood floors and picture windows overlooking The Gulch and downtown Nashville. $$$$

**Timothy Demonbreun House** 746 Benton Ave Ⓦtdhouse.com. Convivial B&B in a three-storey 1906 mansion located a mile from downtown. Guest quarters are named for wine varietals and outfitted with antiques and gas fireplaces; the enormous swimming pool is an afternoon delight. $$$$

## EATING

**SEE MAP PAGE 106**

Nashville offers a wonderfully diverse array of cuisine, from delicious down-home southern joints **downtown** and trendy eateries in The Gulch to farm-fresh places in historic Germantown to **East Nashville**, which has evolved into a foodie destination. Studenty **Hillsboro Village** and **Elliston Place** in the West End are the domain of hip, inexpensive cafés. Keep an eye out for Googoo Clusters (Ⓦgoogoo.com), a tantalizing confection of caramel, peanuts and milk chocolate that has been a Nashville favourite since 1912.

★ **5th & Taylor** 1411 Rep. John Lewis Hwy Ⓦ5thandtaylor.com. A sculpture of General Francis Nash – from whom Nashville gets its name – rises over this elegantly raw Germantown warehouse with soaring ceilings and an open kitchen. Esteemed Chattanooga chef Daniel James

Lindley has developed an eclectic menu that teases out the flavours of each season, with dishes like duck liver mousse with blueberry jam and beer-can chicken with Swiss chard. Sunday brunch brings forth fried chicken biscuits with buttermilk cheddar. $$$

**Arnold's** 605 8th Ave S, downtown Ⓦarnoldscountry kitchen.com. Classic canteen, just south of downtown, where locals wait in line for tasty meat-and-threes (meat, three veggies and buttery cornbread). The delicious soul food includes fried chicken, ham or pork chops, all served with sides. Get here early. $

**CatbirdSeat** 1711 Division St, midtown Ⓦthecatbirdseat restaurant.com. This foodie hot spot, perched above *Patterson House*, serves a seven-course *prix fixe*, which costs over $150 per person and is determined in advance, for just

1

thirty or so lucky patrons a night (reservations required). Hours vary. 💲💲💲💲

**Josephine** 2316 12th Ave S ⓦ josephineon12th.com. Pennsylvania Dutch comfort food meets Southern flourishes at this inviting, spacious restaurant with rustic woods and abundant natural light. The seasonal menu includes beef tongue with caramelized onions; heirloom tomatoes on grilled bread with bacon mayonnaise; and duck breast with black-eyed peas. Top it off with peach cobbler for two. 💲💲💲💲

**Loveless Café** 8400 Hwy-100, 20 miles southwest of town ⓦ lovelesscafe.com. This vintage roadhouse is a local institution for its country cooking. The fried chicken is amazing and breakfast superb: hunks of salty ham with gravy, eggs, toast and fluffy, secret-recipe biscuits. 💲💲

**Margot Café & Bar** 1017 Woodland St, East Nashville ⓦ margotcafe.com. Impeccably fresh European-style food in a cosily converted former service station, run by the owners of the much-lamented neighbouring Marché Artisan Foods. Come to enjoy entrées like cornmeal-crusted trout or yoghurt-marinated chicken. 💲💲💲💲

**Mas Tacos Por Favor** 732 McFerrin Ave, East Nashville ☎ 615 543 6271. A trip to East Nashville wouldn't be complete without a tortilla soup, fried avocado taco and fresh watermelon juice from this slender *taqueria* with indigo walls, a chalkboard menu and a devout set of followers. Cash only. 💲

★ **Monell's** 1235 6th Ave N, Germantown ⓦ monellstn.com. Superb Southern cooking – crispy fried chicken, corn pudding, buttery green beans and piping hot biscuits – served family style at communal tables. Gut-busting, affordable and utterly delicious. 💲💲

**Prince's Hot Chicken Shack** 423 6th Ave S, downtown ⓦ princeshotchicken.com. Nashville is famed for its tradition of "hot chicken" wherein you choose your meal's level of spiciness – and this beloved hole-in-the-wall, in business for more than thirty years, is the place to try it. Be prepared to see stars if you order the hottest level of chilli. 💲💲

**The Southern Steak & Oyster** 150 3rd Ave S, downtown ⓦ thesouthernnashville.com. A great option just off Broadway (close to the Johnny Cash Museum), this snazzy steak and oyster joint offers great food around the clock, a bygone-era feel and a stunning patio with skyline views. 💲💲💲

## DRINKING AND NIGHTLIFE

SEE MAP PAGE 106

Nashville has a burgeoning microbrewery scene, great places to be when tours are running and the taprooms flowing: try Yazoo (ⓦ yazoobrew.com), Jackalope (ⓦ jackalopebrew. com) and Blackstone (ⓦ blackstonebrewery.com). The two obvious ways to experience live country music in Nashville are either to head for the cluster of **honky-tonks** on Lower Broad or to buy a ticket for a **Grand Ole Opry** show, which will feature a mix of stars and newcomers (Thurs–Sat, sometimes Tues; ⓦ opry.com). However, it's worth making the effort to catch up-and-coming or more specialized acts at places like the *Bluebird Café* and the *Station Inn*; look out, too, for special events, including **bluegrass** nights, at Ryman Auditorium (see page 108). Nightlife-packed East Nashville is building a strong local scene, with weekly indie concerts at local bars.

**The Basement** 1604 8th Ave S, Music Row ⓦ thebasementnashville.com. Alt-country, rock and raw indie rule the roost in this tiny, rough-round-the-edges, smoke-free venue south of downtown.

**Basement East** 917 Woodland St, East Nashville ⓦ thebasementnashville.com. This sister venue to *The Basement* (see page 110) features an equally top-notch line-up of acts.

**Bluebird Café** 4104 Hillsboro Rd, Green Hills ⓦ bluebirdcafe.com. Having launched the careers of superstars including Garth Brooks and Taylor Swift, this intimate café, 6 miles west of downtown in the Green Hills district, is *the* place to see the latest country artists, and as a result it made frequent appearances on the popular TV show *Nashville*. The first of the two nightly shows tends to be open-mic or up-and-coming songwriters. Reservations recommended.

**Exit/In** 2208 Elliston Place, West End ⓦ exitin.com. Venerable venue for rock, reggae and country, with the occasional big name.

**Patterson House** 1711 Division St, midtown ⓦ thepattersonnashville.com. There's no sign hanging in front of this 1920s-style speakeasy, but inside, you'll find some of Music City's finest cocktails, mixed with seasonal ingredients.

**Robert's Western World** 416 Broadway, downtown ⓦ robertswesternworld.com. Some of the best country music on Broadway, plus rockabilly and Western swing, in a lively honky-tonk that doubles as a cowboy boots store. No cover.

★ **Station Inn** 402 12th Ave S, Music Row ⓦ stationinn.com. Long-standing, intimate bluegrass, swing and acoustic venue near Music Row, with a euphoric crowd that sings along with popcorn and cheap beer. Shows 8pm and 9pm nightly; cover charge.

**Tootsie's Orchid Lounge** 422 Broadway, downtown ⓦ tootsies.net. Central, touristy, enjoyable honky-tonk, with a raucous atmosphere, plenty of memorabilia and good, gutsy live performers. Generally no cover.

## ENTERTAINMENT

For music at the classical end of the spectrum, Nashville's Neoclassical Schermerhorn Symphony Center (ⓦ nashvillesymphony.org) has a world-class orchestra, which gives nearly 150 performances a year.

**Ascend Amphitheater** 310 1st Ave S ⓦ ascendamphitheater.com. This open-air theatre rises over the banks of the Cumberland River, seats around 6800 and features a superb concert series throughout the year. Performers have included everyone from Journey to Jack White to Goo Goo Dolls. The theatre also serves as the summer home of the Nashville Symphony.

**Ernest Tubb Record Store Midnight Jamboree** Texas Troubadour Theatre, 2414 Music Valley Drive, Opryland ⓦ ernesttubb.com. Old-time radio show recorded every Saturday at 10pm, and broadcast from midnight to 1am, in a theatre adjoining the Music Valley branch of the Tubb store (the main store is on Broadway). Features promising newcomers as well as major Opry stars. Free.

## Jack Daniel's Distillery

182 Lynchburg Hwy • Daily 9am–4.30pm; tours depart at various times • Charge • ⓦ jackdaniels.com

The change-resistant village of **LYNCHBURG**, 75 miles southeast of Nashville, is home to **Jack Daniel's Distillery**. Founded in 1866, this is the oldest registered distillery in the country. A wide variety of **tours** lead you through the sour-mash whiskey-making process, many of which offer a sampling of whiskey flights. Ironically, you can't order the stuff in town, as this is a dry county. Lynchburg itself is tiny, laid out around a neat town square with a red-brick courthouse and a number of old-fashioned stores.

## Pigeon Forge and Sevierville

For anyone who loves kitschy themed **attractions**, there's plenty to do on the double-lane highway that makes up **Pigeon Forge** – ranging from Dollywood (see page 111) through to "Jurassic Jungle" boat rides and the upside-down WonderWorks house; anyone else should arrive with low expectations. Neighbouring **Sevierville** has a more relaxed setting, and a key site on any **Dolly Parton** pilgrimage: a barefoot bronze statue of the superstar, set beside the nineteenth-century courthouse (125 Court Ave). This is Parton's hometown, and she has said that this local recognition is the monument of which she's the most proud.

**EATING**      **PIGEON FORGE AND SEVIERVILLE**

**Applewood Farmhouse** 240 Apple Valley Rd, Sevierville ⓦ applewoodfarmhouserestaurant.com. A Smokies institution, famed for its fritters, served warm with fresh apple butter and "juleps" (a mix of apple and pineapple juices) at the start of each meal. Good Southern cooking, too, served in a rambling house that dates to the 1920s. ⑂⑂

---

### DOLLYWOOD

Born in 1946, one of twelve children with very limited means, music legend **Dolly Parton** was delivered in Locust Ridge, Tennessee, by a doctor who arrived on horseback and left with a sack of homegrown cornmeal as compensation. As a child she sang every week on local radio, before leaving for Nashville the day after she finished at Sevier County High School. Her first success, duetting with Porter Wagoner, came to an end in the early Seventies, but she scored a major country hit in 1973 with *Jolene*. She then crossed over to a poppier sound, and, with her charismatic presence, was a natural in Hollywood films including *9 to 5* (the beat for whose theme song she came up with by tapping on her fingernails) and *The Best Little Whorehouse in Texas*. Always a strong-minded and inspirational figure, Dolly has sold more than 100 million records, written more than three thousand songs, been awarded ten Grammys and performed around the world. More recently, she donated a million dollars to research for a Covid-19 vaccine. **Dollywood**, her "homespun fun" theme park at 2700 Dollywood Parks Blvd in Pigeon Forge (mid-March–Dec, schedules vary; summer hours usually daily 10am–10pm; charge; ⓦ dollywood.com), blends mountain heritage with roller coasters and the merriment of its celebrity shareholder. One section showcases Appalachian **crafts**; a museum looks at Dolly herself in entertaining detail; music shows are constantly on the go and the thrill rides offer plenty for adrenaline-junkies and kiddies alike. A water park, **Dolly's Splash Country** (late May to early Sept, hours vary; charge), is adjacent.

**1**

## Gatlinburg

If you want to stay overnight, try **GATLINBURG**, squeezed amid the foothills of the Smokies a few miles south of Pigeon Forge on US-441. As well as being a fraction more upmarket than Pigeon Forge, it's more compact, with a walkable centre; that said, it's also bursting with overpriced, gimmicky tourist attractions. A couple of chairlifts sweep visitors up the surrounding peaks; one climbs to the year-round Ober Gatlinburg **ski resort** and **amusement park** (ⓦobergatlinburg.com).

### ACCOMMODATION, EATING AND DRINKING                              GATLINBURG

★ **Ole Smoky Moonshine Holler** 903 Pkwy ⓦolesmokymoonshine.com. You can't pay a visit to Tennessee without sampling its famous moonshine. This, the state's first legal distillery, sells six flavours of liquor, including cherry and "white lightning", all born from family recipes. Various other locations nearby – see website.

**Zoder's Inn & Suites** 402 Pkwy ⓦzoders.net. With Gatlinburg being the closest town to the Smokies, accommodation can be pricey. Central, good-value *Zoder's* has basic motel-style rooms with balconies that overlook a rushing stream. $$

## Great Smoky Mountains National Park

Open 24hr • Free

Stretching for seventy miles along the Tennessee–North Carolina border, **GREAT SMOKY MOUNTAINS NATIONAL PARK** lies just two miles south of Gatlinburg on US-441. Don't expect immediate tranquillity, however: the roads, particularly in the fall, can be lined almost bumper-to-bumper, and if you're not staying in Gatlinburg it's best to use the bypass rather than drive through the town.

Located within a day's drive of the major urban centres of the East Coast and the Great Lakes – and of two thirds of the entire US population – the Smokies attract around fourteen million visitors per year, almost three times as many as any other national park. These spectacularly corrugated peaks are named for the **bluish haze** that hangs over them, made up of moisture and hydrocarbons released by the lush vegetation – the park is home to the largest swath of old-growth forest left standing in the east, and is one of the most biodiverse places on earth. Since the Sixties, however, **air pollution** has been adding sulphates to the mix, which has cut back visibility by thirty percent. Sixteen peaks rise above 6000ft, their steep elevation accounting for dramatic changes in climate.

While late March to mid-May is a great time to visit for spring flowers, the **busiest periods** are midsummer (mid-June to mid-Aug), and, especially, October, when the hills are shrouded in a canopy of red, yellow and bronze. During June and July, rhododendrons blaze fiercely in the sometimes stifling summer heat. The best way to escape the crowds is to sample the park's eight hundred miles of **hiking** trails. Just inside the park on US-441, **Sugarlands Visitor Center** has details of hikes, driving tours and various ranger-led tours and activities (see page 113). Many visitors, however, do no more than follow **US-441**, here known as the Newfound Gap Road, all the way to North Carolina. From the gap itself, ten miles along on the state line, a spur road to the right winds for seven more miles up to **Clingman's Dome**, at 6643ft the highest point in Tennessee. A spiral walkway on top affords a panoramic view of the mountains.

### Cades Cove

The main focus of visitor activity is in the **Cades Cove** area, which can be reached either by branching west at Sugarlands along the scenic **Little River Road**, or directly from Townsend via **Rich Mountain Road** (closed in winter). The eleven-mile driving loop here, jam-packed with cars in summer and fall, passes deserted barns, homesteads, mills and churches that stand as a reminder of the farmers who carved out a living from this wilderness before National Park status was conferred in 1934. Halfway along, there's

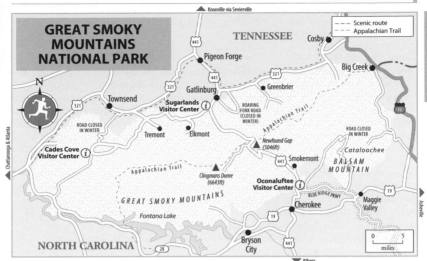

another **visitor centre**. The loop is reserved for **cyclists** on Saturday and Wednesday mornings in summer.

| INFORMATION AND TOURS | GREAT SMOKY MOUNTAINS NATIONAL PARK |
|---|---|

**Sugarlands Visitor Center** Two miles south of Gatlinburg on US-441 (daily: June–Aug 9am–7pm; April, May, Sept & Oct 9am–6pm; March & Nov 9am–5pm; Dec–Feb 9am–4.30pm; ⓦ nps.gov/grsm).

**Cades Cove Visitor Center** Midway along the Cades Cove Loop Rd (daily: June–Aug 9am–7pm; April, May, Sept & Oct 9am–6pm; March & Nov 9am–5pm; Dec–Feb 9am–4.30pm; ⓦ nps.gov/grsm).

**Tours** A Walk In the Woods (charge; ⓦ awalkinthewoods.com) offers exceptionally informed nature tours of the Smokies.

**Camping** The National Park Service administers ten campgrounds within the park. For details, check ⓦ nps.gov/grsm.

# Chattanooga

Few places are so identified with a single song as **CHATTANOOGA**, in the southeast corner of Tennessee. Though visitors expecting to see Glenn Miller's "Chattanooga Choo-Choo" will be disappointed, the place has a certain appeal, not least its beautiful location on a deep bend in the **Tennessee River**, walled in by forested plateaus on three sides. This setting led John Ross, of Scottish and Cherokee ancestry, to found a trading post here in 1815, and its strategic importance made it a prize during the Civil War.

The centrepiece of Chattanooga's twenty miles of reclaimed riverfront is **Ross's Landing** (the town's original name), a park at the bottom of Broad Street. Here the five-storey **Tennessee Aquarium** (daily 10am–6pm; charge; IMAX 3D Theater extra; ⓦ tnaqua.org) traces the aquatic life of the Mississippi from its Tennessee tributaries to the Gulf of Mexico.

### Hunter Museum of American Art

10 Bluff View • Mon, Tues, Fri & Sat 10am–5pm, Wed & Sun noon–5pm, Thurs 10am–8pm • Charge • ⓦ huntermuseum.org

Perched above the river, the **Bluff View Art District**, where High meets Third, comprises a handful of galleries, museums and cafés in lovely old buildings. The **Hunter Museum of American Art**, linked to the aquarium by a stunning glass walkway, has a changing roster of exhibitions covering photography, painting, sculpture and folk art from the nineteenth century to the present. The museum also

**1**

hosts a unique array of events, including painting classes with wine as well as yoga, chamber music, lectures and more.

## Lookout Mountain

**Tennessee Valley Railroad** 4119 Cromwell Rd • June & July daily; hours fluctuate for rest of year • Charge • ⓦ tvrail.com • **Ruby Falls** 1720 S Scenic Hwy • Daily 8am–8pm • Charge • ⓦ rubyfalls.com • Take Broad St south to Cummings Hwy

The name Chattanooga comes from a Creek word meaning "rock rising to a point"; the rock in question, the 2389ft **Lookout Mountain**, looms six miles south of downtown. To reach the top, either drive the whole way along a winding road or catch the world's steepest **incline railway**, which grinds its way up through a narrow gash in the forest from a base near the foot of the mountain, tackling gradients of up to 72.7 percent.

At the top, a short, steep walk through **Point Park** brings you to **Point Lookout**, which commands a view of the city and the Tennessee River below. This forms part of the **Chickamauga and Chattanooga National Military Park**, covering several sites around the city and in nearby Chickamauga, Georgia, that witnessed fierce Civil War fighting in 1863. Among the many memorials in Point Park is the only **statue** in the country to show Union and Confederate soldiers shaking hands.

Inside the mountain itself, **Ruby Falls**, a 145ft waterfall, is heralded by a mock-medieval castle entrance. Numerous experiences are on offer, including Lantern Tours (Friday nights, generally Feb–Sept; charge) through Ruby Falls Cavern.

## Rock City

1400 Patten Rd • Daily: hours vary, but generally Jan to early March & Nov 8.30am–5pm; mid-March to May, Sept & Oct 8.30am–6pm; June–Aug 8.30am–8pm; Dec 8.30am–4pm • Charge • ⓦ seerockcity.com

For a true Americana experience, join generations of road-trippers and "See Rock City" – the iconic sign, painted on roadside barns as far away as Georgia and Texas, was the result of an aggressive 1930s marketing campaign. **Rock City** itself is basically a walking trail along the top of Lookout Mountain that offers not only the pleasure of scrambling through narrow gaps and swinging on rope bridges, but also the weird **Fairyland Caverns**, carved into the rock and populated by grotesque characters that will delight kids and terrify adults.

## ARRIVAL, INFORMATION AND TOURS          CHATTANOOGA

**By bus** Greyhound connections (☏ 423 892 1277) with Nashville and Atlanta arrive at 960 Airport Rd.

**Visitor centre** 215 Broad St (daily 10am–5pm; ☏ 800 322 3344, ⓦ visitchattanooga.com).

**Steam trains** To ride a Chattanooga choo-choo, check out the authentic steam trains of the Tennessee Valley Railroad; they offer a variety of trips, from 55min local jaunts to a stunning 6-mile ride, crossing the river, running through deep tunnels and turning round on a giant turntable (charge, ⓦ tvrail.com).

**River cruises** The aquarium offers catamaran cruises into the Tennessee River Gorge (2–3hr; charge), while the more sedate *Southern Belle* riverboat cruises (charge; ⓦ chattanoogariverboat.com) leave from Pier 2.

## ACCOMMODATION AND EATING

**Big River Grille & Brewing Works** 2020 Hamilton Place Blvd, 12 miles east of downtown ⓦ bigrivergrille. com. Cavernous brewpub and restaurant that has great comfort food such as shrimp and grits ($16) and beer-battered fish and chips ($15), with a stunning location overlooking the Tennessee River. There's also a downtown location, next to the aquarium. $$

**Bluff View Inn** 411 E 2nd St ⓦ bluffviewartdistrict. com. Alluring B&B that offers an assortment of rooms – some with lovely views – spread across three restored houses in the Bluff View Art District. $$$$

**Crash Pad Hostel** 29 Johnson St ⓦ crashpadchattanooga.com. Nearly every hostel in the country could learn a thing or two from the eco-minded *Crash Pad*, where bunk beds are ingeniously outfitted with black-out curtains, outlets and reading lamps; there's also private rooms, a stylish common area with poured concrete floors and stainless-steel appliances, great breakfasts and a gardened courtyard. Dorms $, doubles $$

**Easy Bistro** 801 Chestnut St ⓦ easybistro.com. For creative New Orleans-influenced cuisine, try this upmarket restaurant and cocktail bar. Its menu is built upon locally sourced produce and seafood, and there's a fabulous raw bar for the adventurous eater. $$$

# Alabama

Just 250 miles from north to south, **ALABAMA** ranges from the fast-flowing rivers, waterfalls and lakes of the **Appalachian foothills** to the bayous and white sand beaches of the **Gulf Coast**. Away from the water's edge, agriculture, dominated by pecans, peaches and watermelons, flourishes on the gently sloping coastal plain. Industry is concentrated in the **north**, around **Birmingham** and **Huntsville**, first home of the nation's space programme, while the farmlands of middle Alabama envelop **Montgomery**, the state capital. Away from the French-influenced coastal strip around the pretty little town of **Mobile**, fundamentalist Protestant attitudes have traditionally backed right-wing demagogues, such as **George Wallace**, the four-time state governor who received ten million votes in the 1968 presidential election, and Alabama Chief Justice **Roy Moore**, who was suspended in 2003 for not obeying a federal court order to remove a monument of the Ten Commandments from the rotunda of the state judicial building in Montgomery. While times have moved on since the epic **civil rights** struggles in Montgomery, Birmingham and **Selma** – monuments and civic literature celebrate the achievements of the campaigners throughout the state – a visit to Alabama offers a crucial reminder of just how recently those struggles were fought, and continue to be fought.

## Birmingham

The rapid transformation of farmland into **BIRMINGHAM** began in 1870, with speculators attracted not by the scenery, but what lay under it – a mixture of iron ore, limestone and coal, perfect for the manufacture of iron and steel. The expansion of heavy industry was finally brought to an abrupt halt by the Depression and today iron and steel production account for just a few thousand jobs. But, the spirit of those times lives on, in the form of the mighty Vulcan (see page 116) – the world's largest cast-iron statue – which looms over the city from Red Mountain.

During the **civil rights** era Birmingham was renowned for the brutality of its police force. An intense civil rights campaign in 1963 was a turning point, setting Birmingham on the road to smoother race relations, and after 1979, under five-term black mayor Richard Arrington, the city slowly began to turn itself around. Today, the **Civil Rights Institute** near downtown memorializes the city's turbulent history of race relations. **Downtown Birmingham** extends north from the railroad tracks at Morris Avenue to Tenth Avenue N, between 15th and 25th streets. The main interest is the powerful **Civil Rights Institute** and the **16th Street Baptist Church**. **Five Points South**, its narrow streets packed with bars and restaurants, a mile or so south of the tracks on 20th Street and Eleventh Avenue S, is livelier, thanks to the presence of the university.

### Alabama Jazz Hall of Fame

1631 4th Ave N • Tues–Sat 10am–5pm, guided tours Tues, Wed & Fri 10am–2pm • Charge • ⓦ jazzhall.com

Be sure to call in at the **Carver Theatre for the Performing Arts**, where the **Alabama Jazz Hall of Fame** is a fond memorial to legends ranging from boogie-woogie maestro Clarence "Pinetop" Smith to Duke Ellington to jazzy space cadet Sun Ra. The Jazz Hall also hosts an array of events, including jazz jam sessions, a regular comedy series and more.

### Alabama Sports Hall of Fame

2150 Richard Arrington Blvd N • Mon–Fri 9am–5pm • Charge • ⓦ ashof.org

Northwest of downtown, the Birmingham-Jefferson Civic Center houses the **Alabama Sports Hall of Fame**, a tribute to greats including 1936 Olympic hero **Jesse Owens**, legendary Negro League pitcher **Le Roy "Satchel" Paige** and boxer **Joe Louis**.

**1**

## CIVIL RIGHTS IN BIRMINGHAM

In the first half of 1963, civil rights leaders chose Birmingham as the target of "Project C" (for confrontation), aiming to force businesses to integrate lunch counters and employ more blacks. Despite terrifying threats from Commissioner of Public Safety **Eugene "Bull" Connor**, pickets, sit-ins and marches went forward, resulting in mass arrests. More than two thousand protesters flooded the prisons; one was Dr Martin Luther King, Jr, who wrote his *Letter from a Birmingham Jail* after being branded an extremist by local white clergymen. Connor's use of high-pressure fire hoses, cattleprods and dogs against demonstrators acted as a potent catalyst of support. Pictures of snarling German Shepherds sinking their teeth into the flesh of schoolkids were transmitted around the world, and led to an agreement between civil rights leaders and businesses that June. Success in Birmingham sparked demonstrations in 186 other cities, which culminated in the 1964 Civil Rights Act prohibiting racial segregation. The headquarters for the campaign, the **16th Street Baptist Church**, on the corner of Sixth Avenue, was the site of a sickening Klan bombing on September 15, 1963, which killed four young black girls attending a Bible class. The three murderers were eventually jailed, though it took until 2002. Across the road, Kelly Ingram Park, site of the 1960s rallies, has a Freedom Walk diagramming the events through sculptures of menacing dogs, water cannons and youthful protestors. Next door, the admirable **Civil Rights Institute**, 520 16th St (Tues–Sat 10am–5pm, Sun 1–5pm; charge; ⓦbcri.org), is an affecting attempt to interpret the factors that led to such violence and racial hatred. Exhibits re-create life in a segregated city, complete with a burned-out bus and heart-rending videos of bus boycotts and the March on Washington.

## Birmingham Museum of Art

2000 Rev Abraham Woods Jr Blvd • Tues–Sat 10am–5pm, Sun noon–5pm • Free • ⓦ artsbma.org

On the northern outskirts of downtown, the **Birmingham Museum of Art** is strong on American landscapes, decorative arts and African American works, and boasts one of the most comprehensive collections of Asian art in the Southeast. The museum is surrounded by an expansive sculpture garden. Refuel at on-site restaurant, *Oscar's*.

## Sloss Furnaces

20 32nd St N • Tues–Sat 10am–4pm, Sun noon–4pm • Free • ⓦ slossfurnaces.com

The chimney stacks of **Sloss Furnaces**, which produced pig iron to feed the city's mills and foundries from 1882 until 1970, loom east of downtown. Fascinating self-guided **tours** through the boilers, stoves and casting areas vividly highlight the harsh working conditions endured by the ex-slaves, prisoners and immigrants who laboured here.

## Vulcan Park and Museum

1701 Valley View Drive • Museum open Mon–Sat 10am–6pm, Sun noon–6pm; observation balcony till 10pm • Charge • ⓦ visitvulcan.com

A 50-tonne statue of **Vulcan**, the Roman god of fire and forge, rises over the city on Red Mountain and has become a symbol of Birmingham and of its iron and steel industry legacy. The observation balcony, perched atop the statue's 124ft pedestal offers panoramic views of Birmingham, while the small **museum** features exhibits on local history, geology and industry. The site is also home to an official Birmingham visitor centre (same hours as museum).

## ARRIVAL AND INFORMATION                                    BIRMINGHAM

**By plane** Birmingham Airport (ⓦ flybirmingham. com), 5 miles from downtown, is served by Yellow Cabs (ⓦ birminghamyellowcab.com).

**By bus** The Greyhound station (☎ 205 252 7190) lies at 618 19th St N, between 6th and 7th aves.

Destinations Atlanta, GA (5 daily; 3hr); Montgomery, AL (4 daily; 1hr 50min); Selma, AL (1 daily; 3hr 50min).

**By train** Amtrak pulls in downtown at 1819 Morris Ave.

**Visitor centre** Just off I-20/59 at 2109 Richard Arrington, Jr, Blvd N (Mon–Fri 8.30am–5pm; ☎ 205 458 8000, ⓦ birminghamal.org). There's also a branch at Vulcan Park and Museum.

## ACCOMMODATION

**Grand Bohemian Hotel** 2655 Lane Park Rd ⓦ marriott. com. This landmark property, one of the state's premier luxury boutique hotels, is more than just a place to rest your head – it also features the luxurious Poseidon Spa, an art gallery, a cooking school, wine-blending classes and a seasonal restaurant, *Habitat Feed & Social*. The hotel overlooks the Birmingham Botanical Gardens and has snazzy, contemporary rooms with marble bathrooms. $$$$
**Hampton Inn & Suites Downtown – Tutwiler** 2021

Park Place ⓦ hamptoninn.hilton.com. Handsome restored 1920s hotel near the Civil Rights Institute. Comfortable rooms have huge windows looking out onto downtown. $$$
**Hotel Indigo Birmingham Five Points South** 1023 20th St S ⓦ ihg.com. Modern boutique hotel in a well-maintained Art Deco-style building within walking distance of Five Points South. Enjoy comfortable suites, well-stocked bathrooms and a fitness centre. $$$$

## EATING, DRINKING AND NIGHTLIFE

**Bottega** 2240 Highland Ave S ⓦ bottegarestaurant. com. Elegant 1920s clothing store in Five Points South that houses one of the city's classiest restaurants, serving luscious, garlic-rich Italian cuisine. Try grilled duck breast with couscous, and salmon with local figs. For a more casual atmosphere (and less pricey fare), try the adjoining café. $$$$
**Chez Fonfon** 2007 11th Ave S ⓦ fonfonbham.com. Good French-influenced cooking in a romantic, Five Points South bistro with fixtures and furniture flown in all the way from Paris. Enjoy dishes like trout amandine with brown butter, and tasty mussels. $$$
**Niki's West** 223 Finley Ave W ⓦ nikiswest.com. In

business since 1957, this Birmingham institution falls somewhere between a Greek diner and a down-home Southern café. The speedy lunchtime buffet has delicious fried green tomatoes, butter beans and pork chops. $$
★ **Ovenbird** 2810 3rd Ave S ☎ 205 957 6686, ⓦ ovenbirdrestaurant.com. Award-winning Southern chef Chris Hastings has a winner with the rustic, brick-walled *Ovenbird*, which celebrates global cuisines – from Spain, Argentina and elsewhere – with Southern flair. The menu showcases superb, shareable dishes such as braised octopus with fennel and lemon vinaigrette, and blistered okra with saffron yogurt. The flower-strewn patio is perfect for a cool summer evening. $$$

# Montgomery

**MONTGOMERY**'s location, ninety miles south of Birmingham and 160 west of Atlanta, made it a natural political centre for the plantation elite, leading to its adoption as state capital in 1846 and temporary capital of the Confederacy fifteen years later. In recent years, thanks in part to the ten-year term of progressive mayor Todd Strange, who stepped down in 2019, it's experienced a resurgence, with artists and professionals moving into downtown's historic buildings, an inspiring urban farm (ⓦ eatsouth.org) settling into its outskirts, and a brand-new stadium and baseball team (ⓦ biscuitsbaseball.com) in the heart of the city. Add in the incredible Civil Rights sights, and this is a destination that should not be left off any Southern itinerary.

### Dexter Avenue King Memorial Baptist Church

**Church** 454 Dexter Ave • Tours (booked online) Tues–Fri 10am–3pm, Sat 10am–1pm • Free • ⓦ dexterkingmemorial.org • **Parsonage** 309 S Jackson St • Same hours and website

Following the bus boycotts, Martin Luther King, Jr. remained pastor at the **Dexter Avenue King Memorial Baptist Church**, in the shadow of the Capitol, for a few years. The upstairs sanctuary, left much as it was during his ministry, contains his former pulpit. You can also tour the **Parsonage** where King lived with his family (and gawk at the small crater on the front porch where it was hit with a bomb in 1956) until their move back to his hometown of Atlanta in 1960.

### The State Capitol

600 Dexter Ave • Mon–Fri 8am–4.30pm • Free • ⓦ alabama.gov

On the front steps of the **State Capitol**, a bronze star marks the spot where Jefferson Davis was sworn in as president of the Confederacy on February 18, 1861. The Capitol's lovely Greek Revival facade was immortalized in photographs of the 1965 Voting Rights March, which culminated at its doorstep.

**1**

### Civil Rights Memorial

**Civil Rights Memorial Centre** 400 Washington Ave • Mon–Fri 9am–4.30pm, Sat 10am–4pm • Charge • ⓦ splcenter.org

In front of the **Southern Poverty Law Center**, the moving **Civil Rights Memorial**, designed by Maya Lin (of Vietnam Veterans Memorial fame), consists of a cone-shaped black granite table. It's inscribed with a timeline of events structured around the deaths of forty civilians murdered by white supremacists and police; the circle ends with the assassination of Dr King. You can run your hands through the cool water that pumps evenly across it, softly touching the names while being confronted with your reflection. The wall behind, also running with water, is engraved with the quotation employed so often by Dr King: "(We will not be satisfied) until justice rolls down like waters and righteousness like a mighty stream". Displays in the **Civil Rights Memorial Centre** tell the stories of those killed during the movement.

### Memorial for Peace and Justice and The Legacy Museum

**The Legacy Museum** 115 Coosa St • Wed–Sun 9am–5pm • Charge • ⓦ museumandmemorial.eji.org • **National Memorial for Peace and Justice** 417 Caroline St • Wed–Sun 9am–5pm • Charge • Same phone and web as museum

In 2018, the Equal Justice Initiative (EJI) unveiled the powerful **Memorial for Peace and Justice** – the first memorial in the U.S. dedicated to African American victims of lynching. The memorial, which rises over a Montgomery hilltop, is populated by more than 800 steel columns engraved with the names of victims. The memorial and museum lie just a mile apart and are designed to be visited on the same day. The museum's full name is **The Legacy Museum: From Enslavement to Mass Incarceration**, and it sprawls on the site of a former slave warehouse. Deeply researched displays explore racial inequality through a wide array of exhibits, including first-person accounts, videography and photography, art, sculpture and more.

### Rosa Parks Museum

252 Montgomery St • Mon–Fri 9am–5pm, Sat 9am–3pm • Charge • ⓦ troy.edu

A few blocks west of the memorial, the exceptional **Rosa Parks Museum**, in front of the corner where Parks was arrested, commemorates "the mother of the Civil Rights movement". Exhibits cover the bus boycott and the resulting events that shook the nation.

### Freedom Rides Museum

210 S Court St • Tues–Sat noon–4pm • Charge • ⓦ freedomridesmuseumfriends.org

The small **Freedom Rides Museum** preserves the Greyhound bus terminal where, in 1961, an interracial group of 21 "freedom riders", attempting to desegregate private bus lines, was met with a violent mob of nearly a thousand.

### Hank Williams Museum

118 Commerce St • Mon–Fri 9am–4pm (till 6pm in summer), Sat 10am–4pm, Sun 1–4pm • Charge • ⓦ thehankwilliamsmuseum.net

Montgomery was jammed with mourners in 1954 for the funeral of 29-year-old country star **Hank Williams**, who died of heart failure on his way to a concert on New Year's Eve 1953. An Alabama native, Williams was as famous for his drink-and drug-fuelled lifestyle as he was for writing classics like *I'm So Lonesome I Could Cry*. Fans will thrill to the **Hank Williams Museum**, stashed with the singer's cowboy boots and hand-painted ties, personal notes (including a letter to Hank Williams Jr, imploring him to make a guitar "ring and talk in our good old family way") and the 1952 Cadillac in which he made his final journey. The **Hank Williams Memorial** dominates the Oakwood Cemetery Annex, at 1304 Upper Wetumpka Rd, near downtown.

## CIVIL RIGHTS IN MONTGOMERY

In the 1950s, Montgomery's **bus system** was a miniature model of segregated society – as was the norm in the South. The regulation ordering blacks to give up seats to whites came under repeated attack from black organizations, culminating in the call by the Women's Political Council for a mass boycott after seamstress and civil rights activist **Rosa Parks** was arrested on December 1, 1955, for refusing to give up her seat, stating that she was simply too tired. Black workers were asked to walk to work, while black-owned "rolling churches" carried those who lived farther away. The protest attracted huge support and the Montgomery Improvement Association (MIA), set up to coordinate activities, elected the 26-year-old pastor **Dr Martin Luther King, Jr** as its chief spokesperson. Despite personal hardships, bomb attacks and jailings, protestors continued to boycott the buses for eleven months, until in November 1956 the US Supreme Court declared segregation on public transport to be illegal.

### Blount Cultural Park

Just off Woodmere Boulevard, ten miles southeast of the city, verdant, 300-acre **Blount Cultural Park** is home to the acclaimed **Alabama Shakespeare Festival** (Ⓦasf.net) and the slick **Montgomery Museum of Fine Arts** (Tues–Sat 10am–5pm, Sun noon–5pm; free; Ⓦmmfa.org), which spans more than two hundred years of American art and has an impressive collection of European masters.

### F. Scott & Zelda Fitzgerald Museum

919 Felder Ave • Wed–Sun 10am–3pm • Charge • 334 264 4222, Ⓦ thefitzgeraldmuseum.org.

Set in the last surviving home, built in 1910, in which the Fitzgeralds lived as a family, the delightful, well-curated **F. Scott & Zelda Fitzgerald Museum** features a series of galleries that celebrate the various decades of Fitzgerald's life, from his time at Princeton University to the Roaring Twenties to the Depression era and his wife Zelda's eventual breakdown and hospitalization.

### ARRIVAL AND INFORMATION                                  MONTGOMERY

**By plane** Montgomery Airport (Ⓦiflymontgomery.com) is 11 miles southwest of town on US-80.
**By bus** The Greyhound station (Ⓣ 334 286 0658) is at 950 W South Blvd.

**Destinations** Atlanta, GA (5 daily; 3hr); Birmingham, AL (4 daily; 1hr 50min); Selma, AL (3 daily; 1hr)
**Visitor centre** 300 Water St (Mon–Sat 8.30am–5pm, Sun noon–4pm; Ⓣ 334 262 0013, Ⓦ visitingmontgomery.com)

### ACCOMMODATION

**Hampton Inn & Suites Downtown** 100 Commerce St Ⓦ hamptoninn.hilton.com. Clean, comfortable rooms and a substantial continental breakfast at this cheerful hotel in an historic building at the centre of town. $\overline{55}$

**Red Bluff Cottage** 551 Clay St Ⓦ redbluffcottage.com. Friendly B&B near the Capitol, with comfortable, antique-laden rooms, a big porch with rocking chairs and delicious food. $\overline{55}$

### EATING AND DRINKING

Montgomery's **downtown** has a good range of restaurants, a microbrewery and a handful of watering holes. A few minutes' drive southeast, suburban **Cloverdale** offers a selection of fancier restaurants and has a number of bars and jazz clubs.

★ **Central** 129 Coosa St Ⓦ central129coosa.com. This lively restaurant, set in a former historic warehouse on the riverfront, has become a beloved fixture in the Montgomery dining scene. The open kitchen allows a glimpse into the creativity that fuels the cuisine, like pork belly with wickles

(spicy pickles born in Dadeville, Alabama) and scallops with Meyer lemon and parmesan herb risotto. $\overline{555}$
**Derk's Filet and Vine** 431 Cloverdale Rd Ⓦ filetandvine.com. Very popular neighbourhood deli/grocery/wine store serving hearty, varied lunches including pork chops or sweet potato casserole, deli sandwiches, wraps and salads. $\overline{55}$
**Leroy** 2752 Boultier Ave Ⓦ leroylounge.com. Slender, hip, dimly lit drinking den in the Cloverdale neighbourhood with a retro feel, a nice selection of craft and import beers and a relaxed, starlit patio.

**1**

## Selma

The market town of **SELMA**, fifty miles west of Montgomery, became the focal point of the civil rights movement in the early Sixties. Black demonstrations, meetings and attempts to register to vote were repeatedly met by police violence, before the murder of a black protester by a state trooper prompted the historic **march from Selma to Montgomery**, led by, among others, **Martin Luther King, Jr**. Nowadays, Selma has fallen on hard times, but it's worth making a day-trip here from Montgomery to visit the fascinating **Voting Rights Museum** and take the historic walk across the Pettus bridge.

### National Voting Rights Museum

6 US Hwy-80 E • Mon–Thurs 10am–4pm, Fri–Sun by appt only • Charge • ⓦ nvrmi.com

On "Bloody Sunday", March 7, 1965, six hundred unarmed marchers set off across the steep incline of the imposing, narrow **Edmund Pettus Bridge**. As they went over the apex, a line of state troopers fired tear gas without warning, lashing out at the panic-stricken demonstrators with nightsticks and cattle prods. This violent confrontation, broadcast all over the world, is credited with having directly influenced the passage of the **Voting Rights Act** the following year. The full story – packed with personal testimony – is told in the **National Voting Rights Museum**, located beside the bridge.

## Mobile

**MOBILE** (pronounced "Mo-beel") traces its origins to a French community founded in 1702 by Jean-Baptiste Le Moyne, who went on to establish the cities of Biloxi and Nouvelle Orleans. These early white settlers brought with them **Mardi Gras**, which has been celebrated here since 1704, several years before New Orleans was even dreamed of. With its early eighteenth-century Spanish and colonial-style buildings, parallels with New Orleans are everywhere, from wrought-iron balconies to French street names, but there the comparisons end. It's a pretty place – especially in spring, when ablaze with delicate azaleas, camellias and dogwoods – but there's little to actually do.

A good starting point for exploring the town is **Fort Condé** at 150 S Royal St (daily 8am–5pm; free), a reconstruction of the city's 1724 French fort. Dioramas cover local history; don't miss the atmospheric old photos of carnival, the old city and local African American figures. North of the fort is the **Church Street Historic District**, full of pre-Civil War buildings.

The **History Museum of Mobile**, across from Fort Condé at 111 S Royal St (Mon–Sat 9am–5pm, Sun 1–5pm; charge; ⓦ historymuseumofmobile.com), tells the story of the town from its earliest days, while the small **Mobile Carnival Museum**, 355 Government St (Mon, Wed, Fri & Sat 9am–4pm; docent-led tours offered at 9.30am, 11am, 1.30pm; charge; ⓦ mobilecarnivalmuseum.com), set in a historic house embellished with an elaborate wrought-iron balcony, has quirky exhibits covering the arcane rituals of Mardi Gras. You can also tour the World War II battleship **USS Alabama** (daily: April–Sept 8am–6pm; Oct–March 8am–5pm; charge; ⓦ ussalabama.com), particularly fun if you're travelling with kids.

### ARRIVAL AND INFORMATION
MOBILE

**By bus** The Greyhound station (☎ 251 478 6089) is centrally located at 2545 Government St.

**Visitor centre** In the History Museum, 111 S Royal St (daily 8am–4.30pm; ☎ 251 208 7304, ⓦ mobile.org).

### ACCOMMODATION AND EATING

★ **Dumbwaiter Restaurant** 167 Dauphin St ⓦ dumbwaiterrestaurant.com. This convivial dinner-only restaurant, with exposed brick walls, warm lighting and a buzzing bar, is New Southern cuisine at its best. Witty, modern interpretations of traditional favourites include Creole seafood pasta with sausage, crab and shrimp, and deep-fried pork chop with goat cheese scallion mashed potatoes. $$$$

**Malaga Inn** 359 Church St ⓦ malagainn.com. Comprised

of two townhouses, this 1862 property has spacious rooms set around a pretty courtyard. Breakfast is included in the rate. $$$

**NoJa** 6 N Jackson St ⓦ nojamobile.com. This worldly restaurant serves upmarket takes on Mediterranean and Asian cuisine, for dinner only. With its open kitchen, exposed brick walls and stylish scene, *NoJa* would be right at home in Manhattan's Greenwich Village, though its romantic Greek Revival exterior looks like it could have been airlifted from New Orleans. $$$$

# Mississippi

Before the Civil War, when cotton was king and slavery remained unchallenged, **MISSISSIPPI** was the nation's fifth wealthiest state. Since the conflict, it has consistently been the poorest, its dependence on cotton a handicap that leaves it victim to the vagaries of the commodities market. The state has an undeniable pull, especially for blues fans, drawn to the **Mississippi Delta** – a land of scorching sun, parched earth, flooding creeks and thickets of bone-dry evergreens – as the fabled home of the blues. Technically speaking, the so-called Delta is not in fact a delta at all, but an alluvial flood plain, a couple of hundred miles short of the mouth of the Mississippi. The name stems from its resemblance to the fertile delta of the Nile (which also began as a city named Memphis); the extravagant meanderings of the river on its way down to Vicksburg deposit enough rich topsoil to make this one of the world's finest cotton-producing regions. Devotees of the blues are drawn irresistibly to sleepy Delta settlements such as Alligator or Yazoo City, and to **Clarksdale** above all, with its juke joints, festivals and atmospheric accommodation.

South of the Delta, the rich woodlands and meadows of central Mississippi are heralded by steep loess bluffs, home to engaging historic towns. Driving is a pleasure, especially along the unspoiled Natchez Trace Parkway – devoid of trucks, buildings and neon signs. The largest city is the capital, **Jackson**, but there's little reason to stop here when you could stay in quaint river towns like **Vicksburg** and **Natchez** instead. In the north, literary **Oxford** has a lively college scene and should not be missed; Elvis fans will want to make a beeline for **Tupelo** and the King's humble birthplace.

### Brief history

From Reconstruction onwards, Mississippi was known as the greatest bastion of segregation in the South. It witnessed some of the most notorious incidents of the **civil rights** era, from the lynching of Chicago teenager Emmett Till in 1955 to the murder of three activists during the "Freedom Summer" of 1964, which exposed the intimate connections between the Ku Klux Klan and the state's law enforcement officers. Not until the Seventies did the church bombings and murders end. The legalization of gambling in the 1990s stimulated the economy somewhat, with the hulking **casinos** of Biloxi and Tunica pulling considerable revenues across the state line from Tennessee and Alabama. The Gulf shoreline suffered appalling devastation from Hurricane Katrina in 2005, however, and though most of the casinos had reopened, the coast was still undergoing reconstruction when hit by the BP oil spill in 2010. The impact on marine life and the environment was catastrophic, and though containment efforts went into effect immediately, it wasn't until 2014 that the "active cleanup" was considered complete. Only in 2020 did Mississippi become the last state to remove the Confederate battle flag from its state flag.

## Clarksdale

**CLARKSDALE**, the first significant town south of Memphis, has an unquestionable right to claim itself as the **home of the blues**. It has a phenomenal roll call of former residents, stretching from Son House, Muddy Waters, John Lee Hooker, Howlin' Wolf and Robert Johnson up to Ike Turner and Sam Cooke.

**1**

Clarksdale's music festivals are a major draw, among them the free **Sunflower River Blues and Gospel Festival** (⊚sunflowerfest.org) in August, and the **Juke Joint Festival** in April (⊚jukejointfestival.com); for these you'll need to book accommodation months in advance. Some seventy miles south of Clarksdale, down-at-heel **Greenville**, the largest town on the Delta and an important riverport, hosts the **Mississippi Delta Blues and Heritage Festival** (⊚deltabluesms.org) in mid-September.

Delta Blues Museum

1 Blues Alley • Mon–Sat: March–Oct 9am–5pm; Nov–Feb 10am–5pm • Charge • ⊚ deltabluesmuseum.org

The superb **Delta Blues Museum** celebrates Clarksdale, "the land where blues began". Its fascinating collection is housed in the restored passenger depot of the Illinois Central Railroad, where many black Mississippians started their migration to the cities of the North. As well as featuring exhibits on the history of the blues, including historic photos, album art, instruments and memorabilia, it hosts events from book signings to concerts.

## THE DELTA BLUES

As recently as 1900, much of the Mississippi Delta remained an impenetrable **wilderness** of cypress and gum trees, roamed by panthers and bears and plagued with mosquitoes. In 1903, **W.C. Handy**, often rather spuriously credited as "the Father of the Blues", but at that time the leader of a vaudeville orchestra, found himself waiting for a train in Tutwiler, fifteen miles southeast of Clarksdale. At some point in the night, a ragged black man carrying a guitar sat down next to him and began to play what Handy called "the weirdest music I had ever heard". Using a pocketknife pressed against the guitar strings to accentuate his mournful vocal style, the man sang that he was "Goin' where the Southern cross the Dog". This was the **Delta blues**, characterized by the interplay between words and music, with the guitar aiming to parallel and complement the singing rather than simply provide a backing.

The blues started out as young people's music; the old folk liked the banjo, fife and drum, but the younger generation were crazy for the wild showmanship of bluesmen such as **Charley Patton**. Born in April 1891, Patton was the classic itinerant bluesman, moving from plantation to plantation and wife to wife, and playing Saturday-night dances with a repertoire that extended from rollicking dance pieces to documentary songs such as *High Water Everywhere*, about the bursting of the Mississippi levees in April 1927. Another seminal artist, the enigmatic **Robert Johnson** was rumoured to have sold his soul to the Devil in return for a few brief years of writing songs such as *Love in Vain* and *Stop Breakin' Down*. His *Crossroads Blues* spoke of being stranded at night in the chilling emptiness of the Delta; themes carried to metaphysical extremes in *Hellhound on My Trail* and *Me and the Devil Blues* – "you may bury my body down by the highway side/So my old evil spirit can catch a Greyhound bus and ride."

In addition to towns such as Clarksdale and Helena in Arkansas (see page 128), blues enthusiasts may want to search out the following rural sites:

**Stovall Farms** Stovall Road, 7 miles northwest of Clarksdale. Where tractor-driver Muddy Waters was first recorded; a few cabins remain, though Muddy's own is now in the Clarksdale blues museum.

**Sonny Boy Williamson II's grave** Prairie Place, outside Tutwiler, 15 miles southeast of Clarksdale.

**Parchman Farm** Junction US-49 W and Hwy-32. Mississippi State penitentiary, immortalized in song by former prisoner Bukka White.

**Dockery Plantation** Hwy-8, between Cleveland and Ruleville. One of Patton's few long-term bases, also home to Howlin' Wolf and Roebuck "Pops" Staples.

**Charley Patton's grave** New Jerusalem Church, Holly Ridge, on Holly Ridge Rd off US-82 6 miles west of Indianola.

**Robert Johnson's grave** Little Zion Church, off Money Rd, roughly 4 miles northwest of Greenwood.

## ACCOMMODATION CLARKSDALE

**The Loft at Hopson Plantation** 8141 Old Hwy-49S, 4 miles south of town ⓦ hopsonplantation.com. In 1935, the Hopson Plantation became one of the first fully mechanized cotton operations in the world, and was held up as a shining example of Delta farming. Today, the Hopson Plantation Commissary – which served the many labourers who worked the cotton fields – functions as part mini-museum (filled with historical items and photographs), part bar (regular blues concerts), part barbecue restaurant and part lodging, with the rustic *Loft*, which has a full kitchen, bedroom, living room and, best of all, a front porch with rockers. $$$

**Riverside Hotel** 615 Sunflower Ave ⓦ riversideclarksdale.com. Assuming it has managed to reopen following storm damage sustained during its Covid-era closure, this iconic hotel offers basic, clean rooms (shared bath) in the old hospital building where Bessie Smith died after a car crash in 1937. The owner, daughter of previous innkeeper and local legend Frank "Rat" Ratliff, will happily recount the "true history of the blues". $$

★ **Shack Up Inn** 1 Commissary Circle, 4 miles south on US-49 ⓦ shackupinn.com. This unique option, on the former Hopson cotton plantation, offers six old sharecroppers' cabins with kitchenette and porch, along with ten slightly plusher rooms in the cotton gin. It's hard to imagine a more evocative place to stay in the Delta. $$

### EATING, DRINKING AND NIGHTLIFE

**Abe's** 616 State St ⓦ abesbbq.com. Famed barbecue joint, in business since 1924, located at the iconic blues crossroads of Hwy-61 and 49. $$

**Ground Zero Blues Club** Zero Blues Alley ⓦ groundzerobluesclub.com. Part-owned by Morgan Freeman, this venerable blues haunt – its walls packed with memorabilia and customer scribbles – is an excellent place to catch live music. The kitchen turns out solid Southern fare including grits, pulled pork sandwiches and fried green tomatoes. Don't miss the homemade peach cobbler. $

★ **Red's** 395 Sunflower Ave ☎ 662 627 3166. Authentic juke joint and a Clarksdale must-do for soulful performances staged in a smoky, scruffy lounge. There's divine, slow-cooked barbecue fired up out front. Cover charge.

# Indianola

Every summer **INDIANOLA**, 23 miles east of Greenville on US-82, continues to stage a "Homecoming" celebration in honour of its most famous son, **B.B. King**, who until his death in 2015 would indeed return home to play along with other local blues bands. The **B.B. King Blues Museum**, at 400 2nd St (April–Oct Mon & Sun noon–5pm, Tues–Sat 10am–5pm; Nov–March closed Mon; charge; ⓦ bbkingmuseum.org), tells the story of the blues by tracing King's sixty-year career from sharecropper in the cotton fields via Memphis to international success.

## ACCOMMODATION, EATING AND NIGHTLIFE INDIANOLA

**The Blue Biscuit** 501 2nd St ☎ 662 645 0258,. Across from the B.B. King Blues Museum, this down-home restaurant and juke joint is a good time for all, with beer flowing, burgers grilling, catfish frying and the live music hopping. The *Biscuit* also has rustic bungalows ($$). $$

**The Crown** 112 Front Ave ⓦ tasteofgourmet.com. The name fits the bill at this superlative Southern café, which cooks up the region's best catfish dishes (order it poached with parmesan cheese), gumbo and Mississippi fudge pie in a peach-coloured dining room with local art. $$

# Greenwood

Sleepy **GREENWOOD**, on the shady Yazoo River forty miles east of Indianola, is the country's second largest cotton exchange after Memphis. It has an odd atmosphere nowadays, the huge, aseptic surrounds of the Viking kitchen goods corporation and its associated **Alluvian** hotel and spa creating a wealthy enclave entirely out of keeping with the rest of the Delta. Legend has it that bluesman Robert Johnson died here after drinking a bottle of whiskey poisoned by an admirer's jealous husband.

## ACCOMMODATION AND EATING GREENWOOD

**Crystal Grill** 423 Carrollton Ave ⓦ crystalgrillms.com. Family-owned since 1932, this local favourite serves classic Delta fare such as broiled catfish, veal cutlets and mile-high meringue pie in a 1900s dining room with its original tile floor. $$

**Tallahatchie Flats** 58458 Hwy-518 (Money Rd), 3 miles

**1**

north of town ⓦtallahatchieflats.com. Six renovated, appealingly dilapidated old Delta shacks; porches look out over the river and nothing disturbs the peace but the whistle of the lonesome railroad. $\overline{\underline{\$\$}}$

# Oxford

Twenty-five thousand residents and twenty-four thousand students enable **OXFORD**, an enclave of wealth in a predominantly poor region, to blend rural charm with a vibrant cultural life. Its central square is archetypal smalltown America, but the leafy streets have a vaguely European air – the town named itself after the English city as part of its (successful) campaign to persuade the **University of Mississippi**, known as Ole Miss, to locate its main campus here.

East of the university, in town, life revolves around the central **square**. Here you'll find Neilson's, the oldest department store in the south – little changed since 1897. You can pick up a cool pair of heels in one of the boutiques, have a quick lunch or join students sipping espresso on the peaceful balcony of the splendid **Square Books**.

## Rowan Oak

Old Taylor Rd • Summer Mon–Sat 10am–6pm, Sun 1–6pm; rest of year Tues–Sat 10am–4pm, Sun 1–4pm • Charge • ⓦ rowanoak.com

From Ole Miss, a ten-minute walk through lush Bailey's Woods leads to secluded **Rowan Oak**, the lovely former home of novelist **William Faulkner**, preserved as it was on the day he died in July 1962 (the day after the funeral, his wife added air conditioning to her bedroom, forbidden by Faulkner during his lifetime). Be sure to take a look into his office, where the writer scribbled the outline of *A Fable* directly onto the wall. The fictional Deep South town of Jefferson in Yoknapatawpha County, where the Nobel Prize-winner set his major works, was based heavily on Oxford and its environs.

## INFORMATION

**Visitor centre** Just off the main square, at 1013 Jackson Ave E (Mon–Fri 8am–5pm, Sat 10am–4pm, Sun 1–4pm; ☏662 232 2447, ⓦvisitoxfordms.com); offers lots of information on William Faulkner and local events.

## ACCOMMODATION AND EATING

**Ajax Diner** 118 Courthouse Square ⓦajaxdiner.net. There's a great selection of places to eat on the square; this community hub with vinyl booths and a chequerboard floor serves huge plates of top-notch soul food. Try the signature Ronzo Salad, a mound of catfish, pecans, crumbled blue cheese and corn. $\overline{\underline{\$\$}}$

**Big Bad Breakfast** 719 N Lamar St ⓦbigbadbreakfast. com. This wildly popular breakfast spot, run by the same chef as City Grocery, serves creative takes on traditional brunch items such as the fried oyster scramble with bacon and roast potatoes, and warm biscuits made every which way. $\overline{\underline{\$\$}}$

**Bottletree Bakery** 923 Van Buren Ave ☏ 662 236 5000. Just off the square, this friendly little café serves healthy breakfasts, scrumptious home-baked pastries – including its trademark humble pie – soups and sandwiches. $\overline{\underline{\$}}$

**City Grocery** 152 Courthouse Square ⓦcitygroceryonline.com. For sophisticated Southern cuisine, head to this buzzy landmark, which has a balcony and upstairs bar. $\overline{\underline{\$\$\$\$}}$

★ **McEwen's Oxford** 1110 Van Buren Ave ⓦmcewensoxford.com. Enjoy superb Southern dishes at this elegant, lively restaurant in the heart of town. Start off

---

### INTEGRATING OLE MISS

An appealing place today, in 1962 Oxford was the site of one of the bitterest displays of racial hatred seen in Mississippi – events that Bob Dylan responded to with his contemptuous *Oxford Town*. After eighteen months of legal and political wrangling, federal authorities ruled that **James Meredith** be allowed to enrol as the first black student at Ole Miss. The news that Meredith had been "sneaked" into college by federal troops sparked a riot that left two dead and 160 injured. Despite constant threats, Meredith graduated the following year, wearing a "NEVER" badge, the segregationist slogan of Governor Ross Barnett, upside down. A memorial commemorating his achievement was unveiled in 2002, on the fortieth anniversary of his admission.

with gulf shrimp salad and grilled peaches and brie with pecans, then try the likes of Mississippi catfish with stewed okra. Sunday brunch is deservedly popular, drawing crowds for the hearty platters of chicken and waffles. $\overline{\$\$\$\$}$

**Taylor Grocery** 4A Depot St, Taylor ⓦ taylorgrocery. com. Just 15min south of Oxford, in tiny Taylor, this rickety old shack dishes up amazing catfish and deep-fried oysters to a raucous crowd. $\overline{\$\$}$

# Tupelo

On January 8, 1935, **Elvis Presley** and his twin brother Jesse were born in **TUPELO**, an industrial town in northeastern Mississippi. Jesse died at birth, while Elvis grew up to be a truck driver. Their parents, Gladys and Vernon Presley, who lived in poor, white East Tupelo, struggled to survive. The financial strain was bad enough that Elvis's sharecropper father, in a desperate attempt to raise cash, resorted to forgery and was given a three-year sentence. Their home was repossessed, and the family moved to Memphis in 1948.

Surprisingly, for most of the year Tupelo doesn't go in for Elvis overkill; Main Street is a long, placid stretch of nondescript buildings, with nary a gift shop to be seen. The visitor centre has details of the enjoyable four-day **Elvis Festival** (ⓦ tupeloelvisfestival. com), held in June, when the town fills with jumpsuited tribute artists.

### Elvis Presley Birthplace

306 Elvis Presley Drive • Mon–Sat 9am–5pm, Sun 1–5pm • Charge • ⓦ elvispresleybirthplace.com

The actual **Elvis Presley Birthplace** is fascinating. A two-room shotgun house, built for $150 in 1934, it's been furnished to look as it did when Elvis was born; it's an undeniably moving experience to stand in this tiny building that the Presley family struggled so hard to keep.

Equally poignant is the adjacent family **church**, moved here from one block away; you sit in the pews as wraparound movie screens recreate the kind of barnstorming services that Elvis grew up with, ringing with speechifying, testifying and the emotional gospel music that the King always kept close to his heart. An unmissable small **museum** puts Elvis's early years in fascinating context, illustrating life in the prewar South with lots of old photos and memorabilia.

### EATING                                                                 TUPELO

**Neon Pig** 1203 N Gloster St (Rte-145) ⓦ neonpigtupelo. com. Don't be put off by the location, in a strip mall on the highway; inside, *Neon Pig* is loud, cosy and fun, with a small

but tasty menu of custom-ground burgers, sandwiches and craft beer. There's also a little shop selling fresh veggies, shellfish and local meats. $\overline{\$\$}$

# Vicksburg

The historic port of **VICKSBURG** straddles a high bluff on a bend in the Mississippi, 44 miles west of Jackson. During the Civil War, its domination of the river halted Union shipping and led Abraham Lincoln to call Vicksburg the "key to the Confederacy". It was a crucial target for General Ulysses S. Grant, who eventually landed to the south in the spring of 1863, circled inland and attacked from the east. After a 47-day siege, the outnumbered Confederates surrendered on the Fourth of July – a holiday Vicksburg declined to celebrate for the next 81 years – and Lincoln was able to rejoice that "the Father of Waters again goes unvexed to the sea".

As the Mississippi has changed course since the 1860s, it's now the slender, canalized Yazoo River rather than the broad Mississippi that flows alongside the battlefield and most of downtown Vicksburg. The core of the city, a bare but attractive place of precipitous streets, steep terraces and wooded ravines, has changed little, however, despite the arrival of permanently moored riverfront **casinos**. Downtown, especially **Washington Street**, is being restored to its original late-Victorian appearance, though most of its finest buildings were destroyed during the siege.

**1**

### Old Court House Museum

1008 Cherry St • Mon–Sat 8.30am–4.30pm, Sun 1.30–4.30pm • Charge • ⓦ oldcourthouse.org

Vicksburg's fascinating **Old Court House Museum** covers the Civil War era in depth, even selling genuine minié balls (bullets). Its catch-all exhibits include the tie Jefferson Davis wore at his inauguration, a wartime newspaper – printed on wallpaper because of the conflict – Confederate currency, and a weathered armchair favoured by (a likely very inebriated) General Grant during the siege. The second floor's court chamber feels like it could have been lifted from the set of *To Kill a Mockingbird*.

### Biedenharn Candy Company

1107 Washington St • Mon–Sat 9am–5pm, Sun 1.30–4.30pm • Charge • ⓦ biedenharncoca-colamuseum.com

A small museum at the **Biedenharn Candy Company** marks the spot where Coca-Cola was first bottled, with vivid displays on how it all came about. Out back, you'll find an ancient 1900 soda fountain, dubbed "The Siberian Arctic", presumably because it kept beverages remarkably chilled.

### Vicksburg National Military Park

3201 Clay St • Daily 8am–5pm • Charge • ⓦ nps.gov/vick

Entered via Clay Street (off US-80) just east of town, **Vicksburg National Military Park** preserves the main Civil War battlefield. A sixteen-mile loop drive through the rippling green hillsides traces every contour of the Union and Confederate trenches, punctuated by statues, refurbished cannon and more than 1600 state-by-state monuments. Nearby, in the **Vicksburg National Cemetery**, thirteen thousand of the seventeen thousand Union graves are marked simply "Unknown".

---

**INFORMATION**                                                    **VICKSBURG**

**Mississippi Welcome Center** Exit 1A beside the river (daily 8am–5pm; ☎ 601 638 4269, ⓦ visitvmississippi.org). **Visitor centre** Near exit 4, opposite the battlefield entrance on Clay St (June–Aug daily 8am–5.30pm; Sept–May Mon–Sat 8am–5pm, Sun 10am–5pm; ☎ 800 221 3536, ⓦ visitvicksburg.com).

---

**ACCOMMODATION AND EATING**

★ **Anchuca** 1010 1st East St ⓦ anchuca.com. Housed in the town's first colonnaded mansion, this beautiful B&B boasts a pool and a very good restaurant with outdoor seating. 5̄5̄

**Rusty's** 901 Washington St ⓦ rustysriverfront.com. Tables fill up quickly at this central seafood and steak place with an open kitchen and superlative fried green tomatoes, juicy rib eyes and airy coconut cream pie. 5̄5̄5̄

**The Tomato Place** 3229 Hwy-61 S, just south of Vicksburg ⓦ thetomatoplace.com. Few places in the US excel at quirky roadside Americana like the South – and

*The Tomato Place* is a prime example. Tucked behind a ramshackle fruit and vegetable stand, strewn with flowers and plants, the cheerily painted restaurant serves up mighty fine po-boy sandwiches – try the catfish and sausage – and, of course, lots and lots of tomatoes. Signature sandwiches include the fried green tomato BLT. 5̄5̄

**Walnut Hills** 1214 Adams St ⓦ walnuthillsms.com. This restaurant whips up superb all-you-can-eat "round table" lunches of fried chicken and other Southern delicacies, served in an 1880s house. It also does à la carte. 5̄5̄

## Natchez

Seventy miles south of Vicksburg – at the western end of the pretty Natchez Trace Parkway, the old Native American path that ran from here to Nashville – the river town of **NATCHEZ** is the oldest permanent settlement on the Mississippi River. By the time it first flew the Stars and Stripes in 1798, it had already been home to the Natchez people and their predecessors, as well as French, British and Spanish colonists. Unlike its great rival, Vicksburg, Natchez was spared significant damage during the Civil War, ensuring that its abundant Greek Revival antebellum mansions remained intact, complete with meticulous gardens. Interspersed among them are countless simpler but similarly attractive white clapboard homes, set along broad leafy avenues of majestic oaks, making Natchez one of the prettiest towns in the South. **Horse and carriage** tours (see page 128) explore downtown, while a number of individual mansions are open for tours.

Though Natchez proper perches well above the river, a small stretch of riverfront at the foot of the bluff constitutes **Natchez Under-the-Hill**. Once known as the "Sodom of the Mississippi", it now houses a handful of bars and restaurants, plus the *Magnolia Bluffs* riverboat **casino**.

Natchez's history of **slavery** is chronicled with a rather pitiful display at the **Forks of the Road monument**, a mile east of downtown on Liberty Road at St Catherine, on the site of the second largest slave market in the South.

### Longwood

140 Lower Woodville Rd • Tours daily on the half hour 9am–4.30pm • Charge • ⓦ natchezpilgrimage.com

Fans of HBO's *True Blood* will recognize the elaborate, octagonal **Longwood**, with its huge dome and snow-white arches and columns, as the home of the vampire king of Mississippi. Such was their haste to get north at the start of the Civil War, the Philadelphia builders constructing this six-storey mansion left their tools behind (still on view). Only the first floor of Longwood was ever completed, and it's exciting to go from the elaborately furnished ground level to the raw, unfinished second storey, which spirals upward in an open, unvarnished wooden arc.

### Melrose

1 Melrose Montebello Pkwy • Daily 8.30am–5pm • Charge • ⓦ nps.gov/natc

Unlike many of the town's house tours, which strive to present a Tara-like picture of life in antebellum Mississippi, the 1831 **Melrose** balances facts about the mansion's cotton planter homeowners with hard details on the lives of its slave population, whose quarters have been preserved.

### William Johnson House and around

210 State St • Thurs–Sun 9am–4.30pm • Free • ⓦ nps.gov/natc

Downtown, the fascinating **William Johnson House** relays the history of an African American barber whose sixteen-year diary offers a rare glimpse into the goings-on of a Southern free person of colour. Born a slave in 1809, Johnson became a slaveholder himself during his adult years.

Nearby, at 400 State St, the chapel of the **First Presbyterian Church** (Mon–Sat 10am–4pm; donation; ⓦ fpcnatchez.org) holds an incredible collection of black-and-white photographs depicting all aspects of life in nineteenth-century, riverfront Natchez.

---

#### **DRINK IN THE HISTORY OF NATCHEZ**

Part of the *King's Tavern* – Natchez's oldest structure, dating back to 1769 – the **Charboneau Distillery**, at 617 Jefferson St (distillery tours Fri 5–8pm, Sat noon–6pm; free; ⓦ charboneaudistillery.com) has the distinction of producing the first legally distilled rum in Mississippi, using sugar cane sourced from Louisiana and purified local water. Tours take you through the distillery and include fragrant samples, after which you can stop by the store in the next-door restaurant to pick up a bottle (or three) to take home.

Natchez has, interestingly, become a mini hotbed of locally sourced alcohol. Check out the Natchez Brewing Company, at 207 High St (tours Fri–Sat only; tour times vary, so call ahead; charge; ⓦ natchezbrew.com), which has a tap room where you can sample the brews. And, the long-running Old South Winery, at 65 S Concord Ave (Mon–Fri 10am–5pm; charge; ⓦ oldsouthwinery.com) offers a rich line-up of wines – so now Natchez has rum, beer and wine covered.

**Visitor centre** 640 S Canal St (by the Mississippi River bridge; Mon–Sat 8.30am–5pm, Sun 9am–4pm; ☎601 446 6345, ⍵ visitnatchez.org).

**Tours** The visitor centre is the starting point for various tram (trolley), mansion and bus tours along with carriage rides.

**Natchez Pilgrimage** The mansions can also be seen during fall and spring pilgrimage tours (March–April & Oct; charge; ⍵ natchezpilgrimage.com), led by women trussed up in massive hoopskirts.

## ACCOMMODATION AND EATING

★ **Carriage House** 401 High St, in Stanton Hall ☎601 445 5151. Sunday brunch is a must at this classic Southern restaurant, set on the grounds of an 1857 Greek Revival mansion. The buffet is a luscious cornucopia that may include crab and Brie soup, pork cheeks in grits, flaky biscuits and smothered mustard greens. $\overline{\underline{\$\$\$}}$

**Magnolia Grill** 49 Silver St ⍵ magnoliagrill.com. The glassed-in deck of this local favourite restaurant, facing the Mississippi at the foot of the bridge, makes a hugely atmospheric spot to enjoy all flavours Southern, be it redfish, catfish, fried oysters, shrimp or just a simple grilled steak. $\overline{\underline{\$\$\$}}$

**Pig Out Inn** 116 S Canal St ⍵ pigoutinnbbq.com. Boasting "swine dining at its finest", this downtown haunt has soul records on the wall, barbecue smoking out back and oodles of pig paraphernalia throughout. $\overline{\underline{\$\$}}$

★ **Steampunk Coffee Roasters** 706 Franklin St ☎601 870 6882 ⍵ steampunkcoffeeroasters.com. This shrine to fine coffee is the kind of place you'd expect to see in New York or London. But here it is – a hip and handsome coffee bar serving the finest brews this side of the Mississippi. The ink-black espressos are perfection, as are the iced lattes and dainty baked goods, like biscotti and quiches. $\overline{\underline{\$}}$

**Stone House Musical B&B** 804 Washington St ⍵ josephstonehouse.com. This B&B offers something a little different from the other grand mansions; owned by a professional musician who gives free piano recitals to guests, it also has a billiards room and a store selling antique maps and prints. $\overline{\underline{\$\$\$}}$

# Arkansas

Historically, **ARKANSAS** belongs firmly to the South. It sided with the Confederacy during the Civil War and its capital, **Little Rock**, was, in 1957, one of the most notorious flashpoints in the struggle for **civil rights**. Geographically, however, it marks the beginning of the Great Plains. Unlike the Southern states on the east side of the Mississippi River, Arkansas (the correct pronunciation, following a state law from 1881, is "Arkansaw") remained sparsely populated until the late nineteenth century. What's surprising about the eastern Arkansas delta lands is that they are far from totally flat: **Crowley's Ridge**, a narrow arc of windblown loess hills, breaks up the uniform smoothness, stretching 150 miles from southern Missouri to the sleepy river town of **Helena**, which is an important stop for **Delta blues** enthusiasts. In 1992 local boy **Bill Clinton**'s accession to the presidency catapulted Arkansas to national prominence.

## KING BISCUIT TIME SHOW

In 1941, Helena was the birthplace of the celebrated **King Biscuit Time Show**, broadcast on radio station KFFA (1360 AM). The first radio show in the nation to broadcast live Delta blues, it featured performances from legends including boogie pianist Pinetop Perkins and harmonica great **Sonny Boy Williamson II** ("Rice" Miller) – the local boy who featured Helena in intimate detail in many of his (usually extemporized) recordings. With a huge influence that belies its tiny size – musicians from B.B. King to Levon Helm cited it as a major inspiration – the show is the longest running in history, having been on air continuously ever since and hosted from 1950 onwards by legend "Sunshine" Sonny Payne, who sadly passed away in 2018. **Broadcasts** are recorded from the foyer of the excellent Delta Cultural Center at 141 Cherry St (Tues–Sat 9am–5pm; broadcasts Mon–Fri 12.15–12.45pm; free⍵ deltaculturalcenter.com); observers are welcome. If you miss the show, make sure to stop by the centre's **music exhibit**.

Though Arkansas encompasses the **Mississippi Delta** in the east, oil-rich timber lands in the south, and the sweeping **Ouachita** ("Wash-ih-taw") **Mountains** in the west, the cragged and charismatic **Ozark Mountains** in the north are its most scenic asset, abounding with parks, lakes, rivers and streams, and a couple of alternative little towns that make welcoming places to stay.

# Helena

The small Mississippi port of **HELENA**, roughly sixty miles south of Memphis, was once the shipping point for Arkansas' cotton crop, when Mark Twain described it as occupying "one of the prettiest situations on the river". A compact **historic district** bordered by Holly, College and Perry streets reflects that brief period of prosperity, before the arrival of the railroad left most of the river towns obsolete, but nowadays it feels the strain of living in the shadow of the enormous casinos across the river. Most activity takes place along run-down **Cherry Street** on the levee.

### The Depot

95 Missouri St · Tues–Sat 9am–5pm · Free · Ⓦ deltaculturalcenter.com

The Depot, an event space run by the Delta Cultural Center, is set in a restored train depot. Exhibits cover all aspects of the region's history, from the first settlers of this soggy frontier to contemporary racism, with, of course, lots of good stuff about local musical heritage.

| **ACCOMMODATION AND EATING** | **HELENA** |
|---|---|

**Edwardian Inn** 317 Biscoe St, north of the Mississippi Bridge Ⓦ edwardianinn.com. This 1904 inn is an opulent, reasonably priced B&B with large oak-panelled rooms. $$
**Bailee Mae's** 209 Rightor St ☎ 870 338 8862. This convivial café and restaurant, set in the historic former Lewis Supply Building, offers a little bit of everything: coffee and egg sandwiches, ciabatta sandwiches (try the BLAT – bacon, lettuce, avocado, tomato), home-made cookies and beer and wine. $

### SHOPPING

**Bubba's Blues Corner** 105 Cherry St ☎ 870 338 3501. Blues fans can buy a thrilling assortment of records at this legendary music shop. Owner Bubba Sullivan sadly passed in 2021, but the store remains a mine of information on local music, not least the town's superb King Biscuit Blues Festival (Ⓦ kingbiscuitfestival.com), held every fall, which attracts more than 60,000 visitors for its big-name blues, acoustic and gospel.

# Little Rock

The geographical, political and financial centre of Arkansas, **LITTLE ROCK** stands at the meeting point of the state's two major regions, the northwestern hills and the eastern Delta. Site of one of the key flashpoints of the civil rights era (see box, page 131), the town today has a relaxed, open feel, and still maintains a certain cachet since the election of William J. Clinton to the presidency in 1992.

The library forms an anchor for the vibrant **River Market District**, with its splash of restaurants and bars, farmers' market and eclectic food hall. Along the Arkansas River, **Riverfront Park** runs for several blocks. A commemorative sign under the Junction Bridge marks la petite roche (little rock), for which the city is named.

### William J. Clinton Presidential Library and Museum

1200 President Clinton Ave · Mon–Sat 9am–5pm, Sun 1–5pm · Charge · Ⓦ clintonlibrary.gov

Bill and Hillary are celebrated in the dazzling **William J. Clinton Presidential Library and Museum**, an elevated, glass-and-metal building glinting above the Arkansas River east of downtown. Spearheading the revitalization of a once-depressed district of abandoned warehouses, the environmentally friendly structure forms part of a campus of federally certified "green" buildings.

**1**

### Old State House Museum

300 W Markham St • Mon–Sat 9am–5pm, Sun 1–5pm • Free • ⓦ oldstatehouse.com

Surrounded by smooth lawns and shaded by evergreens, the **Old State House Museum**, in the former Capitol building, backs onto the river. The displays – everything from Civil War battle flags to African American quilts – do an admirable job of covering Arkansas history.

### Historic Arkansas Museum

200 E 3rd St • Mon–Sat 9am–5pm, Sun 1–5pm • Charge • ⓦ historicarkansas.org

The **Historic Arkansas Museum**, a living museum of frontier life, includes the 1827 Hinderliter Grog Shop, Little Rock's oldest standing building. The institute is comprised of five antebellum houses, complete with costumed actors, and a handful of galleries devoted to local art, textiles and, intriguingly, knives, including the local weapon made famous by rapscallion Jim Bowie.

### Arkansas Museum of Fine Arts

MacArthur Park, 9th and Commerce sts • Tues–Sat 10am–5pm, Sun 11am–5pm • Free • ☎ 501 372 4000, ⓦ arkarts.com

The elegant **Arkansas Museum of Fine Arts** has high-profile rotating shows, drawings dating from the Renaissance and a nice selection of contemporary crafts. It also houses a renowned children's theatre – try to catch a performance if you're travelling with kids. As this book went to press, it was about to return to its newly rebuilt premises in MacArthur Park; check online before you visit.

#### ARRIVAL AND INFORMATION LITTLE ROCK

**By bus** Greyhound (☎ 501 372 3007) arrives at 118 E Washington Ave in North Little Rock, across the river. There are two daily services to Hot Springs, AR (1hr).
**By train** Amtrak is at Markham and Victory sts.

**Visitor centre** 615 E Capitol Ave (Mon–Sat 9am–5pm, Sun 1–5pm; ☎ 501 371 0076, ⓦ littlerock.com).
**Listings** For listings, check the free weekly *Arkansas Times* (ⓦ arktimes.com).

#### ACCOMMODATION, EATING AND DRINKING

**Capital Hotel** 111 W Markham St ⓦ capitalhotel.com. A grand pillared lobby gives way to elegant, cool-toned rooms at this historic, central hotel. Plus, there's an array of dining and drinking options, including *One Eleven*, with hearty American cuisine, from steaks to lobster. $\overline{\underline{\$\$\$}}$
**Comfort Inn & Suites Presidential** 707 I-30, near the Clinton Library ⓦ choicehotels.com. Good, centrally located budget option with large modern rooms, a swimming pool, complimentary airport shuttle and a hearty free breakfast. $\overline{\underline{\$\$}}$
**Doe's Eat Place** 1023 W Markham St ⓦ doeseatplacelr. com. This unpretentious landmark serves excellent steak and tamales; it's a long-time favourite of Clinton and still a hot spot for hungry politicos. $\overline{\underline{\$\$}}$
**The Empress of Little Rock** 2120 S Louisiana St ⓦ theempress.com. This lovely inn, in the Governor's Mansion Historic District, lives up to its regal name. Step into a charming Victorian world with cosy rooms that invite curling up on the four-poster bed or around the fire. Greet

the morning with a hearty breakfast served in the elegant dining room. $\overline{\underline{\$\$\$}}$
**River Market** 400 President Clinton Ave ⓦ rivermarket. info. The bustling market hall food court provides a wealth of places to eat, with stalls dishing up organic soups, Middle Eastern salads, barbecue, pad Thai, pizza, burgers, artisan breads and coffee. $\overline{\underline{\$}}$
**Rosemont B&B** 515 W 15th St ⓦ rosemontoflittlerock. com. Bill Clinton was a regular visitor at this luxurious, powder-pink inn with sophisticated guest quarters, breakfasts made from locally sourced ingredients, a relaxing veranda and a manicured garden good for coffee and a paper. $\overline{\underline{\$\$}}$
**Tap Room at Lost 40 Brewing** 501 Byrd St ⓦ lost40brewing.com. This high-ceilinged, boisterous tap room flows freely with the namesake local craft beer, named after Lost 40, a tract of forty acres of untouched forest in Calhoun Country. Settle in at one of the communal tables and enjoy big, bold platters of beer-friendly grub, like smoked kielbasa sausages and pepper brisket. $\overline{\underline{\$\$}}$

# Hot Springs

Fifty miles southwest of Little Rock, the low-key, historic and somewhat surreal spa town of **HOT SPRINGS** nestles in the forested Zig Zag Mountains on the eastern flank of the Ouachitas. Its **thermal waters** have attracted visitors since Native Americans used the area as a neutral zone to mediate disputes. Early settlers fashioned a crude resort out of the wilderness, and after the railroads arrived in 1875 it became a European-style spa; its hot waters are said to cure rheumatism, arthritis, kidney disease and liver problems. The resort reached its glittering heyday during the Twenties and Thirties, when the mayor reputedly ran a gambling syndicate worth $30 million per annum, and players included Al Capone and Bugsy Siegel. Movie stars and politicians, aristocrats and prizefighters flocked, and Hot Springs became *the* place to see and be seen. The resort's popularity waned when new cures appeared during the Fifties; today its faded grandeur and small-town sleepiness give it a distinctive appeal.

Quite apart from its waters, Hot Springs prides itself on its small **galleries**, plenty of which line Central Avenue, along with some wonderfully weird Americana. The town hosts a prestigious documentary **film festival** each October (⦵hsdfi.org), and a well-known **classical music festival** in June (⦵hotmusicfestival.com).

Fordyce Bathhouse

369 Central Ave • Feb–Dec daily 9am–5pm • Free • ⦵nps.gov/hosp

Eight magnificent buildings behind a lush display of magnolia trees, elms and hedgerows make up the splendid **Bathhouse Row**. Between 1915 and 1962, the grandest of them all was the **Fordyce Bathhouse**, which reopened in 1989 as the visitor

## CONFRONTATION AT CENTRAL HIGH

In 1957, Little Rock unexpectedly became the battleground in the first major conflict between state and federal government over **race relations**. At the time, the city was generally viewed as progressive by Southern standards. All parks, libraries and buses were integrated, a relatively high thirty percent of blacks were on the electoral register and there were black police officers. However, when the Little Rock School Board announced its decision to phase in **desegregation** gradually – the Supreme Court having declared segregation of schools to be unconstitutional – James Johnson, a candidate for governor, started a campaign opposing interracial education. Johnson's rhetoric began to win him support, and the incumbent governor, **Orval Faubus**, who had previously shown no interest in the issue, jumped on the bandwagon.

The first nine black students were due to enter **Central High School** that September. The day before school opened, Faubus, "in the interest of safety", reversed his decision to let blacks enrol, only to be overruled by the federal court. He ordered the National Guard to bar the black students anyway; soldiers with bayonets forced Elizabeth Eckford, one of the nine, from the school entrance into a seething crowd, from which she had to jump on a bus to escape. As legal battles raged during the day, at night blacks were subject to violent attacks by white gangs. Three weeks later, President Eisenhower reluctantly brought in the 101st Airborne Division, and, amid violent demonstrations, the nine entered the school. That year, they experienced intense intimidation; when one retaliated, she was expelled. The graduation of Ernest Green, the oldest, seemed to put an end to the affair, but Faubus, up for re-election, renewed his political posturing by closing down all Little Rock's public schools for the 1958–59 academic year – and thereby increased his majority. Today Central High School – an enormous brown, crescent-shaped structure at 1500 S Park Ave – is on the National Register of Historic Places and has been designated a National Park site. Across the street, at 2120 W Daisy L. Gatson Bates Drive, the **Central High Visitor Centre** (daily 9am–4.30pm; free; ⦵nps.gov/chsc), on the spot from which reporters filed stories on the only public payphone in the neighbourhood, has a good exhibition about the crisis.

1

centre for **Hot Springs National Park**. The interior, restored to its former radiance, is an atmospheric mixture of the elegant and the obsolete. The heavy use of veined Italian marble, mosaic-tile floors and stained glass lend it a decadent feel, while the gruesome hydrotherapy and electrotherapy equipment, including an electric shock massager, seem impossibly brutish.

Behind the Fordyce, two small **springs** have been left open for viewing. The **Grand Promenade** from here is a half-mile brick walkway overlooking downtown.

## Buckstaff Bathhouse

509 Central Ave • March–Nov Mon–Sat 8am–11.45am & 1.30–3pm; Dec–Feb closed Sat afternoon • charge • ⓦ www.buckstaffbaths.com

It's still possible to take a "**bath**" – an hour-long process involving brisk rubdowns, hot packs, a thorough steaming and a needle shower – on Bathhouse Row. The only establishment that remains open for business is the 1912 **Buckstaff**, where a thermal mineral bath in a municipal, rather prosaic, atmosphere costs from around $40. Hot Springs' water lacks the sulphuric taste often associated with thermal springs; fill a bottle at any of the drinking fountains near Central Avenue. Most of them pump out warm water – if you prefer it cold, head for the Happy Hollow Spring on Fountain Street.

## Ozark Bathhouse Cultural Center

491 Central Ave • Fri–Sun noon–5pm • Free • ⓦ nps.gov/hosp

The handsome **Ozark Bathhouse** was built in 1922, designed in the Spanish Colonial Revival style by Little Rock architects Mann and Stern. Despite the striking exterior, inside it was a no-frills bathhouse, appealing to those looking for an economic soak. It closed in the late 1970s and, after lying dormant for several decades, reopened in 2014 as a cultural centre, hosting events and other activities.

## Hot Springs Mountain

Trails of various lengths and severity lead up the steep slopes of **Hot Springs Mountain**. To reach the summit, take a short drive or any of several different trails, including a testing two-and-a-half-mile hike through dense woods of oak, hickory and short-leafed pine.

### ARRIVAL AND INFORMATION                                                      HOT SPRINGS

**By bus** Greyhound (☏ 501 623 5574) pulls in at 100 Broadway Terrace.

**National Park Service visitor centre** Located in Fordyce Bathhouse (see page 131).

### ACCOMMODATION, EATING AND DRINKING

**Arlington Resort/Spa** 239 Central Ave ☏ 501 623 7771, ⓦ arlingtonhotel.com. Dominating the centre, this 1920s landmark oozes faded grandeur – Al Capone rented the entire fourth floor and President Clinton attended his junior and senior proms in the ballroom. $\overline{\underline{\$\$}}$

**Gold-Inn Hot Springs** 741 Park Ave (Hwy-7) ⓦ gold-inn.webflow.io. Formerly Alpine Motel, this boutique motor lodge is a mile or so from Bathhouse Row, and offers colourful, bright rooms. $\overline{\underline{\$\$}}$

**Gulpha Gorge Campground** 305 Gorge Rd (Hwy-70B) ⓦ nps.gov/hosp. The nearest place to camp is the first-come, first-served spot in the national park, 2 miles northeast of town. $\overline{\underline{\$}}$

**McClard's Bar-B-Q** 505 Albert Pike, 3 miles south of downtown ⓦ mcclards.com. Famed barbecue joint where the mouth-watering ribs, slaw, beans and tamales are all prepared by hand; it's so good that Bill and Hillary stopped

by on their wedding day. $\overline{\underline{\$\$}}$

**Rolando's** 210 Central Ave ⓦ rolandosrestaurante. com. Hidden among the family restaurants along Central Ave, this festive *Nuevo Latino* place serves up tasty, creative food such as shrimp sautéed in a citrusy tequila sauce and topped with sweet peppers and onions, and tacos stuffed with tilapia. $\overline{\underline{\$\$}}$

**Superior Bathhouse Brewery and Distillery** 329 Central Ave ☏ 501 624 2337, ⓦ superiorbathhouse. com. A brewery in a bathhouse? Yes, Hot Springs' first craft brewery and tasting room is in the historic Superior Bathhouse. A terrific variety of beers are matched with excellent, locally sourced small and big plates, including creamy beer cheese with tortilla chips, roast beet salad with feta cheese and mandarin orange, and a unique desert of pretzel bread pudding with beer caramel. $\overline{\underline{\$\$}}$

# The Ozark Mountains

Although the highest peak fails to top 2000ft, the **Ozark Mountains**, extending beyond northern Arkansas into southern Missouri, are characterized by severe steep ridges and jagged spurs. Hair-raising roads weave their way over the precipitous hills, past rugged lakeshores and pristine rivers. When speculators poured into Arkansas in the 1830s, those who missed the best land etched out remote hill farms, much like those they'd left behind in Kentucky or Tennessee, and lived in isolation until the second half of the twentieth century. A massive tourism boom, while bringing much-needed cash, also created a string of cookie-cutter American towns; the Ozarks are now the fastest-growing rural section of the USA.

The word "Ozark" is everywhere, used to entice tourists into music shows, gift emporia and fast-food restaurants. With all the hype, it's difficult to tell what's genuine – a good reason to visit **Mountain View**, where traditional Ozark skills and music are preserved. The region's most visited town, **Eureka Springs**, just south of the Missouri border, is a pretty Victorian spa resort with a rootsy, bohemian scene. Note that the Lake of the Ozarks, made famous by the *Ozark* TV series, is another 150 miles north, in Missouri.

## Mountain View

Roughly sixty miles north of Little Rock, the state-run **Ozark Folk Centre**, two miles north of the town of **MOUNTAIN VIEW** on Hwy-14, is a good living history museum that attempts to show how life used to be in these remote hills, not reached by paved roads until the Fifties. Homestead skills are displayed in reconstructed log cabins, and folk musicians and storytellers perform throughout. In the evenings you can see Ozark and roots music **concerts** (early April to end Nov Tues–Sat 10am–5pm; charge; ⓦozarkfolkcenter.com).

### ACCOMMODATION AND EATING      MOUNTAIN VIEW

**Buffalo Camping** 1 Frost St, Gilbert ☎870 439 2888, ⓦgilbertstore.com. Near Pruitt Landing, this outfit administers a few log cabins, all of which sleep at least two and up to ten. $$

**Inn at Mountain View** 307 W Washington St ☎870 269 4200. This friendly inn is a pretty B&B owned by folk musicians; they serve a full country break-fast (minimum stay required at weekends and festivals). $$

**Ozark Folk Center** 1032 Park Ave, Mountain View ⓦozarkfolkcenter.com. The Folk Center offers quiet, comfortable cabins year-round. $$

**Tommy's Famous** W Main St (Hwy-66) and Famous Place ☎870 269 3278. Funky little place four blocks west of the town square that dishes up good pizza), ribs and barbecue. Note that Mountain View is a dry town. $$

## Eureka Springs

Picturesque **EUREKA SPRINGS**, set on steep mountain slopes in Arkansas' northwestern corner, began life in the nineteenth century as a health resort. As that role diminished, its striking location turned it into a tourist destination, filled with Victorian buildings and streets linked by flights of stone stairs. Today it's a cool, progressive spot, with kitsch outdoor movie events, diversity weekends, and plenty of places offering alternative therapies.

---

### ACTIVITIES IN THE OZARK MOUNTAINS

In the **Ozark National Forest**, fifteen miles northwest of Mountain View off Hwy-14, you can tour the **Blanchard Springs Caverns** (times vary; charge; ⓦblanchardsprings.org), an eerily beautiful underground cave system with a crystal-clear swimming hole surrounded by towering rock bluffs. The **Buffalo River** – a prime destination for whitewater canoeing – flows across the state north of Mountain View. In the sweet little settlement of Gilbert, off Hwy-65 at the end of Hwy-333 E, **Buffalo Camping and Canoeing** (ⓦgilbertstore.com) rents canoes for trips on the mid-section of the river, at its most spectacular around **Pruitt Landing**.

**1**

Great Passion Play

935 Passion Play Rd • April–Oct • charge • 800 882 7529, ⓦ greatpassionplay.org

Three miles east of town on US-62 E, a seven-storey **Christ of the Ozarks** – a statue of Jesus with a 60ft arm span – sets the tone for a jaw-dropping religious complex known as the **Great Passion Play**, the brainchild of Elna M. Smith, who, worried that the holy sites of the Middle East would be destroyed by war, decided to build replicas in the Ozarks. The play itself, first staged in 1968, re-enacts Christ's last days on earth with a cast of 250, including live animals, in a 4100-seat amphitheatre.

## INFORMATION AND TOURS                                    EUREKA SPRINGS

**Visitor centre** Village Circle (daily 9am–5pm; ☎ 800 638 7352, ⓦ eurekasprings.org).

**Train tours** Take a ride on the Eureka Springs and North Arkansas Railway, whose rolling stock includes a magnificent "cabbage-head" wood-burning locomotive; trips depart from the depot at 299 N Main St (April–Oct Tues–Fri 10.30am, noon & 2.30pm, Sat also 4pm; $17; ⓦ esnarailway.com).

## ACCOMMODATION, EATING AND NIGHTLIFE

Eureka Springs has lots of appealing places to stay; log cabins and B&Bs abound, many with staggering views. The town holds the fine Ozark Mountain Music Festival in January (ⓦ ozarkmountainmusicfestival.com), and an acclaimed blues festival in June (ⓦ eurekaspringsblues.com).

**Chelsea's Corner** 10 Mountain ⓦ chelseascafeeureka. com. This friendly local institution features live music most evenings. The homely no-frills grub is perfect for soaking up beer, including a wide range of pizzas, topped with everything from Thai chicken to hummus and green olives, and juicy burgers. $\overline{\underline{\$\$}}$

**Local Flavor Café** 71 S Main St ⓦ localflavorcafe.net. Dishes up tasty modern American cuisine, such as pear salad topped with pine nuts and parmesan cheese, and pan-seared tilapia in a roasted red-pepper cream sauce, and has lovely balcony seating. $\overline{\underline{\$\$}}$

**Mud Street Café** 22 S Main St ⓦ mudstreetcafe.com. This artsy café serves good espresso, hearty breakfast and lunches, from fat omelettes to juicy burgers, and desserts. $\overline{\underline{\$\$}}$

**Sherwood Court** 248 W Van Buren ⓦ sherwoodcourt. com. This charming and very welcoming inn offers individually decorated cottages and motel-style rooms around flower-filled courtyards. $\overline{\underline{\$\$}}$

★ **Treehouse Cottages** 165 W Van Buren ⓦ treehousecottages.com. At this unique place, you can hide away in one of seven luxury cabins on stilts, set deep in the forest. $\overline{\underline{\$\$\$}}$

NATIONAL CENTER FOR CIVIL AND HUMAN RIGHTS, GA

# Contexts

# History

There is much more to the history of North America than the history of the United States alone, and the history of the region covered in this book is shorter again. In these few pages, however, there's little room to do more than survey the peopling and political development of the eight states that now constitute the southern USA.

## First peoples

The true pioneers of North America, nomadic hunter-gatherers from Siberia, are thought to have reached what's now **Alaska** around seventeen thousand years ago. Thanks to the last ice age, when sea levels were 300ft lower, a "**land-bridge**" – actually a vast plain, measuring six hundred miles north to south – connected Eurasia to America.

Alaska was at that time separated by glacier fields from what is now Canada, and thus effectively part of Asia rather than North America. Like an air lock, the region has "opened" in different directions at different times; migrants reaching it from the west, unaware that they were leaving Asia, would at first have found their way blocked to the east. Several generations might pass, and the connection back towards Asia be severed, before an eastward passage appeared. When thawing ice did clear a route into North America, it was not along the Pacific coast but via a corridor that led east of the Rockies and out onto the Great Plains.

This migration may well have been spurred by the pursuit of large mammal species, and especially **mammoth**, which had already been harried to extinction throughout almost all of Eurasia. A huge bonanza awaited the hunters when they finally encountered America's own indigenous "**megafauna**", such as mammoths, mastodons, giant ground sloths and enormous long-horned bison, all of which had evolved with no protection against human predation.

### Filling the New World

Within a thousand years, ten million people were living throughout both North and South America. Although that sounds like a phenomenally rapid spread, it would only have required a band of just one hundred individuals to enter the continent, and advance a mere eight miles per year, with an annual population growth of 1.1 percent, to achieve that impact. The mass **extinction** of the American megafauna was so precisely simultaneous that humans are widely thought to have been responsible, eliminating the giant beasts in each locality in one fell swoop, before pressing on in search of the next kill.

The elimination of large land mammals precluded future American civilizations from domesticating any of the animal species that were crucial to Old World economies. Without cattle, horses, sheep or goats, or significant equivalents, they lacked the resources to supply food and clothing to large settlements, provide draught power to haul ploughs or wheeled vehicles, or increase mobility and the potential for conquest.

| **c.60 million BC** | **15,000 BC** | **900 AD** |
| --- | --- | --- |
| Two mighty islands collide, creating North America as a single landmass, and throwing up the Rocky Mountains | First nomadic peoples from Asia reach Alaska | Mississippian settlements – city-like conglomerations of earthen mounds – appear throughout the Southeast |

What's more, most of the human diseases that were later introduced from the rest of the world had originally evolved in association with domesticated animals; the first Americans developed neither immunity to such diseases, nor any indigenous diseases of their own that might have attacked the invaders.

### Early settlements

The earliest known settlement site in the modern United States, dating back 12,000 years, has been uncovered at Meadowcroft in southwest Pennsylvania. Nowhere did a civilization emerge to rival the wealth and sophistication of the great cities of ancient Mexico. However, the influence of those far-off cultures did filter north; the cultivation of crops such as beans, squash and maize facilitated the development of large communities, while northern religious cults, some of which performed human sacrifice, owed much to Central American beliefs. The **Moundbuilders** of the **Ohio** and **Mississippi** valleys developed sites ranging from the Great Serpent Mound in modern Ohio to Poverty Point in Louisiana. The most prominent of these early societies, now known as the **Hopewell** culture, flourished during the first four centuries AD. The best-known site settled by such peoples within the area covered by this book is now preserved as the Ocmulgee National Monument, near Macon, Georgia – see page 80 – where Mississippian migrants are thought to have replaced the existing Woodland culture from around 900 AD onwards. Slightly later, **Cahokia**, just outside present-day St Louis, grew to become the largest pre-Columbian city in North America, centred on a huge temple-topped mound, and peaking between 1050 and 1250 AD.

Estimates of the total indigenous population before the arrival of the Europeans vary widely, but an acceptable median figure suggests around fifty million people in the Americas as a whole. Perhaps five million of those were in North America, speaking around four hundred different languages.

## European contacts

The greatest seafarers of early medieval Europe, the **Vikings**, established a colony in Greenland around 982 AD. Under the energetic leadership of Eirik the Red, this became a base for voyages along the mysterious coastline to the west. **Leif Eiriksson** – also known as Leif the Lucky – spent the winter of 1001–02 at a site that has been identified with L'Anse aux Meadows in northern Newfoundland. Climatic conditions may well have been much better than today, though it remains unclear what "grapes" led him to call it **Vinland**. Expeditions returned over the next dozen years, and may have ventured as far south as Maine. However, repeated clashes with the people the Vikings knew as **Skraelings** or "wretches" – probably Inuit, who were also recent newcomers – led them to abandon plans for permanent settlement.

### Early explorations

Five more centuries passed before the crucial moment of contact with the rest of the world came on October 12, 1492, when **Christopher Columbus**, sailing on behalf of the Spanish, reached the Bahamas. A mere four years later the English navigator John Cabot officially "discovered" Newfoundland, and soon British fishermen were setting up makeshift encampments in what became **New England**, to spend the winter curing their catch.

| 1539 | 1619 | 1670 |
|---|---|---|
| A Spanish expedition led by Hernando de Soto sets off across what will later become the southern states, and reaches the Mississippi | Twenty African slaves arrive in Virginia on a Dutch ship | British planters from the West Indies found what soon becomes the major slave-trading port of the South, Charleston |

Over the next few years various expeditions mapped the eastern seaboard. In 1524, the Italian **Giovanni da Verrazano** sailed past Maine, which he characterized as the "Land of Bad People" thanks to the inhospitable and contemptuous behaviour of its natives, and reached the mouth of the Hudson River. Further south, the Spaniards started to nose their way up from the Caribbean in 1513, when **Ponce de León**'s expedition in search of the Fountain of Youth landed at what's now Palm Beach, and named **Florida**. Following the lucrative conquest of Mexico, the Spanish returned in 1528 under Panfilo de Narvaez, who was shipwrecked somewhere in the Gulf. The first Spanish party to explore what's now the South in any depth landed in Florida in 1539. Led by **Hernando de Soto**, it followed a meandering, inland route northwards through what's now Georgia and South Carolina, and then turned southwest upon confronting the Appalachian Mountains in modern North Carolina. In Alabama they encountered a fortified town belong to a sophisticated Mississippian group, and fought a bloody pitched battle. They then reached and crossed the Mississippi River in May 1541, probably in northern Mississippi but possibly at modern Memphis, After further fruitless wandering in what are now Arkansas, Oklahoma and Texas, de Soto himself died of fever in 1542, but around half of the original 700 would-be conquistadors straggled back to Mexico.

Although no treasures were found to match the vast riches plundered from the Aztec and Inca empires, a steady stream of less spectacular discoveries – whether new foodstuffs such as potatoes, or access to the cod fisheries of the northern Atlantic – boosted economies throughout Europe. The Spanish established the first permanent settlement in the present United States when they founded **St Augustine** on the coast of Florida in 1565, only for Sir Francis Drake to burn it to the ground in 1586.

## The growth of the colonies

The sixteenth-century rivalry between the English and the Spanish extended right around the world. Freebooting English adventurers-cum-pirates contested Spanish hegemony along both coasts of North America. Sir Francis Drake staked a claim to California in 1579, five years before **Sir Walter Raleigh** claimed **Virginia** in the east, in the name of his Virgin Queen, Elizabeth I. The party of colonists that Raleigh sent out in 1585 established the short-lived settlement of **Roanoke**, now remembered as the mysterious "Lost Colony", in modern North Carolina (see page 50).

The Native Americans were seldom hostile at first encounter. To some extent the European newcomers were obliged to make friends with the locals; most had crossed the Atlantic to find religious freedom or to make their fortunes, and lacked the skills to make a success of subsistence farming. Virginia's first enduring colony, **Jamestown**, was founded by Captain John Smith on May 24, 1607. He bemoaned "though there be Fish in the Sea, and Foules in the ayre, and Beasts in the woods, their bounds are so large, they are so wilde, and we so weake and ignorant, we cannot much trouble them"; six in every seven colonists died within a year of reaching the New World.

Gradually, however, the settlers learned to cultivate the strange crops of this unfamiliar terrain. As far as the English government was concerned, the colonies were commercial ventures, to produce crops that could not be grown at home, and the colonists were not supposed to have goals of their own. Following failures with sugar

| 1733 | 1775 | 1776 |
|---|---|---|
| James Oglethorpe settles at Savannah and establishes the colony of Georgia, where he intends slavery to be illegal | The Revolutionary War begins; George Washington assumes command of the Continental Army | The Declaration of Independence is signed on July 4 |

and rice, Virginia finally found its feet with its first **tobacco** harvest in 1615 (the man responsible, John Rolfe, is better known as the husband of Pocahontas). A successful tobacco plantation requires two things in abundance: land and labour. No self-respecting Englishman came to America to work for others; when the first **slave** ship called at Jamestown in 1619, the captain found an eager market for his cargo of twenty African slaves. By that time there were already a million slaves in South America.

Between 1620 and 1642, sixty thousand migrants – 1.5 percent of the population – left England for America. Those in pursuit of economic opportunities often joined the longer-established colonies, thereby serving to dilute the religious zeal of the Puritans and other such groups. In 1629, less than ten years after the so-called "Pilgrim Fathers" reached New England aboard the *Mayflower*, English king Charles I established the Province of Carolina, covering a vast territory that extended beyond today's Carolinas into modern Georgia and Tennessee. The economy became increasingly dependent on the importation of enslaved peoples from Africa or existing British colonies in the West Indies, while Native Americans were also enslaved and exported. It was British planters from Bermuda and Barbados who first settled what became Charleston in 1670, which swiftly established as the major slave-trading port. Rice plantations, dependent on slave labour, spread through the Low Country.

North and South Carolina divided to become separate colonies early in the eighteenth century, while Georgia got its start as the 13th of the original colonies when Savannah was laid out in 1733. Early settlers proclaimed their desire to outlaw slavery, but such principles were soon abandoned.

## The American Revolution

The American colonies prospered during the **eighteenth century**, prompting the development of a wealthy, well-educated and highly articulate middle class. Frustration mounted at the inequities of the colonies' relationship with Britain, however. The Americans could only sell their produce to the British, and all transatlantic commerce had to be undertaken in British ships.

Full-scale independence was not an explicit goal until late in the century, but the main factor that made it possible was the economic impact of the pan-European **Seven Years War**. Officially, war in Europe lasted from 1756 to 1763, but fighting in North America broke out a little earlier. Beginning in 1755 with the mass expulsion of French settlers from Acadia in eastern Canada (triggering their epic migration to Louisiana, where the **Cajuns** remain to this day), the British went on to conquer all of Canada. In forcing the **surrender of Québec** in 1759, General Wolfe brought the war to a close; the French ceded Louisiana to the Spanish rather than let it fall to the British, while Florida passed briefly into British control before reverting to the Spanish. All the European monarchs were left hamstrung by debts, and the British realized that colonialism in America was not as profitable as in those parts of the world where the native populations could be coerced into working for their overseas masters.

An unsuccessful insurrection by the Ottawa in 1763, led by their chief **Pontiac**, led the cash-strapped British to conclude that, while America needed its own standing army, it was reasonable to expect the colonists to pay for it. In 1765, they introduced the **Stamp Act**, requiring duty on all legal transactions and printed matter

| 1789 | 1803 | 1831 |
| --- | --- | --- |
| George Washington is inaugurated as the first president of the United States | President Thomas Jefferson buys Louisiana west of the Mississippi for $15 million | Nat Turner leads a slave revolt in Virginia |

in the colonies to be paid to the British Crown. Arguing for "no taxation without representation", delegates from nine colonies met in the Stamp Act Congress that October. By then, however, the British prime minister responsible had already been dismissed by King George III, and the Act was repealed in 1766.

However, in 1767, Chancellor Townshend made political capital at home by proclaiming "I dare tax America", as he introduced legislation including the broadly similar Revenue Act. That led Massachusetts merchants, inspired by **Samuel Adams**, to vote to boycott English goods; they were joined by all the other colonies except New Hampshire. Townshend's Acts were repealed in turn by a new prime minister, Lord North, on March 5, 1770. By chance, on that same day a stone-throwing mob surrounded the Customs House in Boston; five people were shot in what became known as the **Boston Massacre**. Even so, most of the colonies resumed trading with Britain, and the crisis was postponed for a few more years.

In May 1773, Lord North's **Tea Act** relieved the debt-ridden East India Company of the need to pay duties on exports to America, while still requiring the Americans to pay duty on tea. Massachusetts called the colonies to action, and its citizens took the lead on December 16 in the **Boston Tea Party**, when three tea ships were boarded and 342 chests thrown into the sea.

The infuriated British Parliament thereupon began to pass legislation collectively known as both the "Coercive" and the "Intolerable" Acts, which included closing the port of Boston and disbanding the government of Massachusetts. Thomas Jefferson argued that the acts amounted to "a deliberate and systematical plan of reducing us to slavery". To discuss a response, the first **Continental Congress** was held in Philadelphia on May 5, 1774, and attended by representatives of all the colonies except Georgia.

### The Revolutionary War

War finally broke out on April 18, 1775, when General Gage, the governor of Massachusetts, dispatched four hundred British soldiers to destroy the arms depot at **Concord**, and prevent weapons from falling into rebel hands. Silversmith **Paul Revere** was dispatched on his legendary ride to warn the rebels, and the British were confronted en route at Lexington by 77 American "Minutemen". The resulting skirmish led to the "shot heard 'round the world".

Congress set about forming an army at Boston, and decided for the sake of unity to appoint a Southern commander, **George Washington**. One by one, as the war raged, the colonies set up their own governments and declared themselves to be states, and the politicians set about defining the society they wished to create. The writings of pamphleteer Thomas Paine – especially *Common Sense* – were a great influence on the **Declaration of Independence**. Drafted by Thomas Jefferson, this was adopted by the Continental Congress in Philadelphia on July 4, 1776. Anti-slavery clauses originally included by Jefferson – himself a slave-owner – were omitted to spare the feelings of the Southern states, though the section that denounced the King's dealings with "merciless Indian Savages" was left in.

At first, the Revolutionary War went well for the British. General Howe crossed the Atlantic with twenty thousand men, took New York and New Jersey, and ensconced himself in Philadelphia for the winter of 1777–78. Washington's army was encamped not far away at Valley Forge, freezing cold and all but starving to death. It soon became

| **1838** | **1860** | **1861** |
| --- | --- | --- |
| The Cherokee are forced to follow the Trail of Tears across the Mississippi | Lincoln's election as president prompts South Carolina and other Southern states to secede and form the Confederacy | The artillery bombardment of Fort Sumter in South Carolina marks the start of the Civil War |

clear, however, that the longer the Americans could avoid losing an all-out battle, the more likely the British were to over-extend their lines as they advanced through the vast and unfamiliar continent. Thus, General Burgoyne's expedition, which set out from Canada to march on New England, was so harried by rebel guerrillas that he had to surrender at Saratoga in October 1777. Other European powers took delight in coming to the aid of the Americans. Benjamin Franklin led a wildly successful delegation to France to request support, and soon the nascent American fleet was being assisted in its bid to cut British naval communications by both the French and the Spanish. The end came when Cornwallis, who had replaced Howe, was instructed to dig in at Yorktown and wait for the Royal Navy to come to his aid, only for the French to seal off Chesapeake Bay and prevent reinforcement. Cornwallis surrendered to Washington on October 17, 1781.

The ensuing **Treaty of Paris** granted the Americans their independence on generous terms – the British abandoned their Native American allies, including the Iroquois, to the vengeance of the victors – and Washington entered New York as the British left in November 1783. The Spanish were confirmed in possession of Florida.

The victorious US Congress met for the first time in 1789, and the tradition of awarding political power to the nation's most successful generals was instigated by the election of George Washington as the first **president**. He was further honoured when his name was given to the new capital city of **Washington DC**, deliberately sited between the North and the South.

## The nineteenth century

During its first century, the territories and population of the new **United States of America** expanded at a phenomenal rate. The white population of North America in 1800 stood at around five million, and there were another one million African slaves (of whom thirty thousand were in the North). Of that total, 86 percent lived within fifty miles of the Atlantic, but no US city could rival Mexico City, whose population approached 100,000 inhabitants.

It had suited the British to discourage settlers from venturing west of the Appalachians, where they would be far beyond the reach of British power. However, adventurers such as **Daniel Boone** started to cross the mountains into Tennessee and Kentucky during the 1770s. Soon makeshift rafts, made from the planks that were later assembled to make log cabins, were careering west along the Ohio River (the only westward-flowing river on the continent).

### The Louisiana Purchase

In 1801, the Spanish handed Louisiana back to the French, on condition that the French would keep it forever. However, Napoleon swiftly realized that attempting to hang on to his American possessions would spread his armies too thinly, and chose instead to sell them to the United States for $15 million, in the **Louisiana Purchase** of 1803.

British attempts to blockade the Atlantic, primarily targeted against Napoleon, gave the new nation a chance to flex its military muscles. British raiders succeeded in capturing Washington DC, and burned the White House, but the **War of 1812**

| 1862 | 1865 | 1870 |
| --- | --- | --- |
| President Lincoln's Emancipation Proclamation declares that all slaves in states or areas of states still in rebellion to be free 1865 | General Robert E. Lee of the Confederacy surrenders to Union General Ulysses Grant. Lincoln is assassinated | Senator Hiram R. Revels of Mississippi becomes the first black man to sit in Congress |

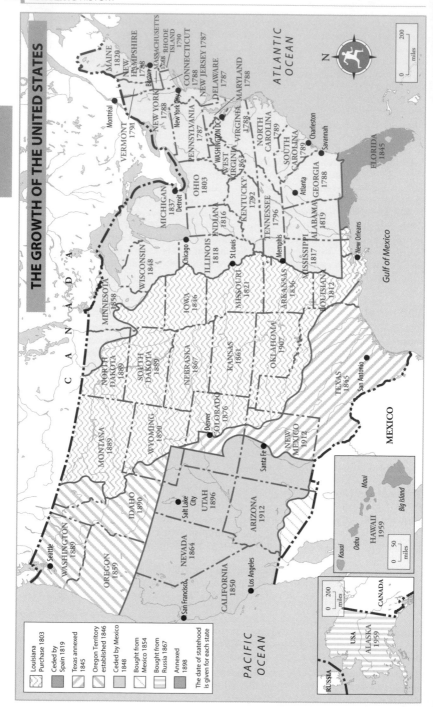

THE GROWTH OF THE UNITED STATES

provided the USA with a cover for aggression against the Native American allies of the British. Thus **Tecumseh** of the Shawnee was defeated near Detroit, and **Andrew Jackson** moved against the Creek of the southern Mississippi. Jackson's campaign against the Seminole won the USA possession of Florida from the Spanish; he was rewarded first with the governorship of the new state, and later by his election to the presidency.

## The Cherokee and the Trail of Tears

During the eighteenth and early nineteenth centuries, the Cherokee were the most powerful tribe in the tri-state region of Tennessee, Georgia, and North Carolina. They forged close links with white pioneers, adopting white methods in schooling and agriculture, intermarrying, and even owning African slaves. The only Native Americans to develop their own written alphabet, they had a regular newspaper, *The Cherokee Phoenix*. They even supplied soldiers for Andrew Jackson's US forces against the Creek Indians and the British in 1814, hoping to buy influence with the federal government.

Thirteen years later, against a background of aggressive territorial claims by settlers, the Cherokee produced a written constitution modelled on that of the US, stating their intention to continue to be a self-governing nation. John Ross, founder of Ross's Landing, and at most one-eighth Cherokee, was elected as their first Principal Chief in 1828 in an effort to appease and negotiate with national and state governments over their lands. However, as white encroachment increased, their former ally Jackson, now US president, was pressured by the Georgians into "offering" the Cherokee western lands in exchange for those they currently held east of the Mississippi. Although the tribal leadership refused, a minority faction accepted, giving the government the opportunity they required.

The Cherokee were ordered to leave within two years, and 14,000 were forcefully removed to what later became Oklahoma in 1838 along the horrific Trail of Tears: four thousand died of disease and exposure on the way. Jackson's goal as president was to clear all states east of the Mississippi of their native populations, and the Cherokee found themselves confined in the barren region known as "Indian Territory" along with the Creek and the Seminole, and the Choctaw and Chickasaw of Mississippi.

In the meantime, Cherokee land in the east was sold by lottery, and Ross's Landing was renamed Chattanooga. Descendants of the one thousand Cherokee who managed to avoid removal by escaping into the mountains now occupy a small reservation in North Carolina.

## The Civil War

From its inception, the unity of the United States had been based on shaky foundations. Great care had gone into devising a **Constitution** that balanced the need for a strong federal government with the aspirations for autonomy of its component states. That was achieved by giving Congress two separate chambers – the **House of Representatives**, in which each state was represented in proportion to its population, and the **Senate**, in which each state, regardless of size, had two members. Thus, although in theory the Constitution remained silent on the issue of **slavery**, it allayed the fears of the less populated Southern states that Northern voters might destroy their economy by forcing them to abandon their "peculiar institution".

| **1896** | **1898** |
|---|---|
| Ruling in Plessy v Ferguson, the Supreme Court creates the doctrine of "separate but equal" provision for whites and blacks | A racist mob overthrows the city government in Wilmington, North Carolina, and murders up to 300 black citizens |

However, the system only worked so long as there were equal numbers of "Free" and slave-owning states. The only practicable way to keep the balance was to ensure that each time a new state was admitted to the Union, a matching state taking the opposite stance on slavery was also admitted. Thus, the admission of every new state became subject to endless intrigue. The 1820 **Missouri Compromise**, under which Missouri joined as a slave-owning state and Maine as a Free one, was straightforward in comparison to the prevarication and chest-beating that surrounded the admission of Texas, while the Mexican War was widely seen in the North as a naked land grab for new slave states. The more the United States fulfilled its supposed "Manifest Destiny" to spread across the continent, the more new states joined the Union for which plantation agriculture, and thus slavery, was not appropriate. Southern politicians and plantation owners accused the North of political and economic aggression, and felt that they were losing all say in the future of the nation.

Abolitionist sentiment in the North was not all that great before the middle of the nineteenth century. At best, after the importation of slaves from Africa ended in 1808, Northerners vaguely hoped slavery was an anachronism that might simply wither away. As it turned out, Southern plantations were rendered much more profitable by the development of the cotton gin, invented in South Carolina, and the increased demand for manufactured cotton goods triggered by the **Industrial Revolution**. However, the rapid growth of the nation as a whole made it ever more difficult to maintain a political balance between North and South.

Matters came to a head in 1854, when the **Kansas-Nebraska Act** sparked guerrilla raids and mini-wars between rival settlers by allowing both prospective states self-determination on the issue. That same year, the **Republican Party** was founded to resist the further expansion of slavery. Escaped former slaves such as Frederick Douglass were by now spurring Northern audiences to moral outrage, and Harriet Beecher Stowe's *Uncle Tom's Cabin* found unprecedented readership.

In October 1859, **John Brown** – a white-bearded, wild-eyed veteran of Kansas's bloodiest infighting – led a dramatic raid on the US Armory at Harpers Ferry, West Virginia, intending to secure arms for a slave insurrection. Swiftly captured by forces under Robert E. Lee, he was hanged within a few weeks, proclaiming that "I am now quite certain that the crimes of this guilty land will never be purged away but with blood".

The Republican presidential candidate in 1860, the little-known **Abraham Lincoln** from Kentucky, won no Southern states, but with the Democrats split into Northern and Southern factions he was elected with 39 percent of the popular vote. Within weeks, on December 20, South Carolina became the first state to secede from the Union; the **Confederacy** was declared on February 4, 1861, when it was joined by Mississippi, Florida, Alabama, Georgia, Louisiana and Texas. Its first (and only) president was **Jefferson Davis**, also from Kentucky; his new vice president remarked at their joint inauguration that their government was "the first in the history of the world based upon the great physical and moral truth that the negro is not equal to the white man". Lincoln was inaugurated in turn in March 1861, proclaiming that "I have no purpose, directly or indirectly, to interfere with the institution of slavery in the States where it exists. I believe I have no lawful right to do so, and I have no inclination to do so". He was completely inflexible, however, on one paramount issue: the survival of the Union.

| 1903 | 1954 |
|---|---|
| In the first recorded mention of the Delta blues, orchestra leader W.C. Handy overhears an itinerant guitarist playing "the weirdest music I had ever heard" in Tutwiler, Mississippi | The Supreme Court declares racial segregation in schools to be unconstitutional. Elvis Presley records That's All Right at Sun Studios, Memphis |

## The coming of war

The **Civil War** began just a few weeks later. The first shots were fired on April 12, when a federal attempt to resupply Fort Sumter, off Charleston, South Carolina (see page 65), was greeted by a Confederate bombardment that forced its surrender. Lincoln's immediate call to raise an army against the South was greeted by the further secession of Virginia, Arkansas, Tennessee and North Carolina. Within a year, both armies had amassed 600,000 men. Robert E. Lee was offered command of both and opted for the Confederacy, while George McLellan became the first leader of the Union forces. Although the rival capitals of Washington DC, and Richmond, Virginia, were a mere one hundred miles apart, over the next four years operations reached almost everywhere south of Washington and east of the Mississippi.

Tracing the ebb and flow of the military campaigns – from the early Confederate victories, via Grant's successful siege of Vicksburg in 1863 and Sherman's devastating March to the Sea in 1864, to Lee's eventual surrender at Appomattox in April 1865 – it's easy to forget that it was not so much generalship as sheer economic (and man-) power that won the war. The **Union** of 23 Northern states, holding more than 22 million people, wore down the **Confederacy** of eleven Southern states, with nine million. As for potential combatants, the North initially drew upon 3.5 million white males aged between 18 and 45 – and later recruited black males as well – whereas the South had more like one million. In the end, around 2.1 million men fought for the Union, and 900,000 for the Confederacy. Of the 620,000 soldiers who died, a disproportionate 258,000 came from the South – one quarter of its white men of military age. Meanwhile, not only did the North continue trading with the rest of the world while maintaining its industrial and agricultural output, it also stifled the Confederacy with a devastating **naval blockade**. The Southern war effort was primarily financed by printing $1.5 billion of paper currency, which was so eroded by inflation that it became worthless.

Even so, the Confederacy came much closer to victory than is usually appreciated. The repeated out-manoeuvring of federal forces by General **Robert E. Lee**, and his incursions into Union territory, meant that in each of three successive years, from 1862 to 1864, there was a genuine possibility that Northern morale would collapse, allowing opponents of the war to be elected to power and agree to peace. After all, the Revolutionary War had shown how such a war could be won: for the Union to triumph, it had to invade and occupy the South, and destroy its armies, but for the South to win it had only to survive until the North wearied of the struggle.

The dashing tactics of Confederate generals Lee and Jackson, forever counter-attacking and carrying the fight to the enemy, arguably contributed to the Southern defeat. The grim, relentless total-war campaigning of Grant and Sherman eventually ground the South down. Ironically, had the Confederacy sued for peace before Lee gave it fresh hope, a negotiated settlement might not have included the abolition of slavery. In the event, as the war went on, with Southern slaves flocking to the Union flag and black soldiers fighting on the front line, emancipation did indeed become inevitable. Lincoln took the political decision to match his moral conviction by issuing his **Emancipation Proclamation** in 1862, though the **Thirteenth Amendment** outlawing slavery only took effect in 1865.

| 1955 | 1963 | 1968 |
|---|---|---|
| Black seamstress Rosa Parks refuses to change her seat on a bus in Montgomery, Alabama, and spurs a citywide bus boycott | Martin Luther King, Jr. delivers "I Have a Dream" speech; President Kennedy is assassinated | The nation is polarized by war in Vietnam; Martin Luther King, Jr. is assassinated |

## Reconstruction

The war left the South in chaos. A quarter of the South's adult white male population had been killed, and two-thirds of Southern wealth destroyed. From controlling thirty percent of the nation's assets in 1860, the South was down to twelve percent in 1870, while the spur the war gave to industrialization meant that the North was booming. Lincoln himself was assassinated within a few days of the end of the conflict, a mark of the deep bitterness that would almost certainly have precluded successful **Reconstruction** even if he had lived.

For a brief period, when the South was occupied by Union troops, newly freed Southern blacks were able to vote, and black representatives were elected to both state and federal office. However, unrepentant former Confederates, spurred in part by allegations of profiteering by incoming Northern Republican "carpetbaggers", thwarted any potential for change, and by the end of the century the Southern states were firmly back under white Democratic control. As Reconstruction withered away, "**Jim Crow**" segregation laws were imposed, backed by the not-so-secret terror of the **Ku Klux Klan**, and poll taxes, literacy tests and property qualifications disenfranchised virtually all blacks. Many found themselves little better off as **sharecroppers** – in which virtually all they could earn from raising crops went to pay their landlords – than they had been when enslaved, and duly left the plantations to build new lives in growing cities like Memphis and Atlanta.

The aftermath of the Civil War can almost be said to have lasted for a hundred years. While the South condemned itself to a century as a backwater, the rest of the re-United States embarked on a period of expansionism and prosperity.

## The Twentieth Century

Following the failure of Reconstruction, racial oppression and segregation became entrenched throughout the South, perpetuating massive economic inequalities. Denied the right to vote in the ballet box, the region's African-American population voted instead with its feet. Between 1916 and 1970, in what became known as the **Great Migration**, more than six million African Americans left the South to make their homes in the urban centres of the North and West.

### The Depression and the New Deal

By the middle of the 1920s, the USA was an industrial powerhouse, responsible for more than half the world's output of manufactured goods. Having led the way into a new era of prosperity, however, it suddenly dragged the rest of the world down into economic collapse. The consequences of the **Great Depression** were out of all proportion to any one specific cause. Within three years of the calamitous **Wall Street Crash** of October 1929, industrial production was cut by half, the national income dropped by 38 percent, and, above all, unemployment rose from 1.5 million to 13 million.

Matters only began to improve in 1932, when the patrician **Franklin Delano Roosevelt** accepted the Democratic nomination for president with the words "I pledge myself to a new deal for America", and went on to win a landslide victory. At the time of his inauguration, early in 1933, the banking system had all but closed down; it took

| **1976** | **1992** | **1996** |
|---|---|---|
| Former Georgia governor Jimmy Carter, a Democrat, is elected president in the wake of the Watergate scandal | Alabama governor Bill Clinton is elected president | Atlanta hosts the Olympic Games |

Roosevelt the now-proverbial "Hundred Days" of vigorous legislation to turn around the mood of the country.

The ensuing **New Deal** took many forms, but was marked throughout by a massive growth in the power of the federal government. Among its accomplishments were the National Recovery Administration, which created two million jobs; the Social Security Act, of which Roosevelt declared "no damn politician can ever scrap my social security program"; and the Public Works Administration, which built dams and highways the length and breadth of the country. Its impact was especially large in the South, and nowhere more so than in rural Tennessee. The creation in 1933 of the Tennessee Valley Authority, which generated electricity under public ownership for the common good, arguably marks the closest the USA has ever come to institutionalized socialism.

## The civil rights years

Not until the landmark 1954 Supreme Court ruling in **Brown vs Topeka Board of Education** outlawed segregation in schools was there any sign that the federal authorities in Washington might concern themselves with inequities in the South. Just as a century before, however, the Southern states saw the issue more in terms of states' rights than of human rights, and attempting to implement the law, or even to challenge the failure to implement it, required immense courage. In the face of institutionalized white resistance, nonviolent black protestors coalesced to form the **Civil Rights movement**, and broke down segregation through a sustained programme of mass action. Rosa Parks' refusal to give up her seat on a bus in Montgomery, Alabama, in 1955, triggered a successful mass boycott (see page 119), and pushed the 27-year-old **Rev Dr Martin Luther King, Jr.** to the forefront of the civil rights campaign. Further confrontation took place at the Central High School in Little Rock, Arkansas, in 1957 (see page 131), when the reluctant Eisenhower had to call in federal troops to counter the state's unwillingness to integrate its education system.

The election of **John F. Kennedy** to the presidency in 1960, by the narrowest of margins, marked a sea-change in American politics, even if in retrospect his policies do not seem exactly radical. Although a much-publicized call to the wife of Rev Martin Luther King, Jr. during one of King's many sojourns in Southern jails was a factor in his election success, Kennedy was rarely identified himself with the **civil rights** movement. The campaign nonetheless made headway, lent momentum by television coverage of such horrific confrontations as the onslaught by Birmingham police on peaceful demonstrators in 1963. The movement's defining moment came when Rev King delivered his electrifying "I Have a Dream" speech later that summer. King was subsequently awarded the Nobel Peace Prize for his unwavering espousal of Gandhian principles of nonviolence. Perhaps an equally powerful factor in middle America's recognition that the time had come to address racial inequalities, however, was the not-so-implicit threat in the rhetoric of **Malcolm X**, who argued that black people had the right to defend themselves against aggression.

After Kennedy's assassination in November 1963, his successor, **Lyndon B. Johnson**, pushed through legislation that enacted most of the civil rights campaigners' key demands. Even then, violent white resistance in the South continued, and only the long, painstaking and dangerous work of registering Southern black voters en masse eventually forced Southern politicians to mend their ways.

| **2005** | **2008** | **2016** |
|---|---|---|
| Hurricane Katrina slams into the Gulf Coast, devastating southern areas of Mississippi and Alabama, as well as New Orleans | Barack Obama wins election as the first black president | To worldwide astonishment, Donald Trump is elected 45th president of the United States |

Johnson won election by a landslide in 1964, but his vision of a "**Great Society**" soon foundered. Dr King's long-standing message that social justice could only be achieved through economic equality was given a new urgency by riots in the ghettoes of Los Angeles in 1965 and Detroit in 1967, and the emergence of the Black Panthers, an armed defence force in the tradition of the now-dead Malcolm X. King also began to denounce the Vietnam War. In 1968, the social fabric of the USA reached the brink of collapse. Shortly after Johnson was forced by his plummeting popularity to withdraw from the year-end elections, Martin Luther King was gunned down in a Memphis motel.

## The New South

Although the Civil Rights movement achieved unquestionable advances, above all in enfranchising black voters and thereby transforming future elections, it would be foolish to assume that all the white citizens of the South simply saw the error of their ways and abandoned their former racist attitudes. As the recent Black Lives Matter have shown, the struggle for civil rights is not yet over.

For the century since the Civil War, the Democrats had been the dominant political force in the South, albeit often in a form that was barely compatible with the Democratic Party elsewhere in the country. On the night he signed the Civil Rights Act, in 1964, President Johnson remarked to an aide that "I think we just delivered the South to the Republican party for a long time to come". That shift did indeed occur. While ever more cities have elected black mayors and transformed urban governments, conservative rural voters have ensured the states as a whole have remained largely in the Republican camp. As of 2022, all but two of the eight states covered in this book – Kentucky and North Carolina – had Republican governors.

There's been talk of the emergence of a "New South" ever since the Civil War, but the term acquired renewed currency during the 1970s. Southern Democratic politicians like Georgia's Jimmy Carter, elected to the presidency in 1976, seemed to herald a changing profile for the South, and a significant number of African Americans have "returned" – or at least migrated to their parents' former home states – to re-shape the Southern world. The decline of the industrial heartlands of the North – around Detroit, Chicago and Indiana for example – have played a role in such moves too, but either way, the South is no longer stuck in the past. One conspicuous symbol of such changes – literally – has been the slow but inexorable disappearance of Confederate monuments, while Mississippi became the final state to remove the Confederate battle flag from its own state flag in 2020.

The biggest success story has been Atlanta, which has boomed to the point that it now holds what's often said to be the world's busiest airport, as well as hosting the Olympics and becoming a major centre for TV and movie production, but similar stories can be told throughout the South, including for example the high-tech "Research Triangle" around Raleigh, North Carolina.

| **2020** | **2022** |
| --- | --- |
| The global Covid-19 crisis hits the US hard; Trump is ousted as president by Joe Biden. Mississippi removes the Confederate battle flag from its state flag, the last state to do so | With increased Covid-19 vaccination rates restrictions are eased and tourism returns |

# Books

Space not permitting a comprehensive overview of the literature of the South, the following list is simply an idiosyncratic selection of books that may appeal to interested readers. Those tagged with the ★ symbol are particularly recommended.

## HISTORY AND SOCIETY

★ **W.E.B. DuBois** *The Souls of Black Folk*. Seminal collection of largely autobiographical essays examining racial separation at the start of the twentieth century.

**John Ehle** *Trail of Tears: The Rise and Fall of the Cherokee Nation*. A gut-wrenching account of the systematic dispossession of the Cherokee people.

**Brian Fagan** *Ancient North America*. Archaeological history of America's native peoples, from the first hunters to cross the Bering Strait up to initial contact with Europeans.

**Tim Flannery** *The Eternal Frontier*. "Ecological" history of North America that reveals how the continent's physical environment has shaped the destinies of all its inhabitants, from horses to humans.

**Shelby Foote** *The Civil War: A Narrative*. Epic, three-volume account containing anything you could possibly want to know about the "War Between the States".

**Eugene D. Genovese** *Roll, Jordan, Roll: The World The Slaves Made*. The classic study of what it actually meant to live under slavery, for both the enslaved and the slave masters.

**Doris Kearns Goodwin** *Team of Rivals*. This detailed story of how Abraham Lincoln marshalled the talents of his unruly cabinet to win the Civil War makes it abundantly clear why he's regarded as the greatest of all US presidents.

**James M. McPherson** *Battle Cry of Freedom*. Extremely readable history of the Civil War, which integrates and explains the complex social, economic, political and military factors in one concise volume.

**Lee Miller** *Roanoke: Solving The Mystery of England's Lost Colony*. A painstaking investigation of the enigmatic fate of Raleigh's failed colony.

**Edmund Morgan** *American Slavery, American Freedom*. Complex and far-reaching historical account of the cunning means by which white working-class conflict was averted by rich Virginia planters through the spread of black slavery.

**David Reynolds** *Waking Giant: America in the Age of Jackson*. Rousing portrait of America in the first half of the nineteenth century, from its clumsy attempt to take Canada in the War of 1812 to its successful Mexican land grab three decades later, with the figure of Andrew Jackson providing the touchstone throughout.

★ **Alan Taylor** *American Colonies*. Perhaps the best book on any single era of American history – a superb account of every aspect of the peopling of the continent, from remote antiquity until the Declaration of Independence.

**Larry E. Tise and Jeffrey J. Crow (eds)** *New Voyages to Carolina*. A fascinating anthology of essays exploring the history of North Carolina from every conceivable angle.

★ **Mark Twain** *Life on the Mississippi* and many others. Mark Twain was by far the funniest and most vivid chronicler of nineteenth-century America, and his memoir of his experiences as a riverboat pilot on the Mississippi is absolutely compelling.

**Timothy B. Tyson** *Blood Done Sign My Name*. The shocking first-person account of a racist murder in North Carolina in 1970, and its impact on the local community.

**Geoffrey C. Ward, with Ric and Ken Burns** *The Civil War*. Illustrated history of the Civil War, designed to accompany the TV series and using hundreds of the same photographs.

**Juan Williams** *Eyes on the Prize*. Informative and detailed account of the civil rights years from the early 1950s up to 1966, with lots of rare, and some very familiar, photos.

**Edmund Wilson** *Patriotic Gore*. Fascinating eight-hundred-page survey of the literature of the Civil War, which serves in its own right as an immensely readable narrative of the conflict.

## BIOGRAPHY AND ORAL HISTORY

**Muhammad Ali, with Hana Yasmeen Ali** *The Soul of a Butterfly: Reflections on Life's Journey*. Thought-provoking and moving autobiography, in the course of which the late boxer's third daughter helped him describe his career and embrace of Sufi Islam.

**Maya Angelou** *I Know Why the Caged Bird Sings*. First of a five-volume autobiography that provides an ulti-mately uplifting account of how a black girl transcended her traumatic childhood in 1930s Arkansas.

**John Berendt** *Midnight in the Garden of Good and Evil*. Thirty years on from its original publication, there's still no resisting Berendt's shocking, gossipy, enthralling tales of Savannah society.

**Taylor Branch** *America in the King Years*. Brilliant three-volume series tracing, through the life story of Martin Luther King, Jr, the sweeping transformation of the USA during the civil rights struggle of the 1950s and 60s.

**Frederick Douglass, et al** *The Classic Slave Narratives*. Compilation of ex-slaves' autobiographies, ranging from Olaudah Equíano's kidnapping in Africa and global wanderings to Frederick Douglass's eloquent denunciation of slavery. Includes Harriet Jacobs' story of her escape from Edenton, North Carolina.

★ **U.S. Grant** *Personal Memoirs*. Encouraged by Mark Twain, the Union general and subsequent president wrote his autobiography just before his death, in a (successful) bid to recoup his horrendous debts. At first the book feels oddly downbeat, but the man's down-to-earth modesty grows on you.

**Gary Younge** *Stranger In A Strange Land* and *No Place Like Home*. Black British journalist Gary Younge is an acute observer of contemporary America; his experiences in the self-proclaimed New South make fascinating reading.

## MUSIC

**James Dickerson** *Goin' Back To Memphis*. A hundred-year romp through the extraordinary music of twentieth-century Memphis, heavily rooted in personal interviews with the major players.

**Jonathan Gould** *Otis Redding: An Unfinished Life*. Unfinished indeed – the story of Otis Redding ended all too soon, but this absorbing biography celebrates his prodigious talent and charts his course through the dynamic world of Memphis' own Stax Records.

**Michael Gray** *Hand Me My Travellin' Shoes*. Detailing his career as a street musician in and around Atlanta in the first half of the twentieth century, this biography of legendary blues guitarist Blind Willie McTell throws much light on everyday life in Georgia.

★ **Peter Guralnick** *Lost Highways*, *Feel Like Going Home* and *Sweet Soul Music*. Thoroughly researched personal histories of black popular music, packed with obsessive detail on all the great names. His twin Elvis biographies, *Last Train to Memphis* and *Careless Love*, trace the rise and fall of the iconic star, while also managing to evaluate him seriously as a musician.

**Gerri Hershey** *Nowhere to Run: The History of Soul Music*. Definitive rundown of the evolution of soul music from the gospel heyday of the 1940s through the Memphis, Motown and Philly scenes to the sounds of the early 1980s. Strong on social commentary and political background and studded with anecdotes and interviews.

**Robert Palmer** *Deep Blues*. Readable history of the development and personalities of the Delta Blues.

## TRAVEL WRITING

**James Agee and Walker Evans** *Let Us Now Praise Famous Men*. A deeply personal but also richly evocative journal of travels through the rural lands of the Depression-era Deep South, complemented by Evans' powerful photographs.

**J. Hector St-John de Crèvecoeur** *Letters from an American Farmer and Sketches of Eighteenth-Century America*. A remarkable account of the complexities of Revolutionary America, first published in 1782. His report on Charles Town, South Carolina, is searing: "They neither see, hear, nor feel for the woes of their poor slaves, from whose painful labours all their wealth proceeds".

**Bernard A. Weisberger** (ed) *The WPA Guide to America*. Prepared during the New Deal as part of a make-work programme for writers, these guides painted a comprehensive portrait of 1930s and earlier America. Each of the eight states covered in this book is covered in its own separate volume.

## FICTION

**Wiley Cash** *The Last Ballad* Set amid the labour struggles of North Carolina in the early twentieth century, this gripping historical novel tells the real-life story of activist and songwriter Ella May Wiggins.

**William Faulkner** *The Reivers*. The last and most humorous work of this celebrated Southern author. *The Sound and the Fury*, a fascinating study of prejudice, set like most of his books in the fictional Yoknapatawpha County in Mississippi, is a much more difficult read.

**Charles Frazier** *Cold Mountain* The haunting and beautifully written saga of a disenchanted Confederate deserter attempting to get back to his home in the mountainous west of North Carolina, with some wonderful descriptions of the landscape.

**Zora Neale Hurston** *Spunk*. Short stories celebrating black culture and experience from around the country, by a writer from Florida who became one of the bright stars of the Harlem cultural renaissance in the 1920s.

**Harper Lee** *To Kill a Mockingbird*. Classic tale of racial conflict and society's view of an outsider, Boo Radley, as seen through the eyes of children.

**Cormac McCarthy** *Suttree*. McCarthy is better known for "modern Western" works like *Blood Meridian* and *All the Pretty Horses*, but this beautifully written tale, of a Knoxville, Tennessee, scion opting for a hard-scrabble life among a band of vagrants on the Tennessee River, is his best.

**Carson McCullers** *The Heart is a Lonely Hunter*. McCullers is unrivalled in her sensitive treatment of misfits, in this case the attitude of a small Southern community to a deaf-mute.

**Margaret Mitchell** *Gone With the Wind*. Worth a read

even if you know the lines of Scarlett and Rhett by heart.

★ **Toni Morrison** *Beloved*. Exquisitely written ghost story by the late Nobel Prize-winning novelist, which recounts the painful lives of a group of freed slaves after Reconstruction, and the obsession a mother develops after murdering her baby daughter to spare her a life of slavery.

**Flannery O'Connor** *A Good Man is Hard to Find*. Short stories, featuring strong, obsessed characters, that explore religious tensions and racial conflicts in the Deep South.

**Alice Walker** *In Love and Trouble*. Moving and powerful stories of black women in the South, from the author of *The Color Purple*.

**Eudora Welty** *The Ponder Heart*. Quirky, humorous evocation of life in a backwater Mississippi town. Her most acclaimed work, *The Optimist's Daughter*, explores the tensions between the daughter of a judge and her stepmother.

**Colson Whitehead** *The Underground Railroad* Fantasy combines with appalling truth, in a searing depiction of the horrors of slavery.

# Small print and index

**A ROUGH GUIDE TO ROUGH GUIDES**

Published in 1982, the first Rough Guide – to Greece – was a student scheme that became a publishing phenomenon. Mark Ellingham, a recent graduate in English from Bristol University, had been travelling in Greece the previous summer and couldn't find the right guidebook. With a small group of friends he wrote his own guide, combining a contemporary, journalistic style with a thoroughly practical approach to travellers' needs.

The immediate success of the book spawned a series that rapidly covered dozens of destinations. And, in addition to impecunious backpackers, Rough Guides soon acquired a much broader readership that relished the guides' wit and inquisitiveness as much as their enthusiastic, critical approach and value-for-money ethos. These days, Rough Guides include recommendations from budget to luxury and cover more than 120 destinations around the globe, from Amsterdam to Zanzibar, all regularly updated by our team of roaming writers.

Browse all our latest guides, read inspirational features and book your trip at **roughguides.com**.

## Rough Guide credits

**Editor:** Beth Williams
**Cartography:** Carte
**Picture editor:** Piotr Kala

**Layout:** Katie Bennett
**Head of DTP and Pre-Press:** Katie Bennett
**Head of Publishing:** Kate Drynan

## Publishing information

First edition 2022

**Distribution**

*UK, Ireland and Europe*
Apa Publications (UK) Ltd; sales@roughguides.com
*United States and Canada*
Ingram Publisher Services; ips@ingramcontent.com
*Australia and New Zealand*
Booktopia; retailer@ booktopia.com.au
*Worldwide*
Apa Publications (UK) Ltd; sales@roughguides.com

**Special Sales, Content Licensing and CoPublishing**
Rough Guides can be purchased in bulk quantities
at discounted prices. We can create special editions,
personalised jackets and corporate imprints tailored to
your needs. sales@roughguides.com.
roughguides.com

Printed in Spain

A catalogue record for this book is available from the
British Library

The publishers and authors have done their best to
ensure the accuracy and currency of all the information
in **The Rough Guide to USA: The South**, however,
they can accept no responsibility for any loss, injury, or
inconvenience sustained by any traveller as a result of
information or advice contained in the guide.

## Help us update

We've gone to a lot of effort to ensure that this edition of
**The Rough Guide to USA: The South** is accurate and up-
to-date. However, things change – places get "discovered",
opening hours are notoriously fickle, restaurants and
rooms raise prices or lower standards. If you feel we've got
it wrong or left something out, we'd like to know, and if

you can remember the address, the price, the hours, the
phone number, so much the better.
    Please send your comments with the subject line
"**Rough Guide USA: The South Update**" to mail@
uk.roughguides.com. We'll credit all contributions and
send a copy of the next edition (or any other Rough Guide
if you prefer) for the very best emails.

---

## ABOUT THE AUTHOR

**Greg Ward** has worked on every edition of the Rough Guide to the USA since the very first,
on which he was the commissioning editor. He has also written separate Rough Guides
to the Southwest USA, Las Vegas and the Grand Canyon; is the sole author of many other
Rough Guides, including those to Hawaii and Brittany & Normandy; the joint author of others
including Provence, Spain, Barcelona, Belize and Japan. For more information, visit Ⓦgregward.
info.

## Photo credits

# Index

# Map symbols

The symbols below are used on maps throughout the book

| | | | |
|---|---|---|---|
| International boundary | ✈ International airport | Spring | Boat |
| State/province boundary | Domestic airport/airfield | National Park | Hindu/Jain temple |
| Chapter division boundary | ★ Transport stop | Gate/park entrance | Church (regional maps) |
| Interstate highway | P Parking | State capital | Church (town maps) |
| US highway | Post office | Lighthouse | Cemetery |
| State highway | ⓘ Information centre | Statue | Building |
| Pedestrianized road | Hospital/medical centre | Bridge | Stadium |
| Path | Cave | Battle site | Park/forest |
| Railway | Point of interest | Ski | Beach |
| Funicular | Viewpoint/lookout | Mountain range | Native American reservation |
| Coastline | Campground | Mountain peak | |
| Ferry route | Museum | Swamp/marshland | |
| National Parkway | Monument/memorial | Tree | |
| Ⓜ Metro/subway | Fountain/garden | Gorge | |
| Ⓣ Tram/trolleybus | Waterfall | Arch | |